Also available at all good book stores

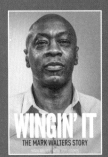

9781785314407

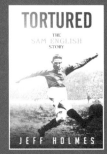

9781785317255

9781785314995

9781785316333

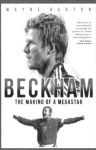

9781785316760

9781785315510

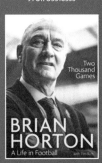

9781785316685

9781785316807

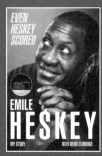

9781785315008

THE QUIET MAN
ROARS
The DAVID ROBERTSON Story

THE QUIET MAN

ROARS

The _____

DAVID ROBERTSON

Story

WITH ALISTAIR AIRD

Forewords by Richard Gough
and Walter Smith OBE

First published by Pitch Publishing, 2021

Pitch Publishing
A2 Yeoman Gate
Yeoman Way
Worthing
Sussex
BN13 3QZ
www.pitchpublishing.co.uk
info@pitchpublishing.co.uk

ISBN 978 1 78531 766 8

Typesetting and origination by Pitch Publishing
Printed and bound in India by Replika Press Pvt. Ltd.

CONTENTS

This book is dedicated to the memory of my mum, Muriel Robertson, who sadly lost her brave battle against cancer while I was writing it

FOREWORD BY
RICHARD GOUGH

I KNEW of David Robertson before he came to Rangers in 1991. He had broken into the Aberdeen team as a young player and was full of energy and possessed a good left foot. You are always aware of the better players that play against you and back then they would either go to Rangers or Celtic or go down to England. And although David came to Rangers for just short of £1m at a time when transfer fees were starting to take a real hike, for me he was worth the money we paid as he was a good servant for the club.

In the late '80s and early '90s Rangers had a few players who had filled the left-back position, guys such as Stuart Munro and John Brown, but when David came to the club you knew almost immediately that if he was fit, he was going to play. He was a good athlete, and I took to him straight away as first and foremost, he was a good defender. You get full-backs now who get criticised for their defending and use of the ball but Robbo always defended really well. He complemented Gary Stevens at right-back and I knew as a central defender that I had two full-backs who would take no nonsense from anyone and who liked to give the wingers they were up against a hard time.

David suited that Rangers team really well. He had tremendous pace and his recovery was phenomenal; he was quick enough to get back and clear things up. I played alongside some marvellous left-backs like Maurice Malpas but he had a more defensive mindset. Tom Boyd, who I played about ten or 15 games for Scotland with, was a great athlete and very powerful. But for me Robertson had the edge. He was really quick and his partnership with Brian Laudrup, in particular, created a lot of goals for the likes of Ally McCoist and Mark Hateley in what was a successful era for Rangers.

When he came to Rangers he had to adapt fairly quickly to how we played. At Aberdeen, Willie Miller and Alex McLeish were deep-lying centre-backs but at Rangers, I preferred us to hold a higher line. I liked my full-backs to be about two or three yards in front of me but it didn't take Robbo long to adapt. With some young players you can tell them something but it doesn't register and mistakes are made. But that was never the case with David. I told him that was the way we played and he was such a good player that he adjusted pretty quickly. And a few years later when Walter Smith decided to go with three at the back rather than a flat back four, that suited David as it encouraged him to get forward even more.

Although he was quiet, David was also good in what was a lively dressing room. He was a strong character and wasn't one to be messed with. He could handle himself and the bottom line was that he was a good professional. I had a huge amount of respect for him as he was a good player and, as captain, that's what I wanted at the football club.

We speak to each other regularly and I admire the fact that he has always wanted to go and work no matter where it was.

When we were team-mates I didn't see him as a future manager as he was so quiet but I take my hat off to him; to go out to Kashmir and do the job he has done tells you a lot about him as a person.

If I was asked to sum up David Robertson in three words it would be tough, good and brave. Exactly what I needed in a defender.

Richard Gough
July 2020

FOREWORD BY
WALTER SMITH OBE

BEFORE RANGERS signed David in 1991 when Graeme was still the manager, we had been actively seeking a left-back. Graeme was happy enough to look beyond Scotland for players but irrespective of where our attention was, good-quality left-backs were thin on the ground. We looked at a few and went to watch David a few times too. Personally I didn't need to go and watch him and I had seen the qualities he had when he had played against Rangers.

When it came to the final decision to sign David, Graeme had left to join Liverpool but it was an easy decision for me as I thought he was the best left-back in Scotland at that time. He performed at a high level consistently and, as a manager, that's one of the key things you look for in a defender. You wanted someone who was reliable and David always was, particularly in terms of his defending and how he went about his job. He was keen to get forward too and we had players in the team who could get the ball and hold on to it, allowing David to go on the overlap. He would then have the opportunity to get in a cross or have a shot at goal. David's attitude was first-class as well.

When David came to Rangers he grew into the position and, helped by the quality of players we had in the team, he developed more confidence and became more decisive, particularly in the attacking part of his game. You have to remember this was a young player who had never made a move before. He was used to the environment at Aberdeen and he was now coming into a club that had a high turnover of staff that year due to the introduction of the three-foreigner rule. But we had a good dressing room, one that made new players feel welcome, and David soon realised that he wasn't out of place.

Ibrox can be an unforgiving environment to play in and some players struggle when they come in while others thrive. I have to say that David thrived and over the period he was at Rangers there weren't many other players who were as consistent as him. He was always prepared to go forward, always prepared to take the ball and, initially, when he played with the likes of Pieter Huistra and Alexei Mikhailichenko, they knew that when they got the ball, David would be around them and, if they could play him in, they knew he would get there.

When I decided to change our system in 1995 and go to a back three with two wing-backs, David had no issues adapting. As he was a full-back there wasn't a massive change – David maybe received the ball a bit further up the pitch than he normally would – but it would have been more difficult for a winger or wide midfielder to take on the role as they would have to look more at the defensive aspect of their game. I had no fears that David could play in that position and it's to his credit that this trait – getting the ball in more advanced positions – improved. His passing got better, his crossing got better and so did his finishing.

David played over 200 games for Rangers and, with the amount of work he put in during each of them, the consistency of his performance separated him from a lot of other players who played in that position. He was terrific over the period he was with us and he played as much of his game in the opposition half as he did in his own. There were very few players who covered the ground he did.

One of the biggest accolades I can give David is that when we sat down to pick the team we didn't need to consider him as, if he was fit or free from suspension, he was already in. The amount of games he played in that time – sometimes 50 or 60 a season – was hard going, particularly for someone like David given the work he did up and down the pitch.

I have already said about David's consistency but that word doesn't tell you about the level of performance. David's performances were of a very, very high level and to do that takes a lot of mental toughness. David had that and during the six years he was with us I don't think there many times I was disappointed with his performances. From the summer of 1991 until he left in the summer of 1997 there was a steady improvement as he became more confident playing in a team filled with exceptionally good footballers. In fact if you were to do a statistical analysis of his play during that time you would find that in every department you wanted a full-back to be good in, he was statistically high up in all of them.

I have to admit that I didn't see him as a manager. David was quiet and usually folk who go into coaching are a bit more outgoing, but he has done, and he's made sure that every bit of it has been an adventure. He's gone from the Highlands to the USA and now to Kashmir, which has made for quite an amazing story and an amazing journey. When he was a player I didn't even think he would go to other countries to work, never mind be a manager, but you can see the enthusiasm and intensity he had as a player coming to the fore again now he is in that role. I wish him the best of luck.

Walter Smith OBE
August 2020

CHAPTER 1

IN THE BEGINNING

MY NAME is David Alexander James Robertson. I was born on 17 October 1968 in Aberdeen and I made my name as a marauding full-back for Aberdeen, Rangers and Leeds United. After my career ended prematurely through injury, I moved into management and had spells in charge at Elgin City and Montrose in Scotland before moving to America. I started in grassroots football out there and eventually became executive director at Sereno Soccer Club. During that time, I had an ill-fated spell as head coach with Phoenix FC and when I left the States, I took on my current role as head coach of the Indian I-League side, Real Kashmir.

But before we get to all that I want to take you back to the beginning and my early years growing up in Aberdeen. My family and I lived in a council house in Inchbrae Terrace in a part of Aberdeen called Garthdee. My dad, Leslie, was a stock taker for breweries such as Ushers and Lorimers and my mum, Muriel, worked in Watt and Grant, which was regarded as one of the most upmarket and expensive department stores on Union Street. My sister Susan, three years my senior, completed the

Robertson family unit at that time and my granny, my dad's mum, and my dad's sister also lived with us.

For both Mum and Dad, family came first. They were very private people and didn't want to impose on anyone. My dad used to travel a couple of times a month with work but every night he was home, he would take me to training. And hail, rain or shine he was there for the majority of games I played too. He was extremely supportive – his favourite phrase when I got out the car was 'remember to turn it on today' – but he would be blunt with me too. After games his feedback would be one of two things: I was either brilliant or murder! He didn't mince his words but never lost his temper once. Between him and my mum there's no doubt he was the soft touch.

I admit I did have a fear of my mum, but it was a fear of letting her down. She was a very warm person, but you knew if you stepped out of line, she would come down on you like a ton of bricks. I once got the belt at school – I can't remember what it was for – and it was a couple of months before a parents' evening. I was terrified of my mum finding out as I knew she would be disappointed, so I didn't tell her when it happened. But about half an hour before she was due to go to the parents' evening, I had to admit it to her as I didn't want her finding out from the teacher. In the end it wasn't mentioned!

I recall a time too when Mum sent me up to the local shop. It was snowing and the shop was at the top of a steep hill. I was despatched to get half a pound of chopped pork and she would always write in capital letters that it had to be cut thin. I picked up the meat and got the change and started to run home, but I fell. I skinned my knees and all the coins I was carrying flew out my hand. When I got home, Mum shouted at me as I had holes in my trousers and she also asked where her change was. I hadn't been able to recover it after my fall so had to explain that I had lost it. But the incident was soon forgotten about and I have a host of good memories of growing up.

Susan and I used to fight a lot – in later years it was usually over who was going to use Mum's car – but we always played together when we were younger. Like me, Susan is very quiet. We would talk a lot when we were in the house but when we ventured outside, we were both a bit shy. I wouldn't say we were scared to talk to other people, it was more that you feared saying something wrong that would see you getting ridiculed.

My brother Michael was a late bloomer, arriving 12 years after I did. My mum told me that both her and my dad were worried about what Susan and I would say when we found out she was pregnant. They had agreed that if I got upset, they would buy me a new pair of football boots. But instead of being upset, when they told me I was delighted so I never got those boots! For my mum and dad, Michael's arrival was like a new chapter in their life and, initially, it was a bit weird having a baby in the house. Susan and I both looked after him, though, taking him out for walks in his pram. And once he grew up, we ended up sharing a room together.

In the house in Garthdee, my dad had erected a dividing wall so Susan and I could have separate rooms. But after Susan moved out that wall came down and Michael and I shared the space. I remember us having bunk beds and he was a typical little brother. By the time I was full-time at Aberdeen I would take him down to Pittodrie and you could tell he was proud of me.

Incidentally, my middle names came from both my grandfathers. Mum and Dad couldn't decide which one to choose so I ended up with both. But over the years the length of name has caused me some problems, notably when filling in forms as my full name is often too long to fit in the boxes provided!

There was a real community spirit in Garthdee. This was a generation where we had no Xbox or PlayStation; in fact we only had two channels to choose from on the TV. Live football was a rarity too and even highlights were confined to either a Wednesday or a Saturday night. Our house phone was one of those old-fashioned dial ones and we didn't have an answering machine. I have often wondered how boys' club coaches communicated with their players back then, but in a similar way to the poverty I've experienced in India, we didn't know any different and we just got on with it. There was no trouble, and everybody got on with each other.

However, initially at least, I didn't have much interest in football. My dad, who played amateur football, was an Aberdeen supporter and he would take me to games at Pittodrie, bribing me with sweeties so I would go along. I think he just wanted me to get involved but I only went to a handful of games. And he would also take Susan and me to Duthie Park most weekends to kick a ball around. I know he wanted me to share his love for the beautiful game and for me to get into the school team, but try as he might, he just couldn't stimulate an interest in football. In fact, my sister would usually kick the ball more often than I did and, for me, the highlight of the trip to the park was getting an ice cream before we went home. But my relationship with football would all change in November 1976 when I fell in love with the game after Aberdeen upset the odds to beat Celtic 2-1 in the Scottish League Cup Final.

Although they were on the cusp of arguably the most successful era in their history, silverware was a rarity at Pittodrie back then. Since their foundation back in April 1903 they had won just four major honours in Scotland: the Scottish Cup twice (in 1946/47 and 1969/70), the league title in 1954/55, and the League Cup a year later. But under the guidance of the eccentric Ally McLeod, the Dons progressed to the final of the League Cup in 1976/77, steamrollering the holders and Treble winners the previous season, Rangers, 5-1 in the semi-final.

Jocky Scott, who would go on to have a successful career as a manager at Dundee and also as co-manager when I was in the first team at Aberdeen, scored a hat-trick in that one, with the other goals coming from wee Joe Harper and Drew Jarvie. And the balding Jarvie was on the mark again in the final against Jock Stein's Celtic at Hampden. Celtic, playing in the final for the 13th successive year, scored first courtesy of a Kenny Dalglish penalty but big Drew equalised to force extra time. And in the additional half-hour substitute Dave Robb grabbed the winning goal for Aberdeen.

Unfortunately, Dad hadn't been able to go to Hampden. It was extremely difficult to get tickets for matches of this ilk in those days and it was commonplace to see hundreds of folk snaking round the streets around Pittodrie as fans queued for tickets for big games. Indeed, when Aberdeen welcomed Liverpool to Pittodrie for a European Cup tie in 1980, Dad queued from 5am and still didn't get a ticket. While he didn't wait in line as long this time, he still missed out on a much sought-after ticket and as the game wasn't televised, we had to content ourselves with listening to the commentary on the radio.

He might have missed out when it came to attending the game but there was no way my dad was going to miss the open-top bus parade when the players returned to the north-east with the trophy. My mum, Susan and I went with him and I remember Mum buying us scarves and flags. Dad was in his element, proudly pointing out the players to me as the bus negotiated its way along a packed Union Street.

After the bus passed, we joined the crowd that followed it to Aberdeen's Pittodrie Stadium. For my dad, going into the stadium wasn't a new experience – he went to the majority of the home games the Dons played – but although I had been before, on this occasion I was awe-struck. The sheer size of the place and the fact it was packed just blew me away. Seeing what winning the cup meant to so many people got me really excited and changed my outlook when it came to football.

I was now hooked, and intoxicated by the game. Whenever I got the opportunity I would be out in the back garden with a ball. What used to be my sister's swing fast became a set of goals, complete with a fishing net which we draped over it. My mum's family are from Peterhead so we managed to get our hands on one of the big nets from the harbour, and night after night I would be out there until darkness descended, battering balls into my makeshift goals. And I would be out on any patch of grass I could find with my mates too, playing anything up to 50-a-side in communal areas with jackets for goalposts. I loved it.

Dad would now have a more willing companion when he went to Pittodrie. And I was so enthused that I didn't just attend first-team fixtures, I would go and watch the reserves too. I remember going to one reserve match against Queen's Park in

February 1977 and although it ended 0-0, the lack of goals did not curb my enthusiasm.

On the rare occasions a game was shown on television, I would be alongside my dad too. Back in the 1970s live football wasn't the big deal it is today. It was usually just international matches and the Scottish and FA Cup finals that were televised live but, when they were on, I would position myself next to my old man on the sofa and drink in everything.

And it wasn't just watching football that appealed to me; I now had a hankering to play the game and perhaps pursue a career as a professional. There were, however, some initial bumps in the road. Only a few weeks after the League Cup Final I got a trial for the school team at Inchgarth Primary but didn't get in. I remember being disappointed and frustrated but, even when I was at Rangers, I always doubted my ability as a player, so I wasn't surprised. However, I stuck at it and eventually got picked. But my debut ended embarrassingly.

I may have made my name as a full-back but in the fledgling days of my career I was a left-winger. And it was on the wing that I played for the school team but, if I'm honest, I was a bit of a one-trick pony. I had lots of pace so all I would do was knock the ball beyond the full-back and use my speed to beat him. I felt I wasn't blessed with a huge amount of technical ability, though, and a few years later Alex Ferguson would tell my dad that I lacked sufficient guile to make it as a winger.

That's maybe why I didn't impress in my initial games for the school team. For my first appearance I was selected as sub after one of the regulars called off as he was ill. But when I came on I had such a poor game that I was actually subbed off! In fact, my mum and Aunt Betty, who were at the game, said they were embarrassed by my performance.

But what I lacked in self-confidence I made up for in determination. I stuck at it and got a run in the team. And I impressed in one game against Cummings Park, setting up our first goal and then scoring our second all within the first five minutes. We won that one 5-1 and I was starting to make a name for myself due to my surging runs down the left wing.

And my development was helped by the fact that I supplemented my games for the school team with appearances for the Boys' Brigade football team. I was a member of the 62nd Company of the Aberdeen and District Battalion and I loved the fact they had a football team. I was now playing three games every weekend. I would play for the school on a Saturday morning, my boys' club team in the afternoon then in tournaments for the Boys' Brigade on the Sunday.

The officer who ran the Boys' Brigade team was a quiet chap called David Wyness, and he had a significant influence on my career. He decided to pen a letter to Aberdeen, wherein he suggested they should send a scout to watch me. They did but I would have to wait a few years before they took me on. There weren't any youth academies back then and the lowest age group at Aberdeen was under-14. That meant I had to content myself with game time in the interim for the school, the Boys' Brigade and my boys' club team.

The boys' club I was playing for was Deeside and that all came about after the second year of playing for Inchgarth Primary. At the end of the year, I was picked for a team called Garthdee Gola who took part in a tournament called Champion Street. That took place in the summer holidays and the idea was that if you lived within a certain radius of a big street – Garthdee Road in my case – you were eligible to get picked. You then played two or three games a week, with the final for the Denis Law Trophy taking place at Pittodrie.

After a convincing 5-0 win over Mastrick Dynamo, Garthdee made it to the final in 1979 and it took place at Pittodrie on 1 September before Aberdeen faced Meadowbank Thistle in the second leg of a second-round League Cup tie. Although the ground wasn't full – there were only about 6,000 there – it was by far the biggest crowd I had ever played in front of and it was such a thrill to play at the home ground of my local team. Our team manager, Adrian Thomson, laid on a double-decker bus to ferry the families to the ground and although we lost 2-0 to a team called Netherview Spurs, we stayed on to watch the senior match. Having won the first leg 5-0 this was about going through the motions for the Dons but they got a bit of a fright when having twice taken the lead through goals from John McMaster and Gordon Strachan, a late goal earned Meadowbank a 2-2 draw. Incidentally, my mum ended up £50 richer too for she was picked out as the face in the crowd in the local paper the following day.

If I ever needed confirmation that a career as a footballer was the one for me then I got it that night at Pittodrie. The whole experience was magical and fuelled my desire to make an impression on any scouts coming to watch Deeside's games. And I must have impressed those that watched the games as both Aberdeen Lads' Club and Deeside Boys' Club came in for me. I didn't think I was good enough to play for either team, but the coach of Deeside was chap called Ian Connell, who lived not far from us. He made me feel at home, so I elected to play for Deeside.

I had a great time with Deeside. I was only ten when I joined but I worked my way through the age groups and there were numerous highlights, including four goals in an 8-0 win over a team called Perth City in the second round of the Scottish Juvenile Under-18 Cup.

But I wasn't just making an impact with Deeside. My form for the school team saw me selected for the Aberdeen Primary School Select side and getting picked for that really thrust you into the shop window. Since Aberdeen's youth teams only started at under-14, they instead brought boys from the Primary School Select in for training, keeping them on for a while as they went on to secondary school then deciding who they wanted to sign and who they didn't.

Under the watchful eye of coaches Lenny Taylor, George Adams and Bobby Clark, we used to train on a Monday night on the red ash pitch that sat opposite Pittodrie and is still used to this day as a car park on matchdays. I had worked with Lenny and Bobby at schoolboy level and Bobby was an Aberdeen legend. He had kept goal for the club for over 15 years and in 1971 went a phenomenal 13 consecutive matches without conceding a goal. As you can imagine, my dad was absolutely buzzing that his son was being coached by such an iconic figure and I'll never forget the lessons I learned in those sessions.

With both Bobby and Lenny being schoolteachers, they were big on discipline and neither of the two of them swore. There was very little shouting; it was all about encouragement and training, and playing games in that system wasn't too dissimilar to being at school. It was more like teaching than coaching.

Unlike Bobby, Lenny didn't have the same playing background, but he was well-liked at the club and he was part of the furniture.

Fergie really trusted him, and they had a very close working relationship. He's just a great guy and there's not one player I know who has a bad word to say about him. When we attend reunions, even the guys he let go, the ones that he didn't think were good enough to make it at Aberdeen, all speak highly of him.

The encouragement he offered didn't stop when I made the first team, particularly if I was going through a hard time. One such occasion came after I cost Aberdeen a point in a league match against Motherwell in October 1986. We were struggling a bit at the time – we had only taken four points from our previous five games – and our cause wasn't helped by the fact the manager had had to call upon 26 players since the start of the season. To put that figure in perspective, he had only used 27 in the entirety of 1985/86.

We fell behind that day when Alex Kennedy scored for Motherwell but goals from Davie Dodds, his first for Aberdeen, and Willie Miller had us 2-1 ahead with 16 minutes to go. It was then that I stepped in and ended up getting slaughtered by Fergie. John Reilly, who had come on as sub, picked up the ball inside the box but there wasn't any danger. However, I must have thought there was as I lunged into a challenge and took John down. The referee awarded a penalty, Andy Walker scored, and Fergie was apoplectic. It was only my fourth league appearance, but Fergie was quoted in the press as saying that he had paid the price for playing a 17-year-old defender. He said that you could have got away with playing a forward at that age, but you were taking a chance with a defender.

I was pretty low after Fergie raged at me and my face was tripping me when I took myself along to my sister Susan's wedding later that night. But Lenny was brilliant afterwards. He simply asked what I had learned and what I would do differently next time. It was pretty much along the lines of, 'You can't change what's happened, but you can use it to your advantage to improve your game going forward.' Even though by that time I had left the youth system, Lenny was still there for me and would always have time for me.

In addition to training we would play games against Highland League teams on a Monday night and the ash park we played on was the only one in Aberdeen. It was a decent pitch but wasn't anywhere near the standard of the ones we would play on when we went to Glasgow. They were beautiful and we would often struggle when we played there.

After leaving Inchgarth Primary in the summer of 1980 I moved on to Harlaw Academy. I'll admit that I was never the best scholar – I left in the winter of 1984 with just a single 'O' Level in arithmetic – but the move to secondary school gave me more opportunities to play football. I was a regular in the school team and became captain too. The team was looked after by the Modern Studies teacher, Mr Ewen, and I really looked up to him. He had made over 100 appearances for Aberdeen between 1957 and 1962 and had been part of the team that lost out to St Mirren in the 1959 Scottish Cup Final.

He stayed next door to us when we moved to Peterculter and all the pupils knew about him playing for the Dons. But he was such a humble guy and never spoke about his career; it was all about him looking out for his team. We all had so much respect for him and his knowledge of the game was first-class. It was a privilege to play for him.

We won a few trophies during my time at Harlaw. I remember being skipper when we lifted the Sportsman's Trophy one year –

we beat a team called Linksfield in the final – and I was starting to catch the eye of scouts who attended our games. I managed to impress them enough to earn a place in Aberdeen Secondary Schools select team and that led to national success.

I started with them initially at under-15 level. I was only 14 at the time but the coaching team reckoned I was good enough to train and play with the older lads. And that offered me the opportunity to be part of the team that won the Scottish Cup when we beat Edinburgh 3-0 at Tannadice in 1983.

The tournament had started in 1901. The last time a team from Aberdeen had won the trophy outright was back in 1947 – in 1978 Aberdeen had been declared joint winners with Ayrshire – and we made it through to the final thanks to a 4-1 win over Dumfries. The coaching team must have rated me as they picked me as part of the XI for the final. Similarly to the experience with Garthdee it was incredible to play on the same turf as a top-tier side. Indeed, this was the ground of the Premier Division champions that year. I was deployed at left-back and Lenny told me I had a storming game. Edinburgh were a good side and had won the trophy in 1979 and 1981 but goals from Laird, Lawrence and Brown gave Aberdeen the victory. I can also recall a torrential downpour at the end and staying on to watch the Dundee United match that was played later the same day.

We retained the trophy the following year with a 2-1 win over Lanarkshire at Blairgowrie. Kincorth Academy's Douglas Baxter scored both goals in that one and the lads made it three in a row in 1985 when they defeated Ayrshire 4-1 in Perth. This was the first time in the history of the competition that a team had won three times in succession but, although I played in the team that retained the cup in 1984, by the time of the win over Ayrshire I had moved to under-18 level and was making good progress at Aberdeen.

I enjoyed success when I progressed to the under-18 school select too and I can recall in one game being denied a hat-trick when I missed a penalty in a 3-1 victory over the North of Scotland in the last eight of the Scottish Cup. I scored the first two goals and after Douglas Baxter, the chap who had scored twice in the Under-15 Scottish Cup Final, made it 3-1, I had the opportunity to net my third. I couldn't beat the goalkeeper from 12 yards, but I played well in the game and, in one of the many newspaper clippings I have, myself and Andy Langridge were singled out as being the star performers.

As an Aberdeen fan I hoped what I was doing for the variety of teams I was playing for would be enough to convince the club's hierarchy to offer me on an 'S' Form. That was how schoolboys were signed back then but little did I know that another opportunity to sign for a club was on the horizon. I had been recommended to a chap called Jack Buchanan, a scout for Manchester United, who were managed at the time by Dave Sexton.

When I found out Jack had been impressed and wanted me to sign for United, I'll be honest, I burst out laughing. I thought there was no chance that a team as iconic as Manchester United would be keen on me, but it transpired that the interest was genuine. Jack even came to my parents' house to persuade me to go.

The club wanted me to go down and train during the summer holidays but there was a stumbling block. At that time, you had to be 14 to sign what were called 'associated forms' in England but, as I was aged 13, I could sign schoolboy forms in Scotland. It was, however, a terrific boost to be coveted by United.

But that wasn't the last time I was given the chance to go to Old Trafford. A few months after Alex Ferguson left Aberdeen, I played for the youth team in the BP Youth Cup tie against Celtic at Parkhead. We lost 2-1 and arrived back in Aberdeen about midnight. I drove home to Garthdee in my Vauxhall Astra GTE, a car I couldn't afford, but en route I noticed a car behind me with its lights flashing. It was getting closer and closer so young and naïve as I was then I decided the best way to give the car the slip was to drive faster. I must have reached 80mph in a 30mph zone, yet the car was still right behind me. I then got a horrible feeling it might be the police, so I pulled over. The car following did likewise and from the driver's seat emerged Alex Ferguson.

I was invited into the passenger seat of his car and he basically said he wanted me to go to Manchester United. I told him I would be interested but nothing materialised. Archie Know eventually went with Fergie to Old Trafford, but he took the team for a couple of games before he left. For the last of those fixtures, in midweek at home to Clydebank, I was left out. I had had a good run in the team before that, starting the previous six league games, so it was a surprise when I found out that John McMaster was coming in for me at left-back. However, I heard from Teddy Scott a few months later that this had been a ploy by Fergie. The new Aberdeen manager, Ian Porterfield, was present that night and Teddy told me I had been left out so Porterfield wouldn't know about me, which would make it easier for Manchester United to come in and sign me. In the end it didn't work out that way and I actually established myself as a regular in the first team under Porterfield.

Back in the early 1980s, though, my eyes were firmly fixed on a move to my local club and I eventually struck gold. We were playing on the ash park one night when out of the corner of my eye I saw a very important spectator. Alex Ferguson was a regular attender at our Monday night sessions but on this occasion as he took up position next to Lenny and George Adams, his presence must have galvanised me as I scored a couple of goals. My dad had been watching the game and afterwards he told me he was sure Fergie had picked me out from the crowd. And that was confirmed a matter of days later when Lenny called and asked me straight out if I wanted to sign for Aberdeen.

All of a sudden, the interest from United paled into insignificance. I was wanted by my team, my dad's team. I had the chance to follow in the footsteps of the players I watched from the terraces at Pittodrie; there was no way I was going to turn that down.

When my dad and I travelled to Pittodrie to sign my schoolboy forms I don't know who was more nervous, him or me! It must have been difficult for him. As a parent he must have been worried about what would happen if I didn't make the grade, but on the other hand, as a dyed-in-the-wool Don, he must have been desperate to see his boy donning that red jersey.

That was the summer of 1982. I had started on the path towards a career as a professional footballer and it happened to begin at the outset of one of the landmark seasons in the history of Aberdeen Football Club.

CHAPTER 2

LIVING THE DREAM

AFTER COMING into the world on 21 June 1982, Prince William was christened William Arthur Philip Louis in August. Several hundred miles away in Aberdeen I was enjoying my own baptism as an apprentice footballer and my early days at Pittodrie were awesome. There were about eight in my 'S' Form intake and we also had a lad called Martin Craig who trained with us even though he was an 'S' Form with Dundee United. But such was the rivalry between the teams at the time, Martin wasn't allowed inside Pittodrie, so he had to get changed in his dad's car!

During my days as an 'S' Form I trained at Pittodrie during the school holidays and often that was with the first team. And after I left school and went full-time, I had several jobs to do in and around the club. My main responsibility was for the kit in the home dressing room. That meant gathering up the dirty training gear and putting it in the washing machine then hanging it up to dry in the sauna. Once it was dry it had to be laid out before you went home so it was ready for the first team the next day.

The home dressing room was the domain of the first team – the reserves changed in the away dressing room – but there was never a 'them and us' attitude. The first-team regulars were great with me. Doug Rougvie was one who took me under his wing and Alex McLeish was also brilliant and looked after me.

I was also tasked with cleaning the floor in the home dressing room. The floor was covered in those old-fashioned hairy carpet tiles and every single blade of grass used to stick to them. But the instruction was clear; you were not to use a hoover, you had to use a brush. The first time I did it, it took forever but you didn't dare question why you were doing it this way. Eventually I developed the knack of how to do it and, although I didn't realise it at the time, doing jobs like that toughened you up and helped develop the mentality you need to succeed as a professional footballer.

But as important as those jobs were, the one I paid most attention too most of the time was that of cleaning Alex Ferguson's car. He was driving a silver Mercedes at the time and it was a car I was familiar with as it would often appear in the car park when I was playing for Deeside. Fergie's son, Mark, was part of the same Deeside team as me and I have to admit I didn't like it when Fergie came to watch his boy. His presence made us all more nervous and I don't think we did too well in the games he came along to.

Keeping his car clean was a hard task. Fergie was seldom at home during the week and would be travelling to places like Wick and Brora to go and watch games. As a result, the front of the Mercedes would be caked with flies. It was almost impossible to get them off. On one occasion, myself, Robert McRobb and Scott Tait were trying hard to de-fly the car, but it was late on a Friday and it was starting to get dark. We decided that rather than scrub away and get the flies off, we would just throw buckets of water over the car and hope Fergie wouldn't notice. Once we had done that, we went back into the stadium to put the buckets and cloths away and got ready to go home.

However, as we got to the back door, we could hear Fergie raging about the state of his car, so we made a run for it. Robert was driving his dad's car that day, so we all piled in. Fergie came out looking for us, but he looked at the bus stop as most of the time we got a bus from Pittodrie into the city centre before getting another bus home from there. On occasion the first-team players would stop and offer us a lift and that was great as it helped youngsters like myself feel part of the team. However, there was one player who shall remain nameless who would pick us up then ask for the 20p bus fare.

Needless to say, we didn't cut corners with car cleaning the next time but it wasn't just keeping Fergie's car spick and span that kept me on my toes; some of the other apprentices left me a bit intimidated too. The 'S' Forms didn't have a dressing room to change in, so we used to get changed around a snooker table. We had some boys from Glasgow like Paul Wright, Stevie Gray and Joe Miller who would change on one side of the table, while the Aberdonians would change on the other side. There was a self-confidence about the Glasgow boys and with Aberdonians, by nature, being very reserved, I was left thinking that I wasn't good enough to be a footballer.

The coaching staff could be brutal too. We weren't given training kit and I turned up one night wearing a pair of black Adidas shorts with three orange stripes. These mirrored those worn by Dundee United so one of the coaches told me I wasn't to wear them. Instead I was handed a pair of shorts that were about five sizes too big for me. It was rare for someone to tell you that you were a good player either. That was the culture in the game in that era and I found it very hard, especially after the encouragement I had had when I was coached by Lenny and Bobby.

But although Fergie and his staff were hard taskmasters, they were excellent with the young players. Fergie essentially put Aberdeen on the football map, not just domestically but in Europe too. As I said earlier, the League Cup win that got me interested in football back in 1976 was only Aberdeen's fifth major trophy. Yet just three seasons later Fergie had the league flag fluttering above the stands at Pittodrie and there would be further title wins in 1983/84 and 1984/85. The Scottish Cup made its way to the trophy room too, courtesy of back-to-back wins over Rangers in 1982 and 1983. And it was after the latter that Fergie famously blasted his players for playing poorly, this coming just minutes after Eric Black's goal had been enough to secure a 1-0 victory after extra time.

The win over Rangers came a matter of days after arguably Aberdeen's most famous triumph, a 2-1 victory over Real Madrid in the European Cup Winners' Cup Final. And I like to think I played a pivotal role in that success. Another job myself and the other 'S' Forms had was that of ball boy and Fergie would always speak to us, particularly if we were on duty for a European tie. Depending on how the game was going we either had to release the ball quickly or take our time. And if you didn't do as he asked or were seen to be slacking he wasn't long in seeking you out and telling you. That summed him up; meticulous, he covered every base. Even though he had such big games on his hands – I was ball boy for the games against Bayern Munich and Waterschei – he still found time to talk to the ball boys.

I wasn't lucky enough to go the final – my dad and I were going to try and go but a bout of German measles meant I had to be content with the coverage on TV – but I was making good progress at Aberdeen and just a few months after the glory in Gothenburg, I was getting game time for the reserves. My debut was late in season 1983/84 against St Johnstone at Pittodrie. However, if I'm being honest, rather than taking the positives from being picked for the second XI, the whole experience left me in a dilemma. I had played as a forward during my schooldays and against the Saints I played up front as I replaced Joe Miller three minutes into the second half. But I really struggled against their experienced centre-back, Don McVicar, and started to question whether I had a future in the game as a forward. Although I had been capped by Scotland at under-16 level, I felt I was okay against players in my age bracket but really struggled when I was up against more experienced defenders. And that's when fate kicked in.

At the start of the following season I was in the reserve squad that took part in the Chivas Regal Tournament. The first games of the four-team tournament took place on the Friday, with the third/fourth-place play-off and the final scheduled for the following day. We faced Keith in our first game, and I came on as sub, replacing a chap called Robert Green. But I couldn't get beyond the full-back I was up against. Although I struggled, we won 1-0 but it had been a bruising encounter so when we met on the Saturday night, it emerged we only had 11 fit players. The coaches were struggling to find someone to play at left-back and as I was the only fit left-sided player in the pool, Teddy Scott suggested I could wear the number three jersey and it was a call that completely changed the trajectory of my career. I played and, although we lost 4-2 to Forfar Athletic after extra time, I was voted man of the match and after that I never looked back. I was no longer a left-winger; for the most part I was now a left-back.

Teddy was a significant influence on my career at that time. Similar to Lenny and Bobby Clark he was more of a mentor than a coach, and it was Teddy who pushed to get me into the reserve team. He also took training, and it was horrendous! There was one occasion when he arranged a practice game at the Gordon Barracks up at Bridge of Don and he asked us to build these portable goals we had at the time. After that we were all set to go but highlighted to Teddy that we had no balls to play with. Calm and assured as you like, Teddy told us that balls weren't required, this was going to be shadow play. That meant I had to run up and down the line and pretend I was crossing balls into the box. Although it is more prevalent in today's game, it wasn't when I started, and it took a bit of time to get used to it. But it helped us develop positional sense, and another of the exercises, the practice of kicking balls against trees, was also excellent as it made your passing more accurate.

The 1984/85 season also saw me get my hands on a national trophy, although it took a half-time tirade from Fergie to ensure we got our act together after an abject first-half display against Celtic in the BP Youth Cup Final at Pittodrie.

Celtic had eliminated us from the competition the previous season – the first time the tournament had taken place – and gone on to beat Rangers 2-0 in the final. I made my debut in the tournament when I came on for Joe Miller when we defeated Brora Rangers 7-0 in the second round at home and I was on the bench again when Celtic came north and beat us 3-1 in round three. I replaced Jim Downie in that one and found myself up against players I would cross swords with numerous times during my career. Lex Baillie, Owen Archdeacon and Tony Shepherd were in the Celtic team, as was Peter Grant. And it was Peter who fired Celtic in front just before half-time. A double from Sandy Fraser finished us off in the second half and the goal I scored with four minutes left was nothing more than a consolation.

Revenge was therefore on the agenda for Aberdeen. Our route to the final had seen us beat Dundee 2-0, St Johnstone 3-1 and Ayr United 6-1 and I had started all of the ties. And I was in the starting XI again for the final, which took place at Pittodrie after the Aberdeen chairman had correctly called the coin toss that decided which team hosted the occasion.

The first team had clinched the league title the previous week so the plan was to present the trophy to the players before kick-off, which made the place pretty buoyant. I think there must have been a crowd of about 6,000 there so Pittodrie was rocking. But we very quickly set about bursting the bubble as we contrived to concede two goals in the first half.

Willie Garner was taking the team, so we expected a bit of a rollicking from him at half-time. But Willie was relatively calm when he started to address us before the dressing room door burst open and Fergie marched in. And he started with the goalkeeper, a lad called Stephen Beckett, and went through each individual player, including the subs. It was brutal, so fierce in fact that there were times where you could see flecks of saliva coming out his mouth.

Yet as hard as it was to hear that criticism, it worked. We went out after the interval and pretty quickly fell 3-0 behind but with Fergie's words still ringing in our ears, goals from our captain, Paul Wright, and Jocky Lawrence – who had scored a hat-trick in the semi-final against Ayr – put us back in contention before wee Joe Miller scored a sublime goal, lobbing the goalkeeper from 35 yards to force extra time. Therein we added another two – Lawrence and Stevie Gray were the marksmen – to secure the trophy.

We then encountered an altogether different Fergie as we celebrated in the dressing room. He came in and congratulated all of us individually and I admired him for doing that. He didn't simply want to win, he wanted you to play well too. And I found this out first-hand when we beat Clydebank soon after I had made it into the first team. We won with relative ease so you might have expected Fergie would be relatively happy, but I had made a mistake during the match and afterwards he slaughtered me for it. Everything was fine again the following Monday morning when he took me into his office and explained things but that showed you how much of a perfectionist he was.

We saw both sides of the manager on the night of that BP Youth Cup Final, but although he could be gruff and harsh, he was excellent with the young players at the club. Fergie would bring all the 'S' Forms in during school holidays to train with the first team. We were training alongside the likes of Mark McGhee, Eric Black and Willie Miller and when I eventually did make the first team, the transition was a lot smoother as I had got to know the players in these sessions.

However, although he placed a lot of emphasis on youth like he did with great success a few years later at Manchester United, that didn't stop you from getting both barrels from him if he saw fit. And yours truly bore the brunt one day when he took a dislike to my hairstyle. Back in my days as an apprentice a lot of folk were sporting the Charlie Nicholas-style mullet, the big side-sweep with the perm at the back. The home and away dressing rooms sat next to each other and there was a wee room across from them where Fergie, Archie Knox and Teddy Scott would sit. If you had done something wrong he would holler, 'Hey Robertson, come here,' as you walked past the door and, on one occasion, I was summoned in such a manner and told to get my hair cut. I went home that evening and did as I was asked but I only got something like a centimetre of the length cut off. Sure enough this wasn't sufficient for Fergie and when I attended training the next day I was ordered to go the barbers immediately to get a haircut.

On another occasion after a reserve game he slaughtered Willie Falconer for missing a couple of sitters. Fergie surmised the reason for Willie's profligacy was his eyesight and ordered him to go and get his eyes tested. Willie didn't think he was being serious but, sure enough, the next morning there was an appointment booked for him at the local opticians.

A few months after the BP Youth Cup victory I was putting pen to paper on my first professional contract. There's no doubt the move to left-back was key to that happening as I feel had I remained on the left wing I would have been a goner. I was only 15 then but it was a turning point and, by the end of my apprenticeship, I was offered a two-year deal with a two-year option. The option in those days wasn't mine, it was up to the club. My weekly wage was to be £65 and that would be the deal on the table two years down the line if Aberdeen still wanted me. There was also a signing-on fee equivalent to £5 for every week you were an 'S' Form, which worked out as roughly £500.

There were clauses in the contract such that your wages rose to £200 per week if you made the first team and there would be a £25 appearance fee too. I was happy enough to sign but I went home and spoke to my dad and he was adamant, it either had to be a four-year deal or a two-year deal, no optional years. I went back in the following day to see Fergie and needless to say I was told to sign the original deal I was offered! I had no issues with that and my advice to players now is the same as it was back then for myself: when it comes to your first contract, you take what you are offered.

I signed the original deal in July 1985 and Fergie didn't give any guarantees. I must have been catching the eye of the first-team coaches, though, as I was picked in the group of players who travelled to face Meadowbank Thistle in a pre-season friendly a month later. I must admit I thought I was just being taken along for the experience. Fergie was never one for naming the team the day before a game and it was only after we had the pre-match meal that I knew I was one of the subs. In fact, when he named the team I was the last name he read out and I was absolutely stunned. But Fergie leaving the team announcement to so late in the day meant I had no time to get nervous and think about what lay ahead.

As it was, I replaced Tommy McQueen in a match that ended 2-2 and my time as a first-team player started then. I earned my first start four days later when we played Dunfermline Athletic at East End Park to mark their centenary year. And that match saw me lose my two front teeth as I was given a robust introduction to first-team football by the flame-haired John Watson. A few minutes shy of the interval, we had an aerial joust in which John's forearm smashed into my face. There was blood everywhere and I trooped off at the interval minus two teeth and with a burst lip. I hoped Fergie would take me off, but he basically told me to stop feeling sorry for myself, that I was in with the big boys now and to get back out for the second half. There was no mollycoddling at all.

The game ended in a 1-0 defeat and I was eventually replaced by Brian Mitchell in the second half. Despite needing an impromptu visit to my dentist, I enjoyed the experience, but the drama of the night didn't end after the final whistle. We got the bus back to Pittodrie and arrived there after midnight. I hadn't long passed my driving test but I was too embarrassed to take the car I was driving, my mum's blue Mini, to the stadium. I needed a way to get home, though, so as Susan and I both took turns driving the car, I arranged for her to bring it to Pittodrie but park it around the corner.

But when I went looking for the car, I couldn't find it. These were the days before mobile phones, so I had to go back to Pittodrie and use a payphone in the main stand to call Susan. She said the car was in Golf Road, but it was so dark that I had walked past it. After hanging up I headed back to the front doors but, when I went to pull them open, they were locked. The corrugated metal shutters had also been pulled down too and it didn't matter how hard I banged on the doors, nobody heard me. I then decided to batter the windows and I did so with such force that the glass eventually broke. That alerted the physio, Davie Wylie, who was just about to get into his car and he unlocked the doors and let me out.

Those two appearances inside four days against Meadowbank and Dunfermline would be the sum total of my first-team outings that season. They ended with me battered, bruised and bleeding but I felt I was making progress. I was on the first-team radar and the following season would see me establish myself as the first-choice left-back.

CHAPTER 3

MAKING THE BREAKTHROUGH

AFTER MY appearances for the first team in pre-season, I spent the rest of the 1985/86 campaign in the reserves. Three players – Tommy McQueen, Ian Angus and Brian Mitchell – vied for the number three jersey but I was happy to train with the first team while learning from the experienced players like John McMaster with the reserves.

The reserves enjoyed a good start to the season. We beat Hibs 6-2 in our opening game and ended August with a 6-1 win over Dundee at home. Paul Wright scored five goals in that match and, like me, he was now pushing for a place in the first team. He was another product of the youth setup at the club and he went on to have a good career, winning the Scottish Cup with Kilmarnock in 1997.

A John McMaster goal gave us a 1-0 win over Celtic at Pittodrie and we were pushing Rangers hard at the top of the Premier Reserve League table. But our interest in the Reserve League Cup was ended at the quarter-final stage when Celtic beat us 5-3 at Parkhead. I was replaced by Brian Grant that night and didn't play for the reserves again until we drew 2-2 at home to Dundee in the middle of January. I was back in contention in time to jet off to Italy in February, though. With the weather in Scotland typically horrendous, we travelled to take part in the Torneo di Viareggio. The tournament had first been held back in 1949 and was one of the top youth competitions in world football. And to illustrate that we were joined in the competition by, among others, Bayern Munich, Nacional from Uruguay, Inter and AC Milan and Napoli.

Aberdeen were drawn in Group B alongside AC Milan, Genoa and the Hungarian side, Ferencváros. But we were met by similar conditions we would have experienced in Scotland for our first match against Genoa. The tie was actually switched to another venue as the original pitch was waterlogged but the surface we played on wasn't much better. It was a bit of a quagmire, but I managed to squelch through it to score the opening goal. The Italians came back to win 2-1, though, one of their goals being from the penalty spot. The award was soft as Ian Robertson lost his footing and the Genoa lad simply fell over. It was a blatant dive, but the referee bought it. A 2-0 defeat by AC Milan ended our interest in the competition prior to the knockout stages but we did return home on the back of a fine 2-0 win over Ferencváros in our last match.

This was the second successive year we had played in the tournament. The previous year we were grouped with Fiorentina, Atalanta and the Romanian side, Universitatea Craiova. We lost 2-0 against Fiorentina before drawing 1-1 with Atalanta. But the last match was the most memorable one as we had to play without a recognised goalkeeper.

The pitch was like a beach and it was pouring with rain. We were all shivering, and nobody really wanted to play. In the warm-up our goalkeeper, David Lawrie, got knocked out when he was struck on the head by the ball. That meant one of our outfield players – it was either Jocky Lawrence or Robert Green – had to go in goal. We had to win to have a chance of qualifying for the knockout stages but, under the circumstances, we did well to hold the Romanians to a 2-2 draw, our goals coming from Willie Falconer and Brian Grant.

Overall, both experiences were incredible. It was the first time I had gone abroad with the team and I remember having a few drinks after one of the games. We were all 16 or 17 at the time but it got a wee bit out of hand and I ended up getting hit in the face with a bottle. My eye swelled up and the next day the coaching staff were asking how I got the injury. I was panicking as I thought this might end my career at Aberdeen as I was about to be sent home for drinking. I told them I had picked it up during the game and, although I'm not sure they believed me, the staff decided to let it go.

Before 1985/86 was over I added a second BP Youth Cup medal to my collection. I scored in our 5-1 win in the opening round against Dundee United and again in our 6-0 victory over Ross County in the next round. That one came from the penalty spot and that was probably the last penalty I took prior to stepping up in the Scottish Cup Final shoot-out in 1990.

An 8-0 hammering of Dundee at Pittodrie in the semi-final took us to Palmerston Park to face Queen of the South in the final. We won 2-0 and although I started to make headway in the first team in the seasons ahead I still played from time to time for the youth team too. I was involved when Celtic stopped us winning a third successive BP Youth Cup at the quarter-final stage in 1986/87 and I also played in a youth tournament in

Switzerland at the end of both 1987/88 and 1988/89, captaining the team in the latter one.

In terms of the first team in 1985/86, there would be a domestic cup double but a third successive league title proved elusive. That was the campaign where it looked as if Hearts would win the league until they lost 2-0 at Dundee on the final day. That coupled with Celtic's 5-0 thumping of St Mirren in Paisley meant the Glasgow side edged it on goal difference. And to compound Hearts' pain, Aberdeen battered them 3-0 in the Scottish Cup Final a week later.

The win over Hearts put the Scottish Cup alongside the League Cup in the trophy room as earlier in the season we had beaten Hibernian 3-0 in the final. I wasn't involved in the squad on either occasion, but the Scottish Cup Final was a great day, although memories are a bit hazy due to the amount of alcohol I consumed. I was still a young laddie, but we got to go to Hampden on the same bus as the players' wives and girlfriends. You weren't allowed to drink on the bus, so everyone had to disguise their tipples in Coke bottles. Suffice to say by the time the bus reached Mount Florida we were hammered. Indeed, I vaguely recall making my way to my seat and tripping up and falling into the lap of the future Scotland manager, Andy Roxburgh.

The 1986/87 season would prove to be my breakthrough, although it was only from late November onwards that I became a first-team regular. The campaign started with the first team on tour in Sweden, but I was up in the Highlands with the reserves playing against the likes of Deveronvale, Keith, Turriff United and Mugiemoss. I got on the scoresheet in the latter game, a 4-2 win for us.

Brian Mitchell started the season at left-back for the first team and I was in that position for the reserves when we opened the season with a 3-1 win over Dundee United at Pittodrie. But I made my league debut when I came on as substitute for Brian against Hamilton at Pittodrie on 16 August. It was a great thrill for me and my family and the 2-0 win thanks to a Billy Stark double was the icing on the cake.

The main differences I noticed that day were the crowd and the size of the pitch. When you played for the reserves at Pittodrie the stadium was empty and that seemed to make the pitch massive. But that day there were over 10,000 in the ground and the pitch appeared smaller. The presence of the crowd also got to me a fair bit in my early games too. You were conscious that they were watching every touch of the ball you had, and it took me a few games before I settled down and calmed my nerves.

You also had a lot less time on the ball in the first team and, if I'm honest, I was also awestruck. Like most youngsters at that time I collected the Panini stickers and all I could think about was that I was now playing against the guys I had collected stickers of for years.

Incidentally, my league debut was also a memorable day for Brian Irvine. With 15 minutes to go Jim Leighton dived bravely at the feet of Willie Jamieson but Willie's boot accidentally caught Jim on the face. He had to leave the field swathed in bandages – I think he ended up with stitches in wounds on his forehead and chin – and with no goalkeepers on the bench then, Brian took the gloves and kept Hamilton at bay for the remainder of the game.

My life changed that day. Across the road from Pittodrie was Bon Accord Golf Club where my dad was a member. As I was only 17 at the time I wasn't allowed in the main bar so even if I was in the squad for the game, I still had to sit with all the other youngsters with a bottle of Coke and a packet of crisps in the locker room. But after the Hamilton game that all changed. As I made my way back to the golf club after the game and headed for the locker room, I was intercepted and taken round to the main door. All of a sudden, I was in the main bar area with folk buying me pints and asking for my autograph. A week earlier I wasn't allowed anywhere near that part of the club but there I was, the new hero for the members.

I made my first start four days later against Alloa Athletic in the League Cup – Fergie praised me in the papers the next day which was a huge boost – but between then and the visit of Rangers to Pittodrie on 22 November, I had to content myself in the reserves, with only sporadic appearances for the first team. It was all good experience, but I was desperate to become the first choice at left-back. There were some memorable reserve games in that spell like the 3-3 draw against Rangers at Pittodrie and a 2-0 win over Celtic at Parkhead.

Rangers came to the north-east in November on the back of an inconsistent start to the Graeme Souness era. Although they had beaten us at Ibrox and won the League Cup, they had lost four of their first 17 league games to sit six points adrift of Celtic in fourth place. And with me filling the left-back berth, we inflicted defeat number five on them that afternoon. It was a scrappy game settled by a Davie Dodds goal after 19 minutes and Rangers' misery was compounded when Dave McPherson was ordered off on the stroke of half-time.

We beat Rangers that day with a new manager in the dugout. Alex Ferguson had been appointed to succeed Ron Atkinson at

Manchester United and Ian Porterfield was brought in to replace him. I found out when the news broke over the radio. I was driving my dad to the golf club and my initial reaction was one of concern. Here was the man who had believed in me, given me my first professional contract and first-team debut gone from the club. There was then uncertainty that the new manager would come in and not take a liking to me.

The next day at Pittodrie the atmosphere was funereal. It was a dull, grey day outside and with everyone on a downer it wasn't any brighter in the corridors inside the stadium. It was eerie, as if there had been a death in the family.

You had to feel for Ian, though. It was a bit like when David Moyes took over from Fergie at Manchester United; it was a real tall order to try and follow on from him after the success he had had. Ian was a great guy, but I don't think he realised that at that time at Aberdeen, you had to win. You had to go to places like Ibrox and Parkhead with the belief you could win down there. But Ian's pragmatic approach was summed up when we were drawing games against the likes of St Mirren and Morton. We would probably have been booed off the park, but Ian would come in and say to us that at least we had one more point than we did when the game kicked off at 3pm.

But Porterfield did have a good start to his tenure and almost completed an Old Firm double when we drew with league leaders Celtic four days after our win over Rangers. The usually reliable Jim Bett had a penalty saved by Pat Bonner after ten minutes, but we went in front four minutes after half-time when Alex McLeish headed in a terrific delivery from Bobby Connor. We held that lead until ten minutes to go when Celtic equalised in controversial circumstances.

Big Alex fouled Alan McInally and the referee, Bobby Cumming, awarded a penalty. Brian McClair took it, but his shot hit the bar. Mo Johnston struck the woodwork again when he pounced on the rebound and that kicked off a good old fashioned 'stramash' in the box that ended with Celtic being awarded a second penalty when Stewart McKimmie was adjudged to have handled the ball. McClair stepped up again and made no mistake this time.

I was praised for my performance that night – writing in the *Evening Times*, John Traynor said I was 'surely a player with a bright future' – and after my initial misgivings the new manager gave me a run in the team. The number three jersey was mine for all but two of the last 29 league matches of the season.

I was also at left-back for an epic Scottish Cup tie with Celtic. Having faced them three times in the league up to this point – each one ended 1-1 – we had also played them in the League Cup earlier in the season. That was at the quarter-final stage, with Celtic winning 4-2 on penalties after a 1-1 draw at Pittodrie. I came on as sub for Stewart McKimmie in that one just before the start of the last period of extra time but wasn't one of our penalty takers. The responsibility for those fell to Jim Bett and Peter Weir, who both scored, and Willie Miller and John Hewitt who missed their respective kicks.

Thus, in four matches we had failed to beat Celtic so we were looking to put that right when we faced them in front of the TV cameras on a freezing Sunday afternoon in February. Like the league fixture at Pittodrie back in November it was another tale of two penalties, with both converted this time. Celtic went ahead when Alan McInally capitalised after Jim Leighton slipped on the treacherous pitch and they doubled their lead eight minutes before half-time. Paul McStay surged into the box and went down under my challenge and the referee, George Smith, awarded a penalty. Brian McClair scored and our reign as Scottish Cup holders looked to be all but over.

But we fought back in the second half and a penalty from Jim Bett and a John Hewitt strike forced a replay at Parkhead the following midweek. That too ended in a draw – 0-0 this time – which sent both teams to Dens Park for a second replay. McClair's goal was sufficient to take Celtic through, a result that ended our 16-match unbeaten run.

As we were also off the pace in the title race – Aberdeen were seven points behind Celtic albeit with two games in hand – the focus after the Scottish Cup exit was to secure a UEFA Cup place for the following season. We managed to do that, and a key point gained came in the penultimate match of the season when Rangers came to Pittodrie.

You could sense the rivalry between the teams. Aberdeen had been at the top of the Scottish game for much of the 1980s but now Rangers were spending big money on the likes of Terry Butcher and Chris Woods and all that did was stoke the fire. Probably before that day our fans could sense the tide was turning and at the end of the 90 minutes that was confirmed.

The thing is, although I played, I have no recollection of it other than what I read in the evening newspaper. The game ended 1-1 and that coupled with Celtic's 2-1 defeat at home to Falkirk handed Rangers the title. But by then I was waking up on a hospital gurney still in my Aberdeen kit, boots and shin pads. I had no idea what had happened to get me there and I was surrounded by Rangers fans who were a bit worse for wear and had obviously hurt themselves.

I had suffered concussion, but it was only later that night when I got home and picked up the evening paper, the *Green Final*, that I found out more. The report in the paper talked about me receiving a yellow card for having a go at Ally McCoist. But what happened was, off the ball, Coisty caught me with a forearm smash. I think I staggered on for a wee while before Brian Grant was brought on to replace me after 31 minutes. The rules over concussions have changed now so I would have had to be out the team for a period of time. But it was different back then and I played in our last match of the season against Falkirk a week later.

In 1986/87 I also made my European debut. We were drawn to face FC Sion from Switzerland in the first round of the European Cup Winners' Cup and I was selected at left-back for the first leg at Pittodrie. I had been to European games at Pittodrie before and it was always packed but the atmosphere seemed to be different.

My direct opponent that night was a chap called Aziz Bouderbala. There was no video analysis in those days, so I was walking out from training the day before the game when Archie asked me if I had watched the World Cup in Mexico. He told me Bouderbala had played well for Morocco in the tournament, but I had no idea who he was. I was still a bit naïve, but I went out and had a good game against him.

This wasn't the first time Aberdeen had faced Sion. We had played them in the first round on the road to Gothenburg in 1982/83, battering them 7-0 at Pittodrie and winning 4-1 in the away leg. Clearly the Swiss didn't want a similar hiding on this occasion, so they played it tight and sat in. In the end a Jim Bett penalty and a goal from Paul Wright gave us a narrow 2-1 lead to take to Sion. But we couldn't hold on when we travelled to Sion two weeks later. I came on as sub for Brian Mitchell, but we had Jim Bett sent off and were hammered 3-0.

All in all, I enjoyed a good first season as part of the first team. I appeared in 34 of the 44 league games – all but two of them were as part of the starting line-up – and was part of a defensive unit that conceded only 29 goals in the league. I missed only two of the last 26 matches – a 1-0 home defeat against St Mirren at the end of March due to chickenpox, and a 1-1 draw against Hearts at Tynecastle in mid-April through suspension.

That run and indeed most of my appearances in 1986/87 had come under Ian Porterfield. At the end of the season, Ian Porterfield was very complimentary about me. He told the press that even though young players usually need a break every now and then, he never once thought of leaving me out the team.

I was flattered too when none other than Kenny Dalglish was rumoured to be interested in taking me to Liverpool. There was speculation that Bob Paisley, who had managed the great Liverpool side of the late 1970s and early '80s, and Ron Yeats, the legendary centre-half from Billy Shankly's team in the 1960s and now chief scout, had come to watch me when we beat Clydebank 5-0 at Kilbowie in January but nothing ever came of it. There was a rumour that Howard Kendall wanted to take me to Everton too but I didn't yet consider myself a regular in the Aberdeen first team so I was quite content making my way in the game with my local team rather than travelling further afield.

Indeed, I was so content that I put pen to paper and signed a four-year contract. The new deal came about as I was at the end of the 'two-year contract with two-year option' that Fergie had offered me. But Porterfield decided against exercising the two-year option and instead he offered me improved terms and a better deal, so I was pleased with that.

On top of all that I gained international recognition too, playing three times for Scotland's under-21s and gaining a cap in the first 'B' international for 30 years when Scotland drew 1-1 with France at Pittodrie in late April. Getting that recognition from my country and my manager was a huge boost. I had made some mistakes in the early games I had played but as tough as that was it was to be expected as I was still so young. It was about learning, and I expected to push on up the learning curve in 1987/88.

After staying close to home for our warm-up matches – we played the likes of Torquay United, Plymouth Argyle and Exeter City, with the Plymouth game particularly memorable for my old youth team buddy Joe Miller as he scored all our goals in our 4-2 win – the season started with an established back five of Leighton, McKimmie, McLeish, Miller and Robertson. And that was the foundation upon which we built an unbeaten start which ran until we faced Hearts at Tynecastle in early October. That was a top-of-the-table clash as we were both tied on 16 points after ten games. But despite going ahead through a Jim Bett penalty, we lost 2-1 and in so doing relinquished top spot in the league table.

I was absent from duty that midweek, though. We had reached the semi-final of the League Cup, beating Celtic 1-0 en route in the last eight, and were drawn to face Dundee at the neutral venue of Tannadice. Robert Connor and Brian Irvine scored in a 2-0 win but during the game I went in for a tackle and hurt my foot. The next day it was still sore, so I was sent for an X-ray, but it came back fine. I missed the next game against Hibs but came back for the second leg of the opening round of the UEFA Cup against Dublin side Bohemians. But I only lasted until half-time and after that a bone scan revealed a fracture. Not only did I miss the Hearts fixture, I also missed out when we faced Rangers at Hampden in the League Cup Final.

That was the first part of the trilogy of League Cup finals against them, but I was gutted to miss out as it would have been my first cup final. I knew if I had been fit, I would have been playing but I travelled down with the squad on the bus which I thought was a nice touch from the manager. It made me feel part of it as I also went into the dressing room before the game but it was still tough when I had to leave the lads and go up into the stand.

I watched an epic tussle that ended with six goals shared and Rangers winning 5-3 on penalties. When we came back from 2-1 down to lead 3-2 with ten minutes to go we looked set to win the trophies – the League Cup was sponsored by Skol who offered their own trophy as well as the traditional one – but Robert Fleck pounced with three minutes left to force extra time. With legs tiring there were chances in that additional half-hour, but it went to penalties. Rangers were flawless from 12 yards, scoring all five of their kicks. But we were not so fortunate and Peter Nicholas, a recent acquisition from Luton Town and one of our stand-out performers on the day, struck the top of the crossbar with his kick and Souness had more silverware to add to his collection.

As you can imagine, the dressing room I returned to when the game was over was subdued. But when I arrived, I was the subject of a lovely gesture from the manager. He gave me his medal and that says a lot about him. As I said, he was a great guy and it's a shame that it didn't work out for him at Aberdeen.

After missing a total of 14 league matches, I made my first-team comeback on 9 December in a 3-1 win over Falkirk at Pittodrie. And when we beat Morton 4-0 at the same venue three days later, we consolidated third place in the league. Celtic, in their centenary season, were leading the way on 37 points, one ahead of Hearts who were a point ahead of us.

We showed our title credentials before the end of the month when we went to Parkhead and drew 0-0 but we then lost twice back to back early in the New Year which was a big blow. The first loss was against Motherwell at Fir Park, but the most damaging defeat was the 2-1 reverse at home to Rangers.

Although we had lost to them in the League Cup Final, we had won the two league encounters – 2-0 at Pittodrie in August and 1-0 at Ibrox in November – and we were level on points going into the fixture. We were both three points behind Celtic – Rangers were ahead of us on goal difference – but goals from Gough and McCoist gave them only their second victory at Pittodrie since league reconstruction in 1975 and I don't think we really recovered after that.

Although we lost only twice in the league thereafter, we ended up fourth. Celtic were champions on 72 points, Hearts were runners-up on 62, Rangers were third on 60 and we ended up with 59. It was disappointing as we had been in contention for most of the season but, ultimately, too many draws and a lack of goals killed us. Out of 44 league games we drew 17 and we only managed 56 goals. In contrast, Celtic scored 79 and Rangers netted 85. Ian Porterfield had recruited Charlie Nicholas to try and add more firepower, but Charlie had managed just three goals in the 14 league games he played. Indeed, only one player, Jim Bett, made it into double figures in the league.

It was a bit of a coup for us to get Charlie. He had shot to fame with Celtic earlier in the decade and ended up at Arsenal. It didn't work out for him in London, so Aberdeen splashed out £400,000 to bring him back to Scotland to try and reignite his career. When he arrived, it was the closest I think we had ever come to seeing a pop star in Aberdeen. He showed up dressed like Bono from U2 and he was a superstar. A lot of people were in awe of him and I don't think we could quite believe that someone like Charlie Nicholas would come to Aberdeen.

From a personal point of view, I had another solid season. After coming back from the foot injury, I missed a further nine matches. The first, against St Johnstone in the Scottish Cup, was through suspension and I wasn't selected when we played Rangers in the league a week later. But my next spell on the sidelines was self-inflicted and I was lucky still to be an Aberdeen player at that time.

I didn't have an agent back then and I heard from a couple of journalists that Terry Venables, manager of Tottenham Hotspur, was interested in signing me. I ended up submitting a transfer request and got sucked into doing a newspaper article that pretty much said I was having a nightmare at Aberdeen and I wanted it to end. I crucified the club, saying that I had been brought up watching a successful Aberdeen team but the team I was in was dying and nowhere near the standard of previous Dons teams.

Understandably I got it tight from my team-mates for what had been written and I was summoned into the manager's office. In his hand he had the envelope containing my transfer request and on his desk was the newspaper article. He said he could deal with the transfer request but couldn't accept what was in print in front of him. I was fined two weeks' wages and dropped from the first team.

I thought I was finished at Aberdeen. I missed a total of four league games – Willie Falconer wore the number three jersey in my absence – before Barbara in the office called and said the manager wanted to see me. We were due to play Dundee United in the Scottish Cup semi-final and the manager asked me how I was feeling. When I said I was fine he told me I was playing against United and all that had happened had been forgotten.

We drew that match 0-0 and the replay ended 1-1 before we lost the second replay 1-0. For a side who had become so accustomed to success, this was now a second season without a major trophy so the pressure on the manager and the players was starting to build.

I managed to make 33 appearances in all, and I now felt I was an established first-team player. Aside from the spell out the team due to the newspaper interview, if I was fit, I was selected. The next three seasons would see me cement my place at left-back as Aberdeen emerged as the main challengers to Rangers' domestic dominance.

CHAPTER 4

WINNER

WE WERE put through our paces on our return for pre-season training ahead of the 1988/89 season at the usual venue of Seaton Park. To start it was almost all running and no ball work which I hated. We would change at Pittodrie and run to Seaton Park, a distance of around one and a half miles. Once there we embarked on something called the 'Seaton Run' which was brutal. It was around tracks and up steep hills and the coaches used to hide behind trees on the route to make sure we kept going. It was a hard shift.

Our warm-up games this time took us to Rothes. As part of the football club's golden jubilee celebrations we were invited to take part in the Mackessack Quaich Jubilee Tournament and we emerged victorious, beating the hosts 8-0 before seeing off Hearts 4-1 in the final. Preparations were complete when we played Feyenoord and Royal Antwerp in the Rotterdam Tournament.

We played in those matches with a new goalkeeper. Jim Leighton had signed for Manchester United, so we went out and spent £300,000 to recruit Theo Snelders from Twente

Enschede. It was a tall order for Theo to take over the gloves from a stalwart like Jim who had been a huge part of the success the club had enjoyed. But the big man rose to the challenge and as part of the back four that played for the majority of the season in front of him, it was reassuring for me to know that we had such a solid and dependable goalkeeper behind us.

It looked like we were still haunted by the affliction that had seen us draw so many games when we started the league campaign with four successive draws. But they formed part of a run that saw us unbeaten in the league until Rangers defeated us 1-0 at Ibrox in late November. That was the third time we had faced Rangers that season. And the first match we played against them is memorable for all the wrong reasons, for that was the game in which Ian Durrant's promising career came to a shuddering halt.

It was a hotly anticipated encounter as both sides had started the season well and there was always a bit of an edge when Aberdeen faced Rangers. I recall the incident happening, but we didn't really know at the time how serious Durrant's injury was. It was only when we got back into training on the Monday that stories and pictures started to appear in the press and we suddenly realised that one of the most talented footballers in the country faced a lengthy spell on the sidelines.

I had my own problems with my knees later in my career but at that point I don't think there was much awareness of cruciate ligament injuries. I was fortunate to play alongside Ian when I went to Rangers and I saw at that time the size his knee had swelled to. The fact he was the player he was after the injury just showed how good he could have become had he not sustained the damage he did that day. I have no doubt he could have gone on to play for the likes of Real Madrid or Barcelona.

The result – a 2-1 win for us – seemed incidental after finding out about Durrant but there was no time to dwell on it as we were set to face each other again 15 days later in the League Cup Final at Hampden.

Having missed out 12 months earlier through injury I was determined to be fit for this one. I had missed a couple of league games at the end of September, but I had been back in the fold for the four matches leading up to the final. I was so excited to play in my first domestic cup final, but I chose this occasion for probably my worst appearance for Aberdeen. I had an absolute nightmare.

I don't know if it was nerves or the big crowd – the official attendance was recorded as 72,122 – but I just didn't play well. I was culpable for the concession of the first goal when my throw-in back to Theo was so poor that the ball barely reached the penalty area. Kevin Drinkell intercepted and rounded Theo who had no option but to bring him down. Ally McCoist scored the penalty and in so doing kicked off another epic joust.

Davie Dodds equalised but shortly afterwards we should have been behind again. I got sucked into a challenge with Drinkell who spun away from me and his ball across the face of goal was palmed away from McCoist by Theo.

Rangers eventually went ahead again ten minutes after the restart when Ian Ferguson scored with a spectacular scissors kick. It was end to end after that and Coisty hit the top of the crossbar before Doddsie scored again to level it up at 2-2 with a looping header. And we had a gilt-edged chance to win it when Jim Bett went through one-on-one with Chris Woods but dragged his shot wide of the far post.

Extra time looked to be beckoning for a second successive year until I intervened again. Gary Stevens burst through from the right-back position and I tried to intercept the pass he made. But the ball ricocheted off my thigh into his path and it took a splendid save from Theo to stop him scoring the winner. The ball spun wide for a corner kick and at that point my infinite wisdom kicked in. Throughout the match I had been picking up Richard Gough at set-pieces for some reason so when Brian Irvine came on as sub for Neil Simpson, I thought it made more sense for him to pick up Goughie. Sure enough the corner came in, Goughie beat Brian in the air and the ball broke to McCoist inside the six-yard box. A predator of Ally's calibre doesn't miss from there and the League Cup was bedecked in red, white and blue ribbons for a third successive season.

After that game was probably the lowest I had ever felt in all my time at Aberdeen. A few weeks earlier I had been ordered off when we exited the UEFA Cup against Dynamo Dresden. We drew 0-0 at Pittodrie in the first leg so the tie was in the balance when we travelled to East Germany for the return leg. And that was an eventful trip on and off the park.

I was sharing a room with the late Stevie Gray and we got duped by a guy outside the hotel we were staying in. We were led to believe that if we gave this man pounds sterling, he would give us in return a significant amount of East German Deutsche Marks. This was what was termed 'black money'. Stevie and I gave him what we had – I think it was something in the region of £100 – and took our marks to a bureau de change on our return home. Our faces must have been a picture when the travel agent told us what we passed over the counter was worthless!

In terms of the game itself, I was up against a striker called Ulf Kirsten. It was a night of torrential rain in Dresden and early in the game, I hit Kirsten hard. That was something I liked to do in every game but on this occasion it earned me a booking. The rain made the playing surface slick, something I liked as I felt it gave me a bit of an edge when timing a sliding tackle. However, later in the first half as I slid in to thwart Kirsten again, he got a little nick on the ball and I couldn't stop. I wiped him out and the inevitable second yellow card was brandished by the Swiss referee.

By then we were 1-0 down so my dismissal left us really up against it. As I trooped up the tunnel there were lines of soldiers either side with bayonets. I have to admit I was a bit scared and my misery was compounded when the vice-chairman, Ian Donald, gave me dog's abuse as I left the field. As if to rub salt into the wound Kirsten scored a second for Dresden midway through the second half and we were out the competition. We stayed over that night and it's fair to say I wasn't the most popular player in the squad. As a youngster that hit me hard and perhaps that had an effect on my performance against Rangers too.

But the manager was excellent with me. Alex Smith had taken charge of the club at the start of the season after Ian Porterfield left and I was used to how he worked as I had been coached by him at youth level with Scotland. I had trained with Alex when he arrived at the club back in April when he put the youth squad through their paces before we went to Switzerland and, given he had won the Scottish Cup with St Mirren in 1986/87, he was a better man for the Aberdeen job than Ian.

Unlike Ian he knew the Scottish game and his man-management was excellent. Alex was actually co-manager with

Jocky Scott, but I always felt Alex had a bit more authority. He was very good with young players like me and wasn't scared to introduce the likes of Eoin Jess and Scott Booth into the first team either. In that respect he was similar to Fergie.

Jocky was a lot tougher. He would be the one to come in at half-time and slaughter you if you weren't playing well and he'd be on your case during the week in training too. But he had a softer side, and the partnership with him and Alex worked really well. They both took time after the final to talk to me and told me it had just been one of those games. Within a couple of days, I was back to my old self again and ready to get my teeth into another tilt at the Premier Division title.

Alex had also shown how much he valued me around that time when he rejected an offer from Coventry City. Their manager John Sillett, who had led them to the FA Cup in 1986/87, had reportedly had a bid of £500,000 turned down before he tried again with a 'name your price' offer. When that was turned down, he offered £300,000 plus the guy who had scored the winning goal in the FA Cup Final, Keith Houchen. But Alex rebuffed them all and stated that there was no chance of me or any other 'quality player' leaving the club. Alex labelling me as a quality player and the fact that Coventry, who were a top club in England at that time, were interested in me certainly boosted my confidence.

But it wasn't long until I was back in the doldrums. Despite suffering our first league defeat of the season at Ibrox a month after the final we were sitting third in the table when we faced Dundee at Dens Park on Hogmanay. On the day we didn't play well, and a Tommy Coyne double consigned us to our second loss. I ended up on the treatment table afterwards too as I injured my knee and needed exploratory surgery.

I came back on 25 February for a league game against Hearts at Pittodrie. We won 3-0 and it was from my cross that Paul Wright scored the opening goal. The second replay against United was scheduled for the following Monday night but I wasn't selected. The knee injury flared up and I didn't see action again until we played Celtic at Pittodrie on 29 April.

That was a pivotal fixture. We needed to win to keep ourselves in the title race, but we drew 0-0 to hand Rangers the championship. We got a wee bit of revenge when we spoiled their title party by winning 3-0 at Ibrox on the final day of the season but it was another barren season at Pittodrie.

So 1989/90 was therefore a huge season for Aberdeen. Our fans were craving a return to the silverware-lined days of the early 1980s and we came very close to delivering a clean sweep of domestic honours for them.

We started with a few games in the Netherlands and a 7-0 thumping of Inverness Clachnacuddin – I scored – but we didn't begin the season at all well. We lost 1-0 to Rangers at Ibrox in our fourth league game, we went out of the UEFA Cup against Rapid Vienna and then lost back-to-back league matches against Dundee United and Hearts. That left us languishing in fifth place in the table, albeit just two points behind leaders Celtic.

The 3-1 defeat against Hearts took place just a week before we were due to face Rangers in the League Cup Final. But despite our recent form, the manager made only two changes, Brian Grant replacing Craig Robertson and Eoin Jess coming in for Ian Cameron who had suffered concussion against Hearts. And that afternoon at Hampden turned our season around.

Our preparation was the same as it had been in the previous two years. We stayed in the old Excelsior hotel at Glasgow

Airport and on the day of the game, we would do some light training at Abbotsinch, not far from the airport. I think that was the management team's way of keeping us relaxed and it wasn't until we left for Hampden about 1pm that they named the team.

I had scored a rare goal – my first for Aberdeen – earlier in the campaign in our 2-0 win over Albion Rovers in the opening round and home wins over Airdrie and St Mirren set up a semi-final against Celtic at Hampden. Ian Cameron, who had arrived from St Mirren, scored the only goal in that one and we edged ahead in the final too. Bobby Connor lobbed the ball into the Rangers penalty area and Paul Mason looped a header back across goal and it crept in at the post.

But we were in front for a mere 12 minutes and the equalising goal came about in controversial circumstances. Ally McCoist and Willie Miller jousted for the ball and, with McCoist backing in, he rolled round Willie and fell to the ground. The referee, George Smith, felt Willie had fouled Coisty and awarded Rangers a penalty. Alex McLeish was booked for protesting the decision, but it mattered little as Mark Walters stepped up and sent Theo the wrong way from the spot.

We were now in the guts of a third classic contest and big Theo kept us level in the second half with a fine one-handed save from a Trevor Steven shot. Rangers struck the woodwork a couple of times too, but we were still level at 1-1 at the end of 90 minutes so the match went to extra time. And we edged it when we won a throw-in on the left after 103 minutes. I hurled the ball into the heart of the penalty area and when it broke to Paul Mason, standing 12 yards from goal, he rifled a shot past Chris Woods.

We clung on a bit after that and Theo had a couple of superb saves, one of which from a McCoist header was world-class, but when the referee blew the final whistle I got such a rush of adrenalin. After the disappointment of my performance the previous year I now had my first medal in one of the major competitions, but it wasn't my first as a professional footballer.

That had come a couple of years earlier when I had been part of the squad that won the annual Tennent's Sixes competition. Held in January each year since its inception in 1984, all the Premier Division clubs took part and in 1987 at the SECC, Aberdeen were drawn in Group 1 with Hamilton Academical and Hibernian. Ian Porterfield selected a really strong squad with the likes of Jim Leighton, John McMaster, Alex McLeish, and Neil Simpson taking part.

I wasn't aware going into the tournament how different it would be, with sin bins and using the walls that surrounded the playing arena to make some of your passes. We topped the group thanks to a 5-1 win over Hamilton and a 4-1 victory over Hibernian and made the last four when we beat Falkirk in the quarter-final. At that stage we beat Hamilton and that set up a final against a Hearts side who had thrashed Dundee 8-1 in their semi-final.

The final comprised two ten-minute periods and we looked to be in for a similar hiding when we fell 3-1 behind. Throughout the weekend the manager had rotated the players such that you would go on for three or four minutes then come off, but you always swapped with the same player. At that stage of the game I was all set to go back on but my performance up to that point must have been really bad as I motioned to go on to the park but Porterfield pulled me back and told me not to bother. It was a good call too as Neil Simpson pulled it back to 3-2 before Paul Wright scored two goals to complete his hat-trick and earn us a 4-3 win and the only silverware under Ian Porterfield.

Shortly after the League Cup Final we bolstered our attacking options when we spent a record fee of £650,000 to bring in Hans Gillhaus from PSV Eindhoven. A Dutch international, he had lost his place at PSV to Romário and he made his Aberdeen debut against Dunfermline at East End Park on 18 November. And inside the opening 15 minutes he showed exactly why the club had seen fit to spend the money they did to get him.

I was involved in his first goal, my cross from the left wing to the back post finding Brian Irvine who headed the ball back across goal. Gillhaus then executed a superb overhead kick to send the ball beyond Ian Westwater. And a few minutes later Brian won the ball in the air again and this time Hans used his head to nod the ball into the net from six yards. The scoring was completed at 3-0 that day when I was afforded plenty of space in the six-yard box to head home a corner from Jim Bett.

That win left us in a three-way tie at the top of the league with Hearts and Rangers. We each had 17 points, but Hearts had played one match more. Our game in hand was the following midweek against Rangers and Hans scored again to give us a precious 1-0 win and take us to the summit. It was a good win for us as Rangers hadn't conceded a goal since losing to us in the League Cup Final and they pounded us in the second half, but we stood firm.

A 5-0 win over St Mirren at home – featuring a Charlie Nicholas hat-trick – kept us out in front but December hit us hard and we lost our place at the top. The month started with a 1-0 defeat at Parkhead and I was culpable for the concession of the only goal of the game. My former team-mate John Hewitt crossed into the box and I rose to meet the ball. However, rather than use my head, I flapped my hand in the air and the ball struck it. It was a clear penalty, and it became even more frustrating when watching the game back as the ball seemed to be drifting harmlessly wide of the goal until my intervention. Andy Walker scored from the spot and now we were only top of the table on goal difference.

A 2-0 win over Dundee United and a 1-1 draw against Hearts at Tynecastle kept us top at the halfway stage but we were toppled on Boxing Day when we faced Hibernian at Pittodrie. Little did I know it at the time, but that match would be my last for Aberdeen for four months.

The festive period is always a busy one and we were due to face Motherwell at Fir Park four days after taking on Hibs. We went into that encounter without Theo who was off to the Netherlands for knee surgery and less than ten minutes in we lost Gillhaus when he damaged ligaments. We lost the match too, former Don Stevie Archibald scoring the opening goal for Hibs in their 2-1 win. Rangers, who had beaten St Mirren 1-0 three days earlier, were now top, two points clear of ourselves with Celtic a further point behind in third place.

We were determined to stay in the hunt, however, and we had an early opportunity to get back on track against Motherwell. In our preparation we played a practice match at Pittodrie on a pitch that was bone hard because of the freezing conditions. After running down the wing to cross the ball into the penalty area I slipped and fell awkwardly. It was a sore one and it was eventually established that I had broken my fifth metatarsal which required surgery. It wasn't an easy procedure. As there is very little blood circulation on the outside of your foot, I had to get a bone graft from my hip and a metal plate put in. I wouldn't see action again until we faced Dundee United in the Scottish Cup semi-final at Tynecastle in April.

My recovery was tortuous. I couldn't do any load-bearing fitness work so a lady by the name of Pamela Smith took me to Robert Gordon's Institute of Technology every day at 6am. That was the place offshore workers undertook survival courses and the water in there is close to North Sea temperatures. It was so deep you couldn't touch the bottom of the pool but as tough as it was at the time, going there got me back on track. That allied to the fact my fitness was so good meant I only needed one reserve game – a 0-0 draw against East Stirling – prior to making my first-team comeback. In fact, I think I only trained for something like four days ahead of the semi-final.

Our run to that match against United had seen us hammer Partick Thistle 6-2 and narrowly beat Morton 2-1 at home before comprehensively beating Hearts 4-1 in the quarter-final. And we were excellent against United too, goals from Brian Irvine and Hans Gillhaus adding to own goals from Paatelainen and Van der Hoorn to book a date with Celtic in the end-of-season showpiece.

We still had an outside chance of catching Rangers in the title race. We had lost 2-0 at Ibrox in January but although our form was pretty erratic after that – we only won six of the remaining 14 league matches – we hung in there. But our hopes ended on 21 April when losing 1-0 against Hearts while Rangers were defeating Dundee United 1-0 at Tannadice. I then missed our penultimate league game before returning for the final fixture against Celtic at Parkhead. This was a dress rehearsal for the

Scottish Cup Final ten days later and, after falling behind early on, we roared back to win 3-1.

We went in without seven players who would be considered first-team regulars. That meant guys like Eoin Jess and Scott Booth made the starting XI. And it was Jess who scored twice to overturn the early lead Celtic had established before Graham Watson completed the win with our third goal.

Celtic were having a dire season and needed a win to ensure European football for 1990/91. Alex Smith was pilloried for what many perceived as the fielding of a weakened team, but we proved yet again how good the youth setup was at Aberdeen. And when Dundee United gained the point they needed to clinch the final UEFA Cup slot through the league, the stakes were now even higher for Celtic at Hampden; they had to beat us to gain a place in the European Cup Winners' Cup the following season.

It was no surprise that most players who had missed the league match with Celtic were back for the final. But Willie Miller, who had played at Parkhead – one of only 15 appearances he made in the Premier Division that season – was absent. It was a blow to lose our captain, but Brian Irvine had been a superb deputy for most of the season and he would have a telling contribution to make on what proved an historic occasion at Hampden.

The game itself was drab and at the end of 120 minutes it was stalemate. That meant for the first time a Scottish Cup Final would be decided on penalties. Not being a renowned marksman from 12 yards, I didn't think I would have to take a kick. We hadn't chosen penalty takers before the game, but I knew when Jocky got his pen and paper out to note down our five at the end of extra time, I wouldn't be one of them. However, it transpired that just about everyone left on the field had to step up.

Celtic went first which immediately put the pressure on the lads taking penalties for Aberdeen. But they missed their kick, so the pendulum immediately swung towards us. And we maintained the advantage when Bett, Connor and Gillhaus all converted their penalties. Peter Grant and Paul McStay did likewise for Celtic. Taking our fourth penalty, Brian Grant had the chance to heap more pressure on Celtic's next taker, but he missed and, when Tommy Coyne netted, it was all-square again at 3-3.

I still didn't think at this stage I would be required to take a penalty. But the quality of the kicks that followed – each one clinically despatched into the corner of the net – meant that I was up. When Paul Elliot slotted away his penalty to make in 7-6 to Celtic all we had left who had not taken penalties were myself, Brian Irvine, a young lad called Graham Watson and big Theo. I remember looking at young Graham and thinking that I would have to grow a set of balls and volunteer as it wasn't fair to put the pressure on him. But as I walked forward towards the Celtic end with the ball in my hands to take the penalty, I genuinely had no idea what I was doing. And when I say walked, I should say limped as I was carrying an injury.

Towards the end of extra time I had suffered a dead leg after a challenge with Mike Galloway, so I essentially limped to the penalty spot and put the ball down. I only took a couple of steps back as I didn't think I was fit enough to take a longer run-up. The plan was to hit the ball to Pat Bonner's right, but I didn't connect well and it went straight down the middle. Had I struck the ball properly I reckon Bonner would have saved it, but my effort trundled into the net and we were level at 7-7.

Young Graham had to step up next and kept cool to draw us level at 8-8 and then Theo got down low to parry Anton Rogan's penalty away. Brian Irvine now had a kick to win the Scottish Cup for Aberdeen. The big man was coolness personified as he stroked the ball into the net, and we surged forward to celebrate with him.

When we won the League Cup earlier on in the season, we had the open-top bus parade, and we had the same again this time. That was pretty special and both occasions took me back to when I was a youngster watching the parade in 1976. Here I was now on the bus showing off the trophy to throngs of supporters that had gathered on the streets of the city.

The bus started out on the Bridge of Dee just before you got into Aberdeen but unlike when I watched the parade some 14 years earlier, we didn't go to Pittodrie. Instead the bus took us to the Town Hall, and we came up to a rapturous reception on a balcony. When I went to Rangers and didn't get the chance to do this kind of thing it made me cherish the memories of these occasions more. It was a real fun time.

There was a real confidence about the club when we gathered ahead of 1990/91. Although our transfer budget and wage bill dwarfed that of Rangers, we had shown that we could compete with them. The management team had been shrewd in the transfer market and had continued to blood young players too. Although Willie Miller retired through injury in the summer, we had a ready-made replacement in Brian Irvine and we set off for the Netherlands for the FC Twente tournament looking to finalise our plans for a push for the Premier Division title.

And it was in that tournament that I suffered one of my biggest embarrassments on a football field. In one of the games the right-winger tore me apart. No matter what I did, I couldn't get near him. After the game both teams got together in the bar for a few drinks and I remember seeing this guy, chain-smoking and necking pints of beer. Lo and behold, when I pointed him out to Theo, the big man told me that this was the same winger that had been running rings round me during the game!

Nevertheless, we won the tournament and burst out the blocks when the league action got under way. After beating Hibs 2-0 at home on the opening day, we went to Parkhead and won 3-0. Paul Mason, Hans Gillhaus and Bobby Connor got the goals and Bobby, in particular, had a great start to the season. He had been the player of the tournament in the Netherlands and this was the second successive league game in which he scored.

Bobby was technically gifted, like Peter Weir who had been part of the team that won the European Cup Winners' Cup a few years earlier. Although he usually played on the left-hand side of midfield, he wouldn't be the type of player to beat the full-back and get crosses in. Instead he would usually go inside and link up the play and his ability meant he could fill in for me at left-back if I was injured. He wasn't afraid to work back either and I knew if I went forward he would sit in. He was a real unsung hero and he helped me a lot.

I scored when we dropped our first point of the season in a 1-1 draw against Dunfermline at East End Park, and another draw against Dundee United and a narrow win over St Mirren kept the confidence high ahead of our League Cup semi-final against Rangers.

All the talk ahead of the game was of the Rangers captain, Terry Butcher, being dropped but his absence didn't affect his team who won 1-0 thanks to a goal from Trevor Steven. And we suffered a real hangover from that defeat as three days later we went to Perth to face St Johnstone and lost 5-0. The Saints had just been promoted so this was a real shock at the time as no one expected us to take such a hiding. I didn't help our cause either as I was given a straight red card for a rash challenge on Allan Moore after just half an hour.

That was my second dismissal of the season. The other had come in more comical circumstances on the pre-season tour in the Netherlands. I was on a yellow card and gave away a free kick. I went to kick the ball away but as I was about to blast it, I realised I would get another yellow so I drew back and chipped the ball instead. However, there was a fence around the pitch and my chip cleared the fence and the referee decided that merited a second yellow card and an early bath for me.

The red card in Perth meant I missed our next league match through suspension – incidentally, the only one I would miss all season – when we drew 0-0 against Rangers at home. We lost Theo that day when he broke his cheekbone following an accidental clash with Ally McCoist, but we were still matching Rangers stride for stride in the title race. We thumped Hearts and Celtic at Pittodrie and chalked up a 4-0 win over St Mirren at Love Street. There was also a thrilling 3-2 win over Dundee United that featured an Eoin Jess hat-trick.

United had been top of the table a couple of weeks earlier, a position they had cemented by beating Rangers 2-1 at Ibrox. But our victory over them took us to the summit, albeit for a mere 24 hours until Rangers defeated Celtic the following day. The only thing separating us was Rangers' superior goal difference.

But a gap started to emerge when we endured a dreadful spell in December and January. We lost 1-0 against Hearts at Tynecastle then drew 1-1 at home with Motherwell. And although we did well to battle back from 2-0 down at Ibrox to draw 2-2, defeats early in the New Year against Dundee United and Celtic left us seven points adrift of Rangers with only 13 games left to play. And when Motherwell eliminated us from the Scottish Cup a week after we lost to Celtic, there were growing calls from the supporters for a change of management. But what followed was a remarkable turnaround.

I don't think anyone genuinely believed we could actually catch Rangers, so we started focusing on picking up points to secure qualification for Europe. With the pressure off we started winning games, beating Hearts 5-0 and following that with a 1-0 win in Perth against St Johnstone. Our next fixture was crucial. We faced Rangers at Pittodrie on 2 March still sitting seven points behind our opponents. In these days of two points for a win this was pretty much win or bust for us.

But we got the victory – Hans Gillhaus scoring the only goal from my cross – and that breathed new life into us. After successive defeats at the end of January we now had three wins in a row, and we would drop just one more point between then and the last match of the season. Slowly but surely, we chipped away at Rangers' lead and all of a sudden when we beat St Johnstone 2-1 in our penultimate game and Rangers lost against Motherwell at Fir Park, we were top of the league on goal difference.

Rangers' game finished later than ours. When we first got into the dressing room Rangers were 2-0 down which meant we would still be in second place and therefore have to go to Ibrox and win to claim the title. However, a matter of seconds later we heard that Motherwell had scored again which pushed Aberdeen into pole position. All we needed to do now was draw at Ibrox in the last game of the season and we would be champions. There was a burst of celebration in the dressing room when the news came through from Motherwell. Rangers were ravaged by injuries, so I think the feeling was that this was going to be it for us. However, although I was still young, I knew going to places like Ibrox looking to play for a draw was a tough ask so I still felt we had a bit to do to get over the line.

We had a good week building up to the final day and there was a confidence that we could do it. Ibrox was getting renovated at the time so, with the away dressing room out of commission, we got changed in a portacabin. And when I came in after my warm-up it was shaking. The Rangers fans had got into the ground early and the place was rocking. The fans were singing and stamping their feet and I recall looking at Paul Mason and saying that we had no chance in an atmosphere like this. It's often said that the fans can be a 12th man and worth a goal of a start when they are on song and I certainly felt that was the case that afternoon.

Yet we had chances early on. Jim Bett volleyed over the bar and Hans Gillhaus and Peter van de Ven had good opportunities too. Had we silenced the crowd by scoring first we might have had a chance but looking back now I feel our attitude that day was that we would just try and hang in there. Had we played the way we had played since beating Rangers in March – on the front foot – with them having so many players playing with injuries the result may have been different.

As it was, Rangers took the lead just before half-time when Mark Hateley towered above Alex McLeish and headed the ball beyond Michael Watt. Theo hadn't played since the end of March and that afternoon Hateley terrorised Michael. He scored again in the second half when Watt fumbled a shot from Mo Johnston. Rangers were champions for the third successive season and Aberdeen once again had to be content with the runners-up spot.

And that was that for me at Aberdeen. My contract was up, and I felt it was time for a change. And ironically the venue where I played my last game for Aberdeen would be the one at which I would be plying my trade for the next few years.

CHAPTER 5

IT'S RANGERS FOR ME

I DIDN'T ask Aberdeen for a transfer, but I felt it was time to go. I had been a first-team regular for five years, yet I was only offered a modest increase in my personal terms. Looking back now, I don't think Aberdeen wanted to keep me and I felt they were starting to become something of a selling club.

To highlight how highly thought of I was, I was the only first-team player who didn't have a club car. As part of the negotiations for a new deal I enquired about getting one only to be told I wasn't a big enough personality. That really stuck in my throat as I knew that some of the players in the reserves had one. And to compound matters, when Theo Snelders' car became available I wasn't given it. Instead the club offered to sell it to me! At that point the penny dropped that I was a marketable asset and Aberdeen were looking to cash in.

My agent, Jim McArthur, had started talking to clubs about me and one man he spoke to was Graeme Souness. Graeme was keen on me moving to Glasgow to join Rangers although I thought I had fucked things up when I got sent off at St Johnstone. As I said, my challenge that day was rash, and I was guilty of doing a few rash things in my days at Aberdeen. I thought Souness might take a dim view of that but when Jim spoke to him, he said that, on the contrary, it showed I had a bit of devil in me and he liked that.

Jim pretty much verbally agreed with Graeme that I would be going to Rangers but all of a sudden it looked like the deal was off. I remember being on the minibus back to Pittodrie after training and the radio was on. There was a breaking news story that Souness was leaving Rangers and going to manage Liverpool. As we were going toe to toe with Rangers for the title, the news was met with whoops of joy from the Aberdeen players. I think some of them thought that this was a pivotal moment in the title race and the odds were now in our favour to bring the Premier Division championship back to Aberdeen for the first time since 1985.

I, however, was the only one not celebrating. Deep down I was thinking that the big move would now be off but only a couple of weeks later I got the reassurance I was looking for. Graeme's assistant, Walter Smith, had taken over the reins from him and he indicated to my agent that he still wanted to sign me. And five days before that decisive Saturday which determined the destination of the league championship trophy, I met with Walter and we shook hands and agreed I would sign for Rangers.

Walter was brilliant. The first thing he said to me was that if I looked after him, he would look after me. He knew it was probably going to take me a bit of time to settle in at Rangers but if he or the team were under any pressure, he never really showed it. I really enjoyed working for him.

In the six years I worked under him I got a bollocking once. That came pretty early in my time there when we lost 1-0 to

Hibs in the League Cup semi-final. He had a real go at me and told me that I was a Rangers player now and there was no place to hide. If I wasn't having a good game – and I had a poor one that night – he told me I still had to look for the ball. If I didn't it would be like playing with ten men and he wouldn't tolerate that. He said that even if I got it and gave it away, I still had to want the ball. I wasn't exactly confident in my ability when I first went to Rangers so when things weren't going well like that night, I admit there were times I didn't want the ball. But strangely Walter's words gave me confidence. He was never one for crucifying you for every mistake you made. That made you feel more at ease.

It wasn't an easy time for the family, though. Given the fractious relationship between Rangers and Aberdeen it was inevitable I was going to get a bit of stick. But my brother Michael, who is 12 years younger than me, ended up getting bullied in school which was really upsetting. And it didn't get any better as the years progressed and Kym and I were abused when we attended the League Cup semi-final between Aberdeen and Celtic at Ibrox in October 1994 to such an extent that we had to leave early.

I decided we would sit in with the Aberdeen fans in the Copland Road Stand. I still didn't think I was anything special and felt I was just a normal guy. I was a bit naïve, though, and I didn't fully understand the intensity of the rivalry between Aberdeen and Rangers. Kym and I were joined by a mate of mine, Sam Kerr, and we were a bit late arriving. Shortly afterwards the abuse started, and it was verbal at first. I was then spat at and coins were thrown too. Eventually the police came over and said that if this continued then we would have to be moved to another part of the stadium for our own safety. Kym was having none of it, though. She was adamant that as we had done nothing wrong we shouldn't have to move – how the police were supposed to relocate 5,000 Aberdeen fans I don't know – but eventually we left and I was back home before half-time.

When I signed in 1991 these were pre-Bosman days, so the transfer fee was settled by a tribunal. Essentially, Rangers argued their case, Aberdeen did likewise, and the tribunal came up with a price. And for me the magic number was £970,000. Was that a burden for me? To be honest, as much as I wasn't the most assured when it came to my ability and being good enough to play at this level, the fee actually boosted my confidence. It was a real boost that the best team in Scotland were prepared to pay that kind of money to get me.

I joined Rangers at the same time as Andy Goram and Stuart McCall. The three-foreigner rule had just been introduced for European football, so Walter's first task was to add more tartan talent to the squad. Goram had the unenviable task of replacing Chris Woods in goal, while Stuart was going to be up against the likes of Trevor Steven for a berth in the midfield.

At left-back my main competition looked like being Stuart Munro. He had been very much an unsung hero after signing from Alloa Athletic in 1984 but not long after I came in, he joined Blackburn Rovers. That only really left youngsters like Chris Vinnicombe and Tom Cowan, so I knew if I kept my form up, I would be on the team sheet most weeks.

I returned after my summer break and reported to Ibrox for pre-season training. I had come down the night before and stayed in the Holiday Inn and when I pushed open the big oak front doors at Ibrox for the first time, I was met by Stan, the commissioner. He made a phone call and the kit man, Jimmy Bell, emerged to take me down to the dressing room. It's only a short walk but it seemed to take forever. And then when I walked into the dressing room, I saw guys like Terry Hurlock, Mark Hateley, Mark Walters and Mo Johnston. My first reaction was that I didn't belong there.

I was overawed but then Jimmy gave me my training number – this was the era before squad numbers – and I was handed number six. The previous occupier of that position had been Terry Butcher, the cornerstone of the Rangers revolution. Jimmy put it mildly when he said I had big shoes to fill! But I must have done okay as when I left Rangers in the summer of 1997, Jimmy said that I certainly filled Terry's shoes which meant a lot.

Upon signing for Rangers, you are immediately taken by the traditions of the club. You had to report every day wearing collar and tie – something that dated back to the days of Bill Struth – but what also struck me was that no one thought they were better than anyone else. This was a squad full of superstars, but you wouldn't have known it. And where I changed was near the 'lively' corner of the dressing room that contained the likes of Ian Durrant and Ally McCoist. We didn't have a lot of bad spells when I was at Rangers but even when we did those lads never changed, the humour and the banter continued and that was excellent for team spirit.

Soon after I arrived at Ibrox – 13 July to be exact – I found myself in the Tuscan Hills. Graeme Souness had had experience of the Il Ciocco complex when he was playing at Sampdoria and when he became Rangers manager he took the players there. Walter was now in charge and he decided to follow suit. And with the site being situated 700 metres above sea level, the training there was among the toughest I ever experienced in my career.

It was solid running, and we didn't see much of the ball until we faced a team of waiters on the last day. It was a real slog and although the sessions at Aberdeen were very good, it wasn't anything like this as all the physical conditioning was done in Scotland. But the tough training wasn't the only challenge I faced. We were there for a fortnight and in those days there were no mobile phones or WiFi and the training base had limited internet access. That left you feeling as if you were shut off from the world and the only way I could really contact Kym was through the phone in the hotel room.

When training was done – and most days we did double sessions – it was difficult to pass the time. I roomed with our Dutch winger, Pieter Huistra, and until he left to go to Japan in 1995, we always shared a room on away trips. Sharing with Pieter was good for me as, like me, he was a shy guy. I have to admit I was intimidated by some of the big personalities in the squad so the similarity in our characters helped me a lot at the time. Pieter spent his spare time watching the Tour de France but most of the TV channels were in Italian which wasn't ideal.

Mo Johnston and Terry Hurlock were still part of the squad then and, although both would soon be off to pastures new, wee Mo was responsible for my first pummelling as a Rangers player. After the last training session, we were allowed a night out and en route to a pub called The Skylab I had to go through my initiation on the bus. That involved going to the front and singing a song. To be honest that had preyed on my mind for most of the week due to the fact I couldn't sing and was so quiet. But Mo stitched me up as he recommended I sing 'The

Northern Lights of Old Aberdeen'. I think I managed to belt out the first line before I was booed off and taken up the back of the bus for a bit of a beating up.

When we came back to Scotland, we played a few friendlies. These are great for getting match sharpness, but they also gave me a chance to get to know my new team-mates better. Although we lost 3-1 to Dundee United in a testimonial for Maurice Malpas, I scored my first goal for Rangers in an 8-2 win over Queen's Park and was on the spot to send us into the final of a warm-up tournament that included Kilmarnock and Coventry City. We drew 1-1 with Coventry, who were managed by Terry Butcher, so the match went to penalties. And it was yours truly who stepped up to net the decisive spot kick.

We beat Kilmarnock 3-1 in the final and then started the season with a 6-0 hammering of St Johnstone. Mark Hateley scored a hat-trick and wee Mo scored two penalties. And before the end of August I had netted my first competitive Rangers goal – I thumped home a left-footed shot from the edge of the box in our 2-0 win over Partick Thistle in the League Cup at Firhill – and tasted victory on my Old Firm debut when we won 2-0 at Parkhead.

But it wasn't all plain sailing. Andy Goram shipped a couple of cheap goals, one in a 1-0 defeat at Tynecastle, and there was a fumble that led to Sparta Prague scoring to eliminate us from the European Cup. That was a huge disappointment and gave me a bit of perspective as to the different expectations now I was a Rangers player. I had suffered early European exits in my days with Aberdeen but that was just the norm. However, at Rangers you soon realised that you were expected to win every game.

There were no excuses; no matter who the opposition were, you had to go out and win.

We had a sticky end to September too. After beating Hearts in the League Cup quarter-final courtesy of a tremendous goal from the returning Ally McCoist, we lost 1-0 to their Edinburgh rivals, Hibernian, at Hampden in the last four in the game I mentioned earlier. And three days later my first encounter against Aberdeen ended badly when we lost 2-0 at Ibrox in the Premier Division. I was voted man of the match but took a bit of stick from the Aberdeen fans. It was something I would get used to in my time at Rangers.

But we were soon back on track and keeping pace with the league leaders, Hearts. What helped was having a settled back four. For the majority of the games it was myself, Richard Gough, Gary Stevens and either Scott Nisbet or Oleg Kuznetsov who played week in, week out. After the New Year John Brown claimed the number six jersey which made us even more solid.

Gary was the model of consistency and he missed only one league match that season, the penultimate fixture against Hearts. Along with Trevor Steven he was very quiet and I learned a lot from him. He was the epitome of the attacking full-back and I used to watch how he timed his runs and my own game improved as a result. This was, after all, a guy who had been capped for England, played in World Cups, faced the likes of Maradona and won the First Division with Everton so the fact that I played so regularly on the opposite side of the park suggested to me that Rangers must have felt I was of a similar standard to Gary. That was another huge boost to my confidence.

'Bomber' Brown and Goughie were fantastic and, although I had played alongside Willie Miller and Alex McLeish at

Aberdeen, that pair were the best centre-back partnership I played with. What struck me at first about Richard was his athleticism. As a captain he wasn't a bawler like Miller, but he led by example and his stature meant he had the respect of everyone in the squad.

As for Bomber, he gave everything he had. He suffered so many injuries but always came back and his spirit typified what it meant to be a Rangers player. He wasn't the quickest of players but was hard as nails and his attitude to each game and training was exactly the same. He rarely got beaten in a one on one, was great in the air and his distribution was excellent. He would provide cover for me when I attacked and that gave me more confidence to go forward. He was a good, solid Rangers man and arguably one of the best players never to have been capped by Scotland.

Back on the pitch there were a couple of stumbles – we lost 3-2 at Tannadice and 1-0 at home to St Mirren – but we entered December only a couple of points behind Hearts. And the first game of the month was a significant one for me, my return to Pittodrie. I knew what to expect when we went up there but, on the night, we scored three superb goals and won 3-2.

I was settling down off the field too. I had got married in the summer of 1990 to my long-time girlfriend, Kym Buchan, and she was pregnant with our first child. We eventually found a house in Erskine which meant we could move out of the hotel. Kym missed Aberdeen but most weekends we had folk visiting like my sister Susan and brother Michael, Kym's brothers, James and Scott, and both sets of parents.

Kym and I were high school sweethearts. She lived in an area of Aberdeen called Broomhill which is about four miles from Garthdee. We both went to Harlaw Academy and caught the same bus, the number 1, to school. And that's where it all started for us. I got on about seven or eight stops before Kym did and when I saw her I immediately took a shine to her. We sat next to each other a couple of times but, with me being so shy and quiet, I didn't have the courage to ask her out on a date. Instead, I got a mutual friend who played in the school football team with me, Donald McLeod, to ask for me!

When he asked she said yes and Donald came back up the bus with Kym's house phone number – there were no mobile phones then – and after that we would speak on the phone for hours. We eventually had our first date, and this was probably the first time we had spoken face to face. Kym arrived with a list of trivia questions – I think that was to break the ice – and we walked around for a while before heading to the carnival at the beach.

I was due to go away with Scotland a couple of days after that, but I found out when we were chatting that Kym's birthday was coming up. I remember I bought her a perfume called Anais Anais – I couldn't pronounce it properly – and we started to see each other more often. And visits to Kym's house used to be great for my fitness levels. I didn't have a car at the time so I would get the bus across to her house. But on numerous occasions if I was there on a Sunday, I would forget that the last bus home was earlier. That meant I would have to either walk or run the four miles back to Garthdee about 11pm.

Kym has been really supportive of everything I have done in my career. She has looked after the financial side of things too and I'm thankful she's sensible with money as in my younger days I may have blown some cash on flash cars and the like. Like all couples we've had our rough patches, notably when I first went to Kashmir, but Kym and I don't hold grudges for too long. And if I'm being honest, the seven months or so we spent together following our return to Aberdeen during lockdown was up there with our best times ever. We've been quite happy with it being just the two of us for the majority of the time and, having been apart for a while when I was in Kashmir, it was just nice to be back in each other's company again.

Rangers started the New Year with a classic win over Celtic at Parkhead on 1 January. That was the match when Bomber netted our third goal in the last minute and hurdled the advertising hoardings to celebrate with the fans. And just a couple of weeks later we supplanted Hearts at the top of the league when we beat Hibernian 2-0.

There was no doubt this was now Walter's team. Of the 11 who had started against Hibernian only five had been involved against Aberdeen on the final day of the previous season. We were starting to gel, but it would take a windy and wet night in March to confirm that one of the greatest teams in Rangers' history had been born. Unfortunately for me I played a very brief part in proceedings.

Our Scottish Cup campaign couldn't have been tougher. We started with a narrow 1-0 win at Pittodrie before eliminating the holders, Motherwell, at Ibrox. A trip to face St Johnstone in Perth ended in a 3-0 win which set up a mouthwatering semi-final against Celtic at Hampden. We would now face them twice in a short space of time with the fourth and final Old Firm league fixture set for 21 March at Ibrox before the Hampden showdown ten days later.

We were on a 19-match unbeaten run when Celtic came to Ibrox. We had won 17 of those games but the sequence came to an abrupt halt when Charlie Nicholas and Gerry Creaney scored to cut our lead at the top of the table to five points. I had had an uncomfortable afternoon as I had picked up an ankle knock after only five minutes and that forced me to withdraw from the Scotland squad. I was desperate to be fit for the semi-final, though, and managed to come through our next league encounter, a 2-1 win over St Johnstone, unscathed. Mark Hateley wasn't so lucky and his back injury counted him out of the action at Hampden.

Paul Rideout replaced Mark up front alongside Coisty and I was relishing the match as I would be up against my former Aberdeen team-mate, Joe Miller. That gave me a bit of an extra edge as I was determined not be outdone by a friend. In those days, and I'm not ashamed to admit it, a full-back like myself would have a wee dig at their opponent inside the opening five minutes to see if they could handle it. Most of the time you would get away with it – on some occasions you would get a yellow card – but I wasn't so fortunate this time around.

Wee Joe had been a thorn in our side in the league match at Ibrox so Archie said to me that I had to make sure as early as possible that he knew he wasn't going to torment us this time. And I got that chance after only six minutes. Pat Bonner threw the ball out and it found its way to Joe on the halfway line. The wee man took a touch that pushed the ball past me, so I thought that this was my chance. I stuck my shoulder and elbow into him – the classic body check – and Joe was stopped in his tracks. I expected a lecture from the referee, Andrew Waddell, or a yellow card so when he brandished a red card, I was astonished. In fairness, in today's game it would have been a straight red and a long suspension, but that kind of incident was the norm back then.

When I got to the dressing room, I was pretty pissed off, so I burst the door open and sat in there on my own. There was no TV in there so when I heard a huge roar and thumping above me later in the first half I didn't know if a goal had been scored or not. My fear was that if it was a goal it would have been for Celtic and it was all going to be my fault. But the next thing I knew George Soutar, or wee Doddie, our kit man came in and told me Coisty had scored to put us 1-0 up right on half-time.

A matter of minutes later the players came in and Walter was brilliant with me. I had snuck into the big, communal bath, trying to hide away but he came in and didn't crucify me as other managers might have. He made me feel a whole lot better about what had happened, and it was that type of man-management that made him the manager he was.

In the second half I was allowed to go and sit in the stand, but I was surrounded by security guards. I virtually kicked every ball as Celtic battered us and it was the most nervous I've been. It was really intimidating as had Celtic won I would have felt it would have been down to me so I reckon I was the most relieved man at Hampden when Mr Waddell blew his full-time whistle.

It was a huge night for the club. Not only had we made it to the final, but we had also laid down a marker. No matter what Celtic threw at us, we stood up to it and after that you felt they never thought they would get the upper hand against us. Most of the times after that when we played them, we would be outplayed, they would have more chances, but we were resilient and were rarely beaten.

Within a few weeks of that victory we beat St Mirren 4-0 at Ibrox to clinch the title. My dismissal ruled me out of the game that followed the semi-final – a 4-0 home win over Falkirk – and I missed only my second league match of the season when we beat the Buddies. But although I wasn't part of the action that day I had more than played my part in this our fourth successive title. I made 42 league appearances – only Goram and Stevens made more – and I thoroughly enjoyed the party that followed. That was my first league winners' medal and, if I'm honest, of the six I won that was the one I enjoyed the most. After that as we edged closer to nine in a row, clinching the title became more of a relief than anything else because of the pressure we were under.

We couldn't afford to take the foot off the gas after sealing the championship as we still had Airdrie to face in the Scottish Cup Final. A win over Motherwell and a draw with Hearts preceded our last league fixture at Pittodrie and it was really satisfying to go back there as a league champion. We won 2-0 and Coisty's first goal that day was our 100th in the league that season.

It was fitting that Ally scored the landmark goal as the campaign was a triumph for him on a personal level. He looked to be on his way out of Ibrox under Souness but he was another in that squad who was resilient. Walter put him back in the team and he repaid the gaffer with 39 goals. Many of them were vital – none more so than his rasping volley in our 1-0 win over our nearest challengers Hearts at Tynecastle in February – and his 34 league goals were enough to earn him the European Golden Boot award.

All that was left was to round off the season in style with a cup final win over Airdrie. But it wasn't a classic. Big Mark and Coisty scored before half-time and we were cruising at 2-0 even though we hadn't played particularly well. I got the assist for Mark's goal, drilling the ball across the six-yard box for him to tap in after Davie Kirkwood and I had clashed. My initial thought was that the referee would penalise me for a foul but he didn't and when Coisty volleyed home a Stuart McCall pass we were seemingly on easy street.

But the second half was pretty flat until Andy Smith smashed one into the top corner with nine minutes left. We were hanging on a bit after that but held firm to complete the Double. Remarkably this was the first time Rangers had won the Scottish Cup since 1981 but you wouldn't have known that inside the dressing room after we returned from parading the trophy on our lap of honour. The place was pretty subdued and there was no real celebration. No disrespect to Airdrie, but we were expected to win comfortably and perhaps we would have been more jubilant had we narrowly beaten Celtic or Aberdeen.

We became spoilt with the success we had but I always remember what Archie said after that match. He told us that we should enjoy winning the cup as 20 years down the line people wouldn't reflect on Rangers winning but not having played well. The record books would show we had won the Scottish Cup and I decided thereafter to try and enjoy our successes as much as I could.

During the close-season there was an addition to the Robertson clan when my daughter, Chelsea, was born. I was there when Kym gave birth and survived almost fainting to witness Chelsea's arrival. Thirteen days late, Chelsea weighed 9lb 4oz but I wasn't like other first-time dads who I knew. They all wanted a boy, but I always wanted a wee girl first. Kym actually calls her 'daddy's princess' because Chelsea and I have such a good, solid bond.

Chelsea was the one, though, who as parents, Kym and I made all the mistakes with. If she cried in her cot at night, we would bring her into our bed. And there were countless occasions when I would be driving round Erskine at 2am with Chelsea in her car seat trying to get her to sleep. However, once my mission was accomplished and I arrived back home with Chelsea asleep, it wasn't long before she was up crying again. I was shattered the next day going into training.

But she's a great kid with a great sense of humour. We'll have a laugh, a joke and a giggle and we're on the same wavelength. We talk regularly on the phone and she sends me sweet messages. She's a great daughter and I feel lucky and blessed to have her.

But initially I had precious little time to enjoy bottle feeding and nappy changing as within a fortnight we were assembling in Glasgow to head back to Il Ciocco to prepare for another challenge for honours on all fronts. We flew from Glasgow to Heathrow where we met Coisty who was only just back from his holiday in the Seychelles. He was his ebullient self when we met him, dressed still in his holiday clothes and carrying a shopping bag. He proudly told us that it contained all he needed for the trip: two shirts, two pairs of shorts, his boots and his Bruce Springsteen and Guns N' Roses CDs!

From there it was on to Pisa and after a two-hour flight we had another hour and a half on a coach to get us to the training complex. To loosen up we had a short training session – Coisty was as sharp as always, scoring a hat-trick in the practice match we had – before we got back to the hotel at about 8pm. We had

One of the first pictures taken of me with my older sister, Susan.

I wasn't really that interested in football until I was about eight years old. After that me and a football were inseparable.

My first taste of silverware as best new recruit in the 62nd Company of the Aberdeen and District Battalion Boys' Brigade.

Proudly wearing my first international cap that I earned at boys' club level in 1983.

Celebrating winning the BP Youth Cup with Aberdeen in 1985 after we came back from 3-0 down to beat Celtic 5-3.

Standing outside the dressing room before I made my debut for the Aberdeen first team against Meadowbank Thistle.

Jousting with Richard Gough in April 1988. Goughie was an inspirational leader and one of the best defenders I played with.

Celebrating after winning my first winners' medal as a professional. We beat Rangers 2-1 in the 1989/90 Scottish League Cup Final.

A few months later I broke a bone in my foot. This is me in the freezing cold swimming pool at RGIT with Pamela Smith who was instrumental in getting me back to full fitness so quickly.

At the 1990 Scottish Cup Final against Celtic. I scored one of the penalty kicks in the shoot-out which Aberdeen won 9-8.

Kym and I on our wedding day in June 1990. My high school sweetheart, she has been a rock throughout my career.

Family is the most important thing to me. This is the Robertson and Buchan families at Loch Lomond after Jordan's christening.

Getting in a cross on my home debut for Rangers against St Johnstone in August 1991.

dinner then a few games of cards before retiring to our rooms about 11pm.

The next morning the training began in earnest and it was no different to the previous year. A typical day saw us enjoy a light breakfast around 9am before we boarded the minibus an hour later for the scary drive up the mountain road to the training pitches. It was pretty steep and the roads were narrow. You were pretty much on the edge of the mountain but, although frightening at the time, some of the journeys I have embarked on since in Kashmir make that trip equivalent to going along the M8.

We trained until noon then returned to the hotel for lunch and a siesta before trekking back up the mountains again for another 90-minute session. Of the double sessions the first was the hardest. It was predominantly running with a bit of ball work and, although there was more running in the afternoon, we saw more of the ball during shooting practice, two-touch practice matches and games of the infamous 'Torro' to sharpen up our first touch.

We left a week later feeling tired but fitter and on our departure from Pisa we met the Liverpool squad who were arriving for their training camp. They had won the FA Cup at the end of the previous season and for most of the lads it was a chance to catch up with Graeme Souness who was looking in great shape after his recent heart bypass surgery.

Back in Scotland the training was still tough, but we were now focussed on sharpening our match fitness. Walter arranged five friendlies, with the calibre of opposition stepping up with each one. I missed the wins over Queen's Park (3-2) and Morton (8-1) but wore number three when we beat

Dunfermline 3-1 thanks to a couple of Paul Rideout penalties. Late goals from Goughie and Bomber earned us a 2-2 draw against Hamilton before we rounded things off with a 2-1 defeat against Marseille at Ibrox. I didn't play well in that one, but our overall performance was good which augured well for the Champions League campaign.

As in the previous season the league flag was unfurled before a match against St Johnstone but there would be a significant absentee from the team sheet. Gary Stevens was ruled out for several months with a stress fracture in his foot, although it was also discovered that he had chipped a bone in his ankle too. Big Dave McPherson, who had returned to the club for a second spell in the close-season, filled in and, although he was a centre-back, Slim proved to be more than adequate cover during Gary's absence.

Inevitably Coisty got the only goal of the game against St Johnstone and that kicked off probably the most memorable season of my career. We fought on all fronts, winning the domestic Treble, going within a goal of making the Champions League Final and embarking on a 44-match unbeaten run. But what made it special for me was that Aberdeen were runners-up in each of the three domestic competitions.

The secret of our success that year was that the games were so close together. For example, in the space of a fortnight in October we played Leeds United home and away in the Champions League, Aberdeen in the League Cup Final and Celtic at Parkhead. We won all those games but you never had time to think in between. I'll admit we had a wee night out after we beat Leeds at Elland Road but it didn't knock us out of our stride as only three days later Durranty got the only goal of the game after we took a pummelling at Parkhead but still claimed maximum points. It was like clockwork.

Andy Goram was the man who defied Celtic that day, but I feel his performance in the second leg against Leeds was his best in a Rangers jersey. We were underdogs that night. Leeds hadn't lost at Elland Road for a while and they had that precious away goal from the first leg at Ibrox.

They had a fantastic side with the likes of Eric Cantona, David Batty, Gary Speed, Lee Chapman and Gordon Strachan but, with only Rangers supporters allowed into the first game at Ibrox, I felt anything was possible with them behind us. It was one of those nights when you emerged from the tunnel and the hairs on the back of your neck stood up – in fairness, it was like that most times at Ibrox – and the noise was phenomenal. Yet within a minute there was an eerie silence.

For some reason I had been designated to pick up Lee Chapman at corner kicks, so I positioned myself next to him at the near post when Leeds won an early corner. Strachan took it and I was really pleased when I met the ball with a good, clean, clearing header. The ball travelled to the edge of the box where it was met in the volley by Gary McAllister. As good as he was, Goram had no chance and barely a minute in we were 1-0 down.

My immediate reaction was that the night was about to turn into a long one for us. But typified by the spirit that had seen off Celtic back in March in the Scottish Cup semi-final, we came back. Maybe Leeds took their foot off the gas after scoring so early but, although we got lucky for the equalising goal, we were worthy winners on the night courtesy of another predatory finish from McCoist. We should probably have scored a third goal as we had a couple of half-chances in the second half but at the final whistle, you would have thought we were out the competition.

We were written off in the English media and they were speculating about how many goals we would be beaten by at Elland Road a fortnight later. But we silenced the cynics as we did so often when we were written off back then. Archie Knox was brilliant and almost every day we would come into the dressing room and find another newspaper clipping from the English press pinned on the notice board. We had a team of seasoned professionals and we used the negativity that was directed towards as motivation.

That night was probably one of my finest in a Rangers jersey. We were under so much pressure but Goram repelled almost everything Leeds threw at him and at the other end we had a dynamic duo that could score goals against anyone. Both goals that night were world-class, and the home fans applauded us off the field at the final whistle. I would have four years with Leeds later in my career, but I can't recall receiving an ovation like that in all my time there.

That took us into the inaugural Champions League group stages. In those days there were only two groups, each made up of four teams. In our section we had Marseille, Club Brugges and CSKA Moscow and the French champions were up first at Ibrox. It was a horrible night weather-wise and we were without Coisty who was out with a calf injury. Goughie and Stuart McCall were also struggling, and Walter had his perennial dilemma at that time of which three foreign players to select. Mark Hateley was a certainty to be one of them and, in the end, Walter went with Trevor Steven and Alexei Mikhailichenko as the other two. Neil Murray made his first appearance at Ibrox that night and fellow youngsters Gary McSwegan and Steven Pressley were on the bench.

Marseille had a fantastic side with the likes of Fabien Barthez, Rudi Vöeller, Marcel Desailly and Alen Bokšić. And it was the latter who put the visitors ahead after half an hour. Although he started the game, it was clear that Goughie was struggling so young Elvis came on for him at half-time. But one of his first involvements was to provide the assist for Marseille's second goal. Franck Sauzée chipped the ball into the penalty area, Goram came out to collect but Pressley slid in and diverted the ball away from Andy and into the path of Vöeller who rolled the ball into the empty net.

I'll be honest, at that stage I thought we were fucked. But the crowd lifted us. At other clubs I have been at a 2-0 deficit would have seen fans flooding for the exits but not at Ibrox. They believed in us and urged us on, but it took an inspired change from Walter to turn the tide. Gary McSwegan had been a regular goalscorer in the reserves for a few years but wasn't a first-team regular due to the form of the likes of McCoist, Johnston and Hateley.

He was on the bench against Marseille and with 13 minutes to go Walter pitched him into the action. He came on for Trevor Steven which allowed Durranty to move back into the central midfield. His first action there was to spray a marvellous pass out to Miko on the left wing and the big man looped a cross into the box. Gary was positioned around the penalty spot and he planted a header from there beyond Barthez. It was his first touch of the ball and Ibrox was absolutely rocking.

Four minutes later we were level. McSwegan was involved again, playing a one-two with Durrant, and when Ian's cross was deflected big Mark flung himself at the ball and sent a diving header into the net. We then went in search of the winning goal, but it wasn't forthcoming. Nonetheless, to come back from 2-0 down without our top goalscorer and captain was a terrific boost for morale.

A 1-0 win over CSKA in Bochum and a 1-1 draw against Bruges in Belgium left us level on points with Marseille at the top of the section at the halfway stage. For me the pivotal match came in the fourth round of fixtures against Bruges at Ibrox. I missed out – the first time that season I didn't start a game – as I had pulled my hamstring in the 3-0 win over Hibernian the previous Saturday so I had to content myself with a seat in the Club Deck. But from my vantage point I got a superb view of the winning goal, scored by Scott Nisbet.

We led 1-0 after Trevor Steven picked out Durrant with a terrific through ball but Bruges were level five minutes after the break when Staelens scored. By then we were down to ten men as Hateley had been ordered off a minute shy of the interval. That decision probably cost us a place in the final. With Mark you didn't realise how good a player he was until he wasn't playing, and we missed his presence when we faced Marseille in a winner-takes-all encounter in the Stade Veldrome.

We went 1-0 down early when I botched a clearance. I tried to play the ball down the line but mishit it and it zipped along the ground to Sauzée who took a couple of strides before lashing his shot beyond Goram. My night was summed up when the injury that had dogged me for a few weeks flared up again and I pulled my hamstring.

There's no doubt we missed Hateley but, typical of that side, we never knew when we were beaten and wee Durrant smashed in a wonderful goal after the interval to keep us in the competition. However, it was advantage Marseille and we effectively had to better their result in Belgium against Bruges when we faced CSKA at Ibrox. That turned out to be one of the most frustrating games I have played in. In fact, we could probably still be playing today and still not have scored. Coisty had numerous chances to score but, for once, spurned them. Goughie hit the bar with a header and Bomber brought the best out in their goalkeeper with a piledriver. In the end the outcome of our game was academic; Marseille won in Bruges and advanced to the final against AC Milan.

There were tears at time up and Goughie had blood streaming from a head wound. But, on reflection, it was such a fantastic achievement to do what we did in Europe that season. After beating the Danish side Lyngby in our first fixture, we ended up winning six and drawing four of the ten ties we played, something that was going to be difficult to repeat.

There was no time to dwell on missing out on a shot at Champions League glory, though. We had the title to clinch and the Scottish Cup Final against Aberdeen to look forward to. Winning both of them would have given us the Treble as we had defeated Aberdeen 2-1 at Hampden to win the League Cup back in late October. That match was a nightmare for my old pal Theo Snelders and I claimed the assist for our winning goal too.

We took the lead after 14 minutes through Stuart McCall. Ian Durrant tried a through ball, but David Winnie cut the pass out and diverted it back to big Theo with his foot. The new back-pass laws had recently been introduced so, caught in two minds, Theo tried to control the ball on his chest but took a heavy touch. The ball broke to Stuart and he stroked it into the net. But Duncan Shearer equalised to force extra time and we looked set for penalties when the ball broke to me on the left-hand side of the pitch six minutes from the end of the extra half-hour. If I'm honest my legs were tired and when Eoin Jess closed me down, I knew I would be hard-pushed to outrun him. As I often did in circumstances like that, I slung a cross into the box looking for Mark Hateley. When I looked up, I saw the big man sliding in to meet the ball, but it didn't reach him. Instead it skimmed off the head of Gary Smith, the Aberdeen centre-half, and ended up in the net. I felt for Gary as he had had a fine match, but we enjoyed the celebrations back at Ibrox after Goughie climbed the stairs at Hampden to collect the trophy.

But if we had relished the party after that one then the one that followed the Scottish Cup Final was even sweeter. We clinched the title with four games to spare when Gary McSwegan, deputising for Coisty who had had his season ended when he broke his leg playing for Scotland in Portugal, scored the only goal against Airdrie and attention turned to Aberdeen at Parkhead.

Hampden was in the throes of reconstruction so the ground of our Old Firm rivals was the chosen venue. And my old club were the opponents and on the verge of ending as runners-up in each of three domestic competitions. Although my family were Aberdeen supporters I used to be spurred on when we played them as I always got a rough time from their fans. Earlier in this chapter I mentioned a couple of incidents, but I can also remember outside Ibrox once an Aberdeen supporter handed me an autograph book to sign as I was getting on the team bus. As I was signing the book, he kicked me on the shin and ran away. And at Pittodrie when I went to take a throw-in the fans would spit on me and throw coins at me. There would be the inevitable name-calling too.

But that cup final wasn't just special because we beat Aberdeen. Not only were we pipping my old team for a trophy for the third time that season, but we were also doing so at Parkhead as the 'home' team. That meant we were celebrating the Treble in the home dressing room and our fans, who were housed on the infamous Jungle terracing, must have revelled in that success more than they did many of the others we enjoyed in that era.

CHAPTER 6

NINE IN A ROW

ALTHOUGH THE club had now won five successive titles, there was no real talk around Ibrox about the fabled nine in a row. Celtic had won nine successive championships between 1966 and 1974 and I'm sure it rankled with the Rangers fans that their club had never managed to match that feat. However, back in the summer of 1993 we were simply taking it one season at a time. Indeed, if anything the emphasis at that time was on being successful in the Champions League.

Having done so well in that competition in its inaugural campaign, you could feel there was increasing pressure when it came to the qualifying ties. We craved the group stages, so the expectation levels were raised as we were drawn to face the Bulgarian champions, Levski Sofia, early in 1993/94. All the pre-season preparations were geared towards this two-legged tie and the pressure on the players ahead of these matches was incredible. An elite club like Rangers were expected to sweep teams like Levski aside but it was never as easy as that. And that was confirmed when we got caught out late on in the first leg at Ibrox.

There was a special moment before the game when Coisty was presented with his second successive European Golden Boot prize and we looked to be comfortable when David McPherson – big Slim – and Mark Hateley put us 2-0 ahead. But they pulled one back with 13 minutes left and, although Mark restored our two-goal lead almost instantly, Nikolay Todorov headed in a second goal for the visitors to leave the tie hanging in the balance.

In truth we weren't in the best of form going into the match. We had succumbed to a late goal at home against newly promoted Kilmarnock – the first time we had lost in the league at Ibrox for a staggering 17 months – and also drawn with Dundee and Partick Thistle. The Kilmarnock match was my first league outing of the season.

Having made 58 appearances in the previous season, a spell on the sidelines is never welcome, but my situation was put into perspective when the news broke that my team-mate Scott Nisbet had been forced to quit the game through injury. Just days after his goal had earned us the 2-1 win over Bruges in the Champions League, he injured his pelvis against Celtic at Parkhead. And a few months later, aged just 25, his career was over. Nissy had originally been advised to rest to try and solve the problem but he soon found it was affecting his hips too. And despite seeing three different specialists in the UK and having his case notes sent to the States, the prognosis was the same; he had to call it a day.

Our erratic start to the season appeared to have been rectified prior to travelling to Sofia. Although we lost 2-0 against Aberdeen at Pittodrie in the league, we beat the Dons after extra time in the last eight of the League Cup and secured a place in the final when we beat Celtic 1-0 at the 'neutral' venue of Ibrox in the semis. Big Mark got the goal that mattered, and we seemed all set to complete the job against the Bulgarians seven days later.

But the Saturday prior to the match I pulled my hamstring in our 2-1 win over Hibernian. I travelled with the squad to Sofia and did a fitness test on the morning of the game but there was no chance I was going to be fit. Fraser Wishart deputised at left-back and we were all set for qualification when Durranty equalised on the night a minute before half-time. Watching from the stands I saw no reason why we wouldn't progress. Slim drew a great save from their goalkeeper and their only threat appeared to be from set-pieces. But just as time was running out, Todorov swung his right foot at the ball 25 yards out and his shot rocketed into the top corner. We were out and, as I made my way down to the dressing room, the feeling was that our season had ended. There must have been a significant impact on the club financially too. I don't know exactly what the figures were but the bonus payments we stood to get if we qualified were massive, so I guess that put into perspective how lucrative making the group stages was.

We suffered a real domestic hangover as a result of the European exit. We drew 1-1 away at Raith and suffered another home defeat, this time at the hands of Motherwell. I missed both those matches but was back in position for arguably our best performance of the season, a 3-1 win over Dundee United at Tannadice. A comfortable 2-0 home win over St Johnstone then set us up nicely for the League Cup Final against Hibernian at Parkhead.

Coisty was now back in contention after recovering from his leg break but he had to content himself with a place on the bench. Hibernian were a decent side but a beautiful lob by Durrant put us 1-0 up ten minutes into the second half. However, just four minutes later a comedy of errors brought Hibs level. Keith Wright pounced on a wayward pass from Gary Stevens and his cross was turned into the net by a spectacular diving header from Dave McPherson.

Enter Ally McCoist.

Walter threw Coisty into the action after 67 minutes and the script, as it was most of the time with Ally, was written. I recall an interview with one of the Hibs players some years later – I can't remember who it was – but he basically admitted that he and his team-mates knew McCoist would score. And nine minutes from time that's exactly what he did.

We won a throw-in on the left and I wound up to take a long one into the penalty area. I had been taking long throws since back in my apprentice days at Pittodrie. You weren't allowed on the pitch so one day we decided to take thrown-ins. The tunnel at Pittodrie is situated at the corner flag so going up the tunnel gave you a long run-up to the touchline. I managed to hurl one to the edge of the six-yard box and Fergie found out about it. He asked me to use it one day in a game and from that day on it was used with great success.

I wouldn't say Walter used it as a tactic, but I always knew with guys like Hateley in the box, he would win the ball nine times out of ten if I could find him. I knew I could consistently get the ball beyond the edge of the six-yard box, although at some stadiums it was more difficult as the track around the pitch wasn't as wide. It was also more difficult on wet days to get the same distance, but we didn't just use it in attack, my long throws got us out of trouble in our defensive third too.

In the match against Hibs I was able to get a decent run-up and I remember the ball skidding off the head of their centre-back, Steven Tweed, and heading towards Coisty. He had his back to goal but he killed the ball on his chest before executing a superb overhead kick. Jim Leighton didn't stand a chance.

But if we thought claiming our sixth successive domestic honour would signal a consistent run of form in the league we were mistaken. Coisty scored again the following weekend against Celtic at Ibrox but an Ally Maxwell fumble allowed John Collins to equalise. And in the dying seconds Brian O'Neill headed in from a corner to inflict upon us our third home defeat of the season. A 2-2 draw four days later against Hearts at Tynecastle left us fourth in the table although we were only two points adrift of Aberdeen.

Another home point was dropped when we followed two successive league wins with a 2-2 draw against Raith. We were relying heavily on Hateley to score goals for us, so Walter did what Walter usually did when we were in a spot of bother, he pulled a rabbit out the hat and signed Gordon Durie from Tottenham Hotspur.

I had played against Jukey when he was at Hibernian and he had carved out a good career south of the border with Spurs and Chelsea. He was a good lad in the dressing room, and he made an immediate impact with a double in just his second appearance, against Motherwell at Fir Park. I claimed the assist for both his goals too. For his first my long ball forward was misjudged by Chris McCart which allowed Gordon a clear run and he showed terrific composure to round Sieb Dykstra in the Motherwell goal before rolling the ball into the empty net. He doubled his tally just after the hour – I made an overlapping run on the left and crossed to the front post from where Jukey headed the ball home – and remarkably that 2-0 win took us top of the table and illustrated perfectly how we could be playing poorly yet still be better than all the rest in Scotland.

A week after the Motherwell win, we welcomed Dundee United to Ibrox. They were sitting seventh in the table so it should have been an opportunity for us to kick on and rack up more points. But we were abject on the day and lost 3-0. We shipped the three goals inside the opening 21 minutes of the game! We were all over the place and considering both Slim and Goughie went off injured in that spell it's a surprise we didn't lose more goals. It was the first time Rangers had lost by such a margin at Ibrox since the Aberdeen side I was part of pooped the championship party on the final day of 1988/89. I was actually voted man of the match by Scottish Brewers that day. It was only the second time I had been given the award since signing for Rangers and the other occasion was after another home defeat, a 2-0 reverse against Aberdeen not long after I had signed for the club. Clearly me being the top man was not a good omen!

We were pretty low afterwards, but it was the shake-up that we needed. It showed us that we weren't invincible and on days like that when we were off form, we could get beaten by anyone. In fact, the defeat galvanised us and the next time we lost in the league was against Motherwell on 26 April, after a run of 17 matches unbeaten. Coisty always used to tell me that the race for the title only started in earnest after Christmas. In several of the title-winning seasons Rangers weren't top of the league at the end of the year but would embark on a run of form that would see them top the table at the end of the season. And as we proved, this one would be no different.

The United match would be my last in a blue jersey for almost a month. With about 15 minutes left I went for a tackle and my left foot met with the studs of the player I challenged. It initially looked as if I had just badly bruised my foot but by the Monday I was still in a lot of pain. I was sent for an X-ray which revealed I had sustained a hairline fracture.

That counted me out of the festive fixtures so Kym, Chelsea and I took ourselves away to Florida for a week on Christmas Eve. And when we came back, we did so to good news: Kym was pregnant, and my son Mason would later become part of the family on 22 July 1994. Unlike Chelsea, Mason was early, arriving a day before Kym's due date weighing 9lb 10oz. Ironically, Kym's labour lasted for 90 minutes.

Incredibly, choosing my son's name made the papers. I'd had a bit of stick over Chelsea's name given the close connection between Rangers and Chelsea but, given the alleged links between the masonic lodge and Rangers, we got hammered for choosing Mason. And being a Rangers player had an impact on the naming of our third child too. We liked the name Kai, but everyone talked about the former Rangers player called Kai Johansen. He was a bit of a cult hero after his goal against Celtic had won the Scottish Cup in 1966 so given the hullaballoo over Chelsea and Mason we decided to go for Jordan and give him the middle name Kai instead. The last of my terrific trio, Jordan was born on 27 October 1995.

Madness like that just showed what living in Glasgow as a Rangers player was like. In Aberdeen you would maybe get noticed walking down Union Street but in Glasgow, no matter where you went, you got stick. There was once Kym and I had to hide out in Next in Argyle Street because I was getting abused by a Celtic fan and there was another occasion when we went looking for a TV in a place called Hutcheson's and they had to ask people to leave and then lock the doors as I was in there. After that, while you don't exactly become a recluse, you just become more careful about where you go in the city.

During my three-game absence there was a welcome return to form for us. I missed our 4-0 win over St Johnstone and 2-2 draw against Hearts and I was suited and booted on the bench at Parkhead on 1 January when we beat Celtic 4-2. As you can imagine, the camaraderie among the subs and the other injured guys was tremendous and I was especially pleased to see Neil Murray, who was deputising for me at left-back, involved in our second goal, his effort being parried into the path of big Miko who scored the first of his two goals that day.

Winning an Old Firm game is special but being on the losing side is painful and for some of the Celtic fans this reverse was too much to take. Celtic had not won a domestic honour since they beat Rangers to win the Scottish Cup in 1989 and they had won just nine of their opening 24 league matches. The club was in disarray and when Miko put us 3-0 up just before the half-hour mark, pockets of the home support vented their fury and hurled objects at the Celtic board members in the directors' box.

Celtic's plight was not a concern for us, though. We were looking to pull away from the chasing pack and seven days after the Parkhead pummelling I was back in action. We comfortably beat Kilmarnock 3-0 and a few weeks later I got my first goal of the season when I lashed home a free kick in our 4-1 win over Dumbarton in the last 16 of the Scottish Cup.

Our team had been bolstered by the return of Goram and McCoist. 'The Goalie' made his first appearance of the season in a 2-0 win over Hibernian in February and Coisty, who had been sidelined with a groin injury, returned in typical fashion, scoring a hat-trick on his first start since November, in a 6-0 win over Alloa in the Scottish Cup. It is testament to the quality and depth of the squad we had that we could afford to go without players of that ilk for long periods and still lead the way.

I was still having trouble with my hamstrings, though. I had started wearing cycling shorts under my shorts as they helped keep my hamstrings warm and eventually, even when my hamstrings weren't troubling me, I wore them for every game because I didn't feel right without them. My pace meant I was more susceptible to pulling my hamstring and I could always sense when it was going to happen. I could feel them getting tighter and tighter, but I was an 'all or nothing' type of player so even if I felt a little niggle I would still play.

Eventually I found that the problem was coming from my back and, after suffering another strain when playing for Scotland against the Netherlands, I decided to go and see a chiropractor. I missed four matches but when I returned I felt a huge difference and I don't recall having any issues with my hamstrings after that. I didn't miss another match that season which meant I was in the thick of the action as we entered the business end of the campaign.

And in that run of games I scored one of the best goals of my career. On 16 April we faced Raith Rovers at Ibrox. We had struggled against the men from Kirkcaldy that season, drawing twice and eking out a narrow 2-1 win but on this occasion, we were comfortable winners. I got the ball, rolling after 17 minutes when I let fly from 25 yards and my shot flew into the top corner. My connection was clean so I knew it had a chance of finding the net and that ranks as the best goal I scored during my career.

Not content with scoring once, I almost doubled my tally later when I rattled a shot off the post. However, that game isn't remembered for my goal, instead it is remembered for an incident that happened some 15 minutes after I scored. The ball was played down the left wing and Duncan Ferguson ended up jostling with Jock McStay. Although we didn't know it at the time the big man had motioned with his head towards McStay and he went down.

The referee, Kenny Clark, didn't even book Duncan and, in his post-match interview with *Scotsport*, Walter didn't even mention the incident. In fact, despite winning 4-0, I recall him saying that it was one of the most uninspiring matches of the season and was only lit up by the goal I scored.

But pretty soon afterwards all hell broke loose. Duncan ended up charged by the police and, because of previous indiscretions, landed himself a three-month jail sentence. To be honest, when you watch it back, there's nothing in the incident. They both squared up and walked towards each other and the next thing McStay was on the deck. I think Duncan's reputation did for him and I actually think my tackle on Joe Miller in the Scottish Cup semi-final was worse than what Duncan did that day.

Ironically, that was the match when Duncan scored his first goal for the club. He posted our third goal a mere 15 seconds into the second half but that is now forgotten due to the events that followed that incident in the first half. And within a matter of months he left Rangers and joined Everton. I think he was too similar to Hateley to be successful at Rangers. He was unfortunate that that season Mark was hardly ever injured, and I think the arrival of who many thought to be the young pretender actually pushed Hateley to another level. I also don't think the move into the Old Firm goldfish bowl was the wisest one for Duncan at the time either.

The win over Raith left us on the cusp of the title – we sat seven points clear of Motherwell with six games left to play – and the result completed a good week for us as a double from Hateley had booked us a place in the Scottish Cup Final. His second goal that night was his 30th goal of the season. With Coisty out injured for most of the campaign, Mark stepped up and scored the goals that put us on the verge of an unprecedented back-to-back Treble.

I don't think I appreciated at the time just how good a player Mark was. He was magnificent in the air, he had a great left foot, he could cross a ball and he was a massive player for us. In addition to his goals, the amount of assists he had was incredible and he made it really easy for players like me. There were times where I felt my use of the ball wasn't the best but if I tried to pick Mark out with a cross I could get away with a poor delivery as he would attack the ball, get a flick-on and create an opportunity for us. He was overshadowed for the most part by McCoist, but he deservedly won the player of the year accolades that season.

Seven days after we defeated Raith we won the Scottish Cup Final dress rehearsal when a Durie double saw off a dogged Dundee United at Ibrox. That maintained our lead at the top but remarkably it would be the last time we would taste victory that season. We limped across the finish line in the title race, drawing two and losing three of our last five games. Was fatigue from the efforts of the previous season a factor? Perhaps, but it's difficult to get back in the groove when you get into a rut like that. And that's why we didn't win the Scottish Cup and become the first side to do a double Treble.

One thing you could be assured of in that era at Ibrox would be that Walter would strengthen the squad every summer. And it was no different in 1994 as we spent big money to bring in the French centre-back, Basile Boli, and the Danish forward, Brian Laudrup. Both had a great pedigree. Boli had been instrumental in the Marseille side that pipped us to the Champions League Final in 1993 and had then headed the winning goal against AC Milan to claim the trophy. And despite having had a torrid time in Italy, Laudrup had been part of the Denmark side that had won the 1992 European Championship and could also count Bayern Munich among the former clubs on his CV.

In the end the signing of Boli was a huge disappointment. Some players arrive at Rangers with a bit of a reputation but they don't fit in and Basile was one of them. He fitted in fine in the dressing room but on the pitch it was a different matter. His style of play didn't suit the Scottish game – although he was a centre-back, he always wanted to charge up the park – and he made a number of mistakes.

As for Laudrup, he was just incredible. Yet at half-time during his first appearance – a pre-season friendly against Clyde at Broadwood – I came off scratching my head wondering what all the hype about this guy was based on. He played in front of me that night and on several occasions he seemed to misplace his passes. I soon realised, however, that Brian was two steps ahead of everyone else and I clicked that where his passes were ending up was where I was meant to be. He was a master at getting himself out of tight spaces and playing the perfect pass and we soon developed a fantastic partnership.

But not long after Brian arrived, he found himself in the midst of a crisis. We had been drawn against the Greek champions AEK Athens in the Champions League qualifiers and the first leg was over there, three days before the domestic season kicked off. For some reason Walter decided to change the system that night and play three at the back, something we had never done before. I had played in that system a couple of times at Aberdeen and must admit found it very difficult.

Although we eventually made the system work it was a strange game to debut it in and we were comfortably beaten 2-0. The system changes aside, we were drained before the start of the game too as it was so hot. It was a huge disappointment and, although we still had the home leg to come, we knew it was going to be a tall order to turn the tie around.

The return leg was the first of three successive home fixtures. After AEK we were due to play Celtic in the league and then Falkirk in the League Cup. And the unthinkable happened – we lost all three. After we were defeated 1-0 by the Greeks, Celtic beat us 2-0 at Ibrox before Falkirk ended our interest in the League Cup with a 2-1 win.

The newspapers had a field day, but it was then that I recognised how good a man-manager Walter was. He shielded us from everything and, although he must have felt the pressure that a run of results like that brings to a Rangers manager, he never showed it in front of the players. This was his first managerial job too so to respond to that pressure the way he did is testament to the type of man he is. I think that was one of the reasons why he enjoyed the amount of success that he did. There was no hint of any nervousness before or after a game or during team talks and for me personally that was great as I think had I picked up on that from the manager it would have affected my performances on the pitch.

Walter wasn't one to chop and change the team either when we weren't doing well. That was another benefit for me as had I been dropped at that time it may well have finished my career. I have played under plenty of managers that take that course of action to try and reinvigorate their team, but Walter wasn't like that and, for the most part, if I was fit I played.

I actually missed the Celtic game with a bruised foot but returned against Falkirk. And I was rarely out of the team prior to Christmas as we set about improving our performances, which we did largely because we became a lot more solid at the back. After losing to Falkirk we kept eight clean sheets in our next 16 games and conceded just 11 goals. We were helped by the purchase of Alan McLaren from Hearts and he slotted in superbly in the back three with Goughie and Boli.

Alan's debut was a memorable one. We faced Celtic in the league at Hampden – Parkhead was still in the throes of redevelopment – and beat them 3-1. Young Charlie Miller was excellent that day, creating the opening goal for Mark Hateley after 25 minutes. The big man scored again on the stroke of half-time when he turned in my driven cross and Laudrup provided the *pièce de résistance* in the second half with a wonderful solo goal.

That was a real statement of intent from us. We had lost at Easter Road and Fir Park in the weeks leading up to the game, but we showed our mettle yet again. The result maintained our two-point lead over Hibs at the top of the league and also stretched the gap between ourselves and Celtic to six points.

A rare Robertson goal had contributed to a 2-0 home win over Kilmarnock a fortnight before we faced Celtic and I was happy with my form going into the festive period. And my good form mirrored that of the team. When we defeated Kilmarnock 2-1 at Rugby Park on 10 December, we moved seven points clear of Motherwell in second place. Under my former team-mate Alex McLeish, the Fir Park side had emerged as our main challengers for the title. And to illustrate how the mighty had fallen, perennial challengers Celtic and Aberdeen were out of contention even though there were still 19 games to go. Celtic sat in fifth place at that stage, 15 points behind us, but my old club were in an even more precarious position. The Dons had won just three of their first 17 games and sat second from bottom, only two points ahead of Partick Thistle who were at the foot of the table.

Our good form continued into the New Year and we cantered to our seventh successive title, clinching it with four games to spare when we beat Hibs 3-1 at Ibrox. By then I was absent from the starting XI. Indeed, I had last played for the first team on 25 February when we defeated Kilmarnock 3-0 at Ibrox.

I was taken off at half-time in that match with a recurrence of a foot injury. Five days earlier we had played Hearts in the Scottish Cup and I had hurt my foot in a challenge with Craig Levein. I didn't train at all until the Friday before we faced Kilmarnock but was passed fit to play. I could hardly walk but I didn't want to miss any games, so I took a painkilling injection. But all that did was numb my foot and I was in agony, so Bomber took over from me for the second half. I'm actually surprised I lasted as long as I did.

I sought advice from a specialist on the injury and it transpired that the challenge from Levein had actually bent and dislodged one of the screws that was holding in place the plate that had been inserted in my right foot in the winter of 1989 while I was with Aberdeen. I ended up in London undergoing surgery to have the plate removed but still expected to be back in action before the end of the season.

The surgeon reckoned I would be back running within a fortnight and playing again within three or four weeks but that wasn't the case. Once the plate and screws were taken out you had to wait for a period of time until the bone calcified again but even after that I was still in agony. I went back down to London and the surgeon suggested that I looked into getting insoles for my boots called orthotics. I recall going to Edinburgh University to get them done but it was a concerning time. Once you have had surgery you think the problem is solved but there seemed to be a few hurdles in the way on that occasion that meant I didn't play again that season.

I was fit for the last game of the season against Partick Thistle at home and thought I might have got a place on the bench, but I didn't. Instead I had to focus on having a good pre-season and when we came back that summer of 1995, I would be joined in the dressing room by one of the best players I have ever played with, Paul Gascoigne.

As a player it was incredible that we had managed to attract someone like him to the football club. There had been rumours in the papers but nine times out of ten they were unfounded. But this time they were spot on, although it was only the day Paul signed and there was a massive gathering of fans outside the stadium that I actually started to believe it was true.

It was another feather in Walter's cap too. He wasn't a renowned manager in world football but he could sell the club and his ambitions to the likes of Laudrup and Gascoigne and they were both a huge part of the success we enjoyed at that time. Paul had had a tough time at Lazio too so I think the move suited him.

He joined what was a lively dressing room but, to be honest, I think he was really nervous at first. And there was a different side to him too. There were many occasions when we were coming back on the bus from games in Edinburgh or Dundee that he would come up and sit next to me and pour his heart out about the problems he was having.

Almost lost in the hullaballoo surrounding Gascoigne was the fact we signed Gordan Petrić from Dundee United. The big Serbian had played well against us after he joined United from Partizan Belgrade, but he was probably best remembered for an incident at the end of the 3-0 home defeat against United back in December 1993. Ian Ferguson was ordered off late in the game after he spat at Gordan but, at the time, we didn't know what had happened. That was commonplace and it was only really on the Monday when we picked up the papers that we knew what had gone on.

I also recall Gordan suffering an infected elbow after an innocuous collision with Andy Goram's teeth! I can vividly remember seeing the pus coming out of the wound and I think he missed a few games because of that injury.

Our other acquisition that summer was a guy I knew very well as I had played with him for three years at Aberdeen. Aged 23, Stephen Wright was one of the best young right-backs in Scotland when he joined us but I knew all about his credentials as I had played alongside him in an under-20 youth tournament in Switzerland when he was just 15. I was sure we would develop an excellent full-back partnership and with Walter looking to make use of a 3-5-2 system, I felt the two of us were tailor-made for the wing-back roles in that set-up.

Pre-season that year took us once again to Denmark – Stephen and I actually roomed together on the trip – and for me the week-long trip was vital to get myself back in shape after spending so long out of the team at the end of the previous campaign. We played three games and I was selected for two of them, wins over Brøndby and Hvidovre. I also started the first match of the Ibrox International Tournament against Steaua Bucharest, which we won 4-0. Gascoigne scored his first goal for the club in that one, but I was rested for the final against Sampdoria the following day.

These matches were all geared towards getting us ready for another Champions League qualifier. Given the chastening experiences against Levski and AEK we were taking nothing for granted when the draw pitched us against the Cypriot champions, Anorthosis Famagusta. We were, however, still expected to sweep them aside with consummate ease. But we laboured to a 1-0 win at Ibrox in the first leg – Jukey scored in the second half – and the return leg was on a knife-edge. The heat was intense, and we really struggled so it was a massive relief when the referee blew his final whistle at the end of a game that finished 0-0.

Domestically we started sluggishly too. It took a late Stuart McCall goal to edge out Kilmarnock on the opening day of the league season and we were booed off the park when we beat Stirling Albion 3-2 in the League Cup at Ibrox. We were cruising when Coisty scored to put us 3-0 up with 19 minutes to go but we shipped two goals in the last ten minutes. We were on a downer in the dressing room after that – although they were the first goals we had conceded that season, we knew we had taken our foot off the gas – but we were still gelling as a team.

The back five were taking time to integrate too. Moving from a flat back four to three at the back with the full-backs pushing forward took a bit of time to get used to. But for Stephen Wright and myself we knew we had in Goughie, Alan McLaren and Gordan Petrić three high-quality centre-backs. That meant as we made forward runs, we had comfort in the fact that it was going to take a very good strike force to breach our defence.

I chalked up my first goal of the season ten days after the Stirling game when I scored our third goal in a 4-0 win over Raith Rovers. It was created by Laudrup and I dinked the ball over Scott Thomson. That must have given me confidence as I tried an audacious shot from 40 yards in the final minute which dipped only a couple of feet off target.

But my run of games came to an end when I missed the first of our Champions League group games against Steaua Bucharest in Romania through suspension. I had been booked in both legs against Famagusta so that counted me out of our 1-0 defeat. Future Ranger Daniel Prodan scored the only goal of the game and we also had Alan McLaren ordered off.

To say we had a tough group would have been an understatement. As well as Steaua we had Borussia Dortmund and Juventus for company in Group C. Matchday two had us at home to Dortmund, but I missed out again, this time through injury. I damaged my hamstring when we beat Celtic 1-0 at Parkhead in the quarter-final of the League Cup and I missed four matches, including another away win over Celtic, this one coming in the league. My replacement at left-back, Alec Cleland, was a hero in that game, scoring the first goal with a header.

But I was back at left-back when we travelled to Turin to face Juventus and it was a night when we were torn apart by Alessandro Del Piero. That was a real eye-opener for me. I had experienced plenty of stadiums playing in Europe for Aberdeen and Rangers but nothing like the Stadio delle Alpi. We went there the night before the game, and it was really imposing and intimidating.

Although we expected to defend for most of the night, and were up against a galaxy of stars, we didn't do anything different tactically for the tie. Walter kept it low-key and the plan was to go out and keep their fans quiet. But that was ripped asunder after just 22 minutes. In that time Fabrizio Ravanelli, the future Chelsea manager Antonio Conte, and Del Piero scored for Juventus. And after we had Cleland sent off after he had been done by a sublime bit of skill by Del Piero, Ravanelli scored again to complete what was a bit of a rout. Goughie's late header was scant consolation for us.

Although I didn't get forward that night as often as I normally would I still felt I had a pretty good game. The Italian league was probably the best in the world then and afterwards the Juventus manager, Marcelo Lippi, said I was one of the few Rangers players who would have made it into their team. For a guy who didn't think he was on a par with the players he was playing alongside at Rangers, getting feedback like that from one of the most renowned managers in the game was a huge boost for my confidence.

I couldn't shake off the hamstring injury, though, and missed out when we exited the League Cup at the semi-final stage against Aberdeen. And I was absent again when Juventus game to Glasgow and battered us again. In fairness we were severely weakened by injury and suspension. Joining me on the treatment table were Brian Laudrup, Craig Moore and Trevor Steven, while Alan McLaren, Gordon Durie and Alec Cleland were suspended. Then, on the night, we lost Stephen Wright to an injury that would severely curtail his Rangers career and Andy Goram didn't reappear for the second half after suffering a hip injury. We were only 1-0 down at that stage but a Moreno Toriricelli goal after 64 minutes gave us a real mountain to climb. We huffed and puffed after that but suffered two sucker punches when our visitors scored a further two goals in the final two minutes.

Our Champions League dreams were all but over for another year – we needed to win our last two games and hope results went our way, only to draw against both Steaua and Dortmund – but I was back in action by then, making my return in a six-goal Old Firm thriller. It was a game that had everything, including a world-class save from Goram, but my memories of the game centre around being denied what would have been my only goal for Rangers against Celtic.

We were trailing 1-0 after 23 minutes when Laudrup played me in on goal with a perfect through ball. I burst clear and struck the ball under Gordon Marshall, but my celebrations were cut short by the linesman's flag. I knew I was onside – I started my run from behind Jackie McNamara – so when the ball hit the net I celebrated accordingly. It was only once I reached the halfway line and the game was restarting with a free kick that I realised the goal hadn't stood.

To be honest getting flagged offside when I was clearly onside happened to me a few times when I was at Rangers. I think a lot of that had to do with my pace but games like that one against Celtic were also incredibly fast. You didn't have time to think and you couldn't hear anything. For most matches at Ibrox it would be raucous for about 10 or 15 minutes but for Old Firm fixtures it was like that for 90 minutes. It was the same when we played them at Parkhead and Hampden too.

Those games were special to play in, but Walter once again didn't do too much different when it came to preparing for them. He was unruffled in the dressing room but for the players it was different. Ahead of other matches in the league and even the Champions League we were, as a whole, relatively calm but when we played Celtic it was fever pitch as we were waiting to go out on to the pitch. In fact, I recall on one occasion that Bomber got himself so pumped up that he started hyperventilating!

When decisions like the goal being ruled out go against you, you must forget about it immediately and get on with the game. We eventually equalised six minutes before the interval when Laudrup scored and, although John Collins restored Celtic's lead with a penalty early in the second half, a header from Coisty and a Tosh McKinlay own goal put us 3-2 ahead with 20 minutes to go. Between those goals Pierre van Hooijdonk had been thwarted by one of the best saves I've ever seen. He met a cross from the left on the volley from six yards but Goram somehow got a hand to it and diverted the ball to safety. The big Dutchman did eventually find a way past Andy to end the scoring at 3-3.

The draw kept us four points ahead of Celtic at the top of the table and we consolidated that lead with a terrific run of results over the festive period. We beat Kilmarnock 3-0 on Boxing Day and followed that with a 7-0 hammering of Hibs. Gordon Durie scored four times in the latter match – my 200th appearance in a Rangers jersey incidentally – and Gascoigne scored a superb solo goal. But the game will also be remembered for the lack of humour shown by the referee, Douglas Hope.

A couple of minutes before half-time one of our attacks broke down and I noticed that the referee had dropped his yellow card on the pitch. I picked it up and handed it to Gascoigne. But rather than simply hand the card back to Hope, Paul decided to 'book' the referee. Hope didn't see the funny side and promptly brandished the yellow card in front of Gascoigne.

I don't think anyone could believe it had happened, but Paul was getting a bit of stick at the time for the number of times he had been booked. For me, though, as a defender a yellow card didn't mean anything. If you accumulate too many you get suspended but I was so focussed on the game that after I was booked, I never really got involved with the referee. I just got on with it.

We started the New Year with a hard-fought 0-0 draw at Parkhead before I had an eventful game against Falkirk at Brockville. Durie had us 1-0 up inside three minutes and I was involved in our second goal after 26 minutes, slipping a pass to Jukey and, when his shot was blocked, Coisty turned in the rebound. And we were 3-0 up before the interval when I rose to head home a cross from Gascoigne. I almost added another to my goal tally that day as I had one chalked off for a tight offside decision and drew a couple of good saves from their goalkeeper, Tony Parks.

Our defensive unit was as tight as it had ever been – we had conceded just ten goals in the 22 league games played – and I was thriving in an attacking sense too. Although I was never going to be a regular goalscorer I became an important weapon in our attacking arsenal and I was in the box again 16 minutes from the end of the Falkirk game when I was felled by their full-back. Coisty did what he did best and despatched the penalty to give us a 4-0 win and a sixth successive clean sheet.

But there was a blip on the horizon. Having built our success that season on defensive solidity we had a bad day at the office when we welcomed Hearts to Ibrox in late January. Allan Johnston scored a hat-trick and we lost 3-0, our first defeat in the league since Hibs had won 1-0 at Ibrox back in September. Our lead over Celtic was now just a single point. Having been also-rans for several years they now had a really good team under Tommy Burns and for the first time for a while they were our closest challengers. We had been the only team to beat them in the league, so we had to make sure that performances like the one against Hearts were few and far between.

The Scottish Cup campaign began at my old stomping ground, Pittodrie, but it wasn't a tough away draw against the Dons. Instead we played Keith from the Highland League and I added my fourth goal of the season in our 10-1 win. My goal – our seventh of the afternoon – was again created by a sumptuous pass from Laudrup but it was my fellow full-back Alec Cleland who hogged the headlines with a hat-trick inside the first 29 minutes. Ian Ferguson, who had been in and out the team all season through injury, also scored three.

A couple of weeks later we grabbed an edge in the title race. We faced a typically dogged Motherwell at Ibrox and looked set to drop a couple of points when we were pegged back twice after taking the lead. But with 18 minutes to go Coisty was brought on and there was an inevitability about what would happen next. The man made a career out of rewriting scripts and when we won a penalty he stepped up and scored with what was his first touch of the ball. It was a vital win and when news filtered through that Celtic had drawn 0-0 at Falkirk our lead at the top was up to three points.

Wins over Aberdeen and Hibs maintained that advantage ahead of the season's final Old Firm league match at Ibrox on 17 March. But after 17 consecutive appearances I wouldn't be wearing the number three jersey as I had picked up a booking in the win over Aberdeen and that took me over the points threshold to earn a two-match ban. That meant I was in the stands when Alan McLaren's header hit the net to give us the lead against Celtic. We should have gone on and won the game, especially after Jackie McNamara was sent off with 13 minutes to go. But we passed up several chances before John Hughes equalised with just three minutes left.

I also missed out when we went to Stark's Park to face Raith Rovers. Looking back now, this was arguably one of the most important matches of all the ones played during the nine-in-a-row run. With my former Aberdeen team-mate Theo Snelders making his debut in goal, we found ourselves 2-1 down with only seven minutes remaining. But we showed real grit to score three times in the short time there was left to eke out a 4-2 win. Coisty was the hero with a hat-trick but he passed up the chance of a fourth goal when we were awarded a penalty in stoppage time. Jukey took it instead and scored and it later emerged that the forever goal-hungry McCoist had allowed Durie to take the spot-kick as he had a bet on with Gascoigne. The wager was based on who would end the season with more goals, Paul or Gordon, and Coisty's generosity edged Durie three goals ahead of our Geordie genius.

I was back in position the following weekend for the Scottish Cup semi-final. Our opponents were, inevitably, Celtic, this being the sixth encounter between the sides that season. We were unbeaten in the previous five and we made it six in a row that afternoon at Hampden. I was involved in the opening goal three minutes before the interval, my shot being parried into the hitting zone of McCoist by Gordon Marshall. In those situations, Ally didn't miss and when Laudrup lobbed in a second midway through the second half we were through to the final. It must have been tough on the Celtic players as this was only their third domestic defeat of the season – all of them at the hands of us. But their re-emergence had reinvigorated Rangers and, after plodding to the previous two titles, we were now racing towards an eighth title in a row and a domestic Double.

There was to be one more bump in the road when we lost 2-0 in a midweek game at Tynecastle but Celtic failed to punish us fully as they could only draw 1-1 at home against Kilmarnock. That set the stage for the penultimate match of the league season and once again Aberdeen stood in our way of the title. So often our closest challengers in the early 1990s, they came to Ibrox a massive 29 points behind us in third place. And although they silenced the stadium by taking the lead, Gascoigne took over and almost single-handed secured eight championships in a row.

With ten minutes to go he picked up the ball on the halfway line and started to run at the Aberdeen defence. As he was making his way towards the left side of the pitch, I made an overlapping run thinking that he might play me in. I'm glad in the end that he didn't. Instead he made his way to the edge of the box and curled the ball beyond Michael Watt. The completion of his hat-trick six minutes later sealed the deal and we were champions again.

When Paul scored that second goal, I was the first to reach him to celebrate. I hauled him to the ground and the rest of the lads piled on top of us. I didn't really over celebrate-goals but in that instance the whole occasion and the fact it was against Aberdeen resulted in a jubilant response. For me, every time we played Aberdeen there was a bit more edge as I didn't want to lose or draw any games against them.

All that remained was to complete the Double and our opponents at Hampden would be Hearts, one of only three teams to beat us domestically that season. But despite scoring five without reply in the previous two encounters they were no match for us that afternoon and the principal reason for that was Brian Laudrup.

Brian tormented Hearts that afternoon, scoring the first two goals and laying three on a plate for Gordon Durie. He was unplayable and after his second goal went in you knew there was no way back for Hearts. We could relax a little and turn on the style and that remains the only cup final I played in that turned into a bit of a party. It was a game you just didn't want to end.

We were now on the cusp of history and the Holy Grail of nine league titles in a row was within our grasp. The pressure was huge, but my season wouldn't start until the end of October. In addition to the hamstring problems I had had during the season I had also been playing with an injury to my right knee. I went in for surgery two days after we beat Hearts and I remember vividly the surgeon telling me he was confident I would play again. Although I had been out for long spells with injury in the past, when the surgeon said that it was the first time I can remember thinking that there was chance I wouldn't play again. I have to admit I became a bit selfish after that.

In total I was out for action for five months. Alan McLaren had also undergone knee surgery – his injury was worse than mine and would eventually end his career – and we were buddies in the gym for months. We would still change with the rest of the squad before training but when they boarded the minibus to go to the training venue – these were the days before the training centre so we would often train at places like the West of Scotland Cricket Ground – we would stay behind to sweat it out in the gym. We were both pretty low but tried our best to motivate each other. I wasn't going to games either as I preferred to stay at home as watching from the stands was never something I enjoyed.

I wasn't even sure that once I was fit I would be a Rangers player. As I started my recovery there were rumours in the media that I was on my way out of Ibrox. I had one year left on my contract and, conscious of the consequences of losing players on a Bosman deal, David Murray was looking to tie up players like myself on long-term contracts. Negotiations had begun with my agent but that didn't stop the press speculating that Rangers were about to cash in on a marketable asset. Manchester United, Newcastle and Arsenal were rumoured to be interested and a fee of around £2m was bandied about. But there was no foundation at that point in any of the rumours. My focus was on fitness and getting back into the Rangers first team and the first I knew of the perceived interest was when I read the stories in the papers.

I eventually came back into the team for the League Cup semi-final against Dunfermline on 22 October but I had to ease myself back in as the doctors felt that too many games in such a short period of time could set me back. That was probably in Walter's thinking when he picked me as sub for the game against Motherwell four days later as we had the small matter of Ajax at Ibrox in the Champions League to think about. We had romped through the qualifying round, defeating Alania Vladikavkaz 10-3 on aggregate, but we had lost our first three group matches against Grasshopper Zürich (3-0), Auxerre (2-1) and Ajax (4-1). Our luck didn't improve at Ibrox and the 1-0 defeat ended our interest in the competition.

My return to action gave me the chance to link up on the left with our new signing, Jorg Albertz. Jorg was unlike a lot of the big-money buys at that time as not too many people had heard of him. He was better in central midfield, but he could fill in in the wide areas too. He was fantastic, good on the ball and very rarely gave it away. But one of the first things I noticed about him was he was a smoker. Although most players smoked in the 1960s and '70s it was very rare for it to happen when I played. The only other guy who did it at that time was Peter van Vossen.

In those days, after Walter had done his team talk and we got stripped, I would grab a towel and go into the shower area and do my stretches. I recall before one game – I think it might have been at Parkhead – going in and seeing Jorg and Peter perched against the sinks lighting a cigarette. It was weird, although I am led to believe that if you smoke at a young age, your body gets used to it and it doesn't adversely affect your fitness levels.

Although we were out of the Champions League, we were now entering a crucial stage of the season domestically, with two fixtures at Parkhead sticking out. We were neck and neck with Celtic at the top of the league so top spot was up for grabs when we faced them. We had beaten them 2-0 at Ibrox earlier in the season and got off to a great start in this one when Laudrup scored after just seven minutes. What followed was an extraordinary game that featured a fox, two missed penalties and a glaring miss from our Dutch striker Van Vossen.

Gazza missed the spot kick we were awarded while Goram did what Goram did best to thwart Pierre van Hooijdonk with only six minutes left. But we should have been out of sight by then. Jorg teed up Peter about eight yards with a gaping goal in front of him. I was right behind him so turned away to celebrate as I was certain he would score. But when I turned back, I saw Van Vossen with his head in his hands and the ball not in the net. There's no doubt that that made it difficult for us, but we did what that team did, hung on and secured a vital three points.

We returned to Parkhead ten days later to face Hearts in the League Cup Final and despite me having made a return to the starting XI, Walter decided to leave me on the bench for this one. I hadn't trained in the early part of the week as I had been laid low by a virus. I came back in on the Thursday but had missed the trip to Turnberry in the week leading up to the final. It was to take place on the Sunday, so I went with the squad to the Moathouse Hotel on the Friday night and trained on the Saturday with no ill effects. I expected I would be in the team when Walter announced it.

Prior to finals we always went from the hotel to Ibrox to get the team bus and we were sitting in the dressing room when Davie Dodds came in and said the gaffer wanted to see me. I went through and he told me that as I hadn't trained much, he was putting me on the bench. While I recognised his rationale my immediate feeling was that I had been dropped. My face was tripping me on the bus journey to Parkhead and even in the warm-up I was still licking my wounds and feeling sorry for myself. And when I was out warming up behind the goals during the first half my head was all over the place and I was miles away.

Coisty was the main man in that first half. Although now in the veteran stages of his career, he was still razor-sharp and scored twice inside the first 26 minutes to put us 2-0 ahead. But he then fell out with Gazza and when Steve Fulton scored to half our lead two minutes before the interval it's fair to say Walter was less than happy in the dressing room.

I came in still feeling sorry for myself, not expecting that I would get on the pitch. But Walter told me I was on. This all came after Gazza and McCoist had to be separated after their on-field disagreement had continued into the dressing room. But that altercation won the League Cup. Gazza needed that at times, someone to have a go at him and push him to a higher level. And in that second half he raised his game to another level, scored two magnificent goals and ensured the trophy was on its way back to the trophy room at Ibrox.

The following week I was back in the starting XI and I marked my return with a goal against Aberdeen for the first time. It was probably the worst goal I ever scored in my career too. After a typical burst of pace from Laudrup, he cut the ball back and there was I, six yards from goal. But I stumbled as the ball arrived and it hit my right foot and spun beyond Nicky Walker in the Aberdeen goal. I was elated but Coisty was very cute as we celebrated. Perhaps thinking I might make a gesture that would get me in trouble, he pinned my arms to my side as he hugged me but, as poor a goal as it was, it was still a real rush scoring at my old stomping ground.

Charlie Miller and Brian Laudrup also scored that day to secure a straightforward 3-0 victory. That win came 24 hours after Celtic had drawn 2-2 with Hearts so we were now five points clear. And we stretched that to eight points six days later when we beat Hibs 4-3 at Ibrox. This was a special day for Coisty as his two goals made him the top post-war goalscorer in Scottish league football.

From a personal point of view, I was just glad to be getting a run of games and I racked up my tenth start in succession when we went to Easter Road and beat Hibs 2-1. That result came just two days after we had beaten Celtic 3-1 at Ibrox. There was virtually nobody fully fit for that one as there was a flu bug going around. In fact, I think it was so bad that I played at centre-back that day. But we got the win thanks to a thunderbolt from Jorg and a late double from an unsung hero.

Jorg's goal has no doubt been seen millions of times on YouTube. I was fouled by Jackie McNamara about 25 yards from goal and when I got back to my feet I stood right behind Jorg and got a great view as he strode forward and hammered the ball beyond Stewart Kerr with his left foot. Celtic equalised but we won the game when our Danish striker Erik Bo Andersen scored late in the game. He wasn't a big-name signing so I think a lot of opponents underestimated him. But he was deceptively quick and glided over the ground and he did that twice to get on the end of passes from Jorg and score to earn us a crucial 3-1 win. And to round off a special night, I was voted man of the match by Sky Sports who were showing the match live.

I also made a goalscoring contribution in the festive fixtures, scoring in successive games against Kilmarnock and Hearts. My goal in the latter game was a favourite as I picked up the ball on the halfway line, ran forward unchallenged then fired the ball beyond Giles Rousset from the edge of the box.

But all was not well at that time. Although negotiations had begun with the club on a new contract, they were stalling. I had hoped to get a four-year deal as that would have secured me a testimonial, but the club were only offering three years. At that time there was interest from a few clubs in Europe and I have to admit that was turning my head.

With my future up in the air all I could do was focus on playing but that was curtailed in March when I was injured in our Scottish Cup defeat against Celtic. That meant I missed out when we returned to Parkhead ten days later in the league and effectively clinched nine in a row. When I was injured or suspended, I didn't like to go to games as I felt it made you feel worse so I would usually stay at home and listen to the games on the radio. This one was live on TV, though, and I was delighted as I watched Laudrup lob Stewart Kerr to give us a 1-0 win.

I missed a total of three matches but came back when we beat Dunfermline 4-0 at home. On the scoresheet that day was Mark Hateley. Bringing Mark back was another stroke of genius from Walter. When he left in 1995, I think most observers thought he was finished so no one expected him to come back. But he did and, although he ended up getting sent off, his physical presence ruffled the Celtic defence and caused havoc.

I scored on my next outing – a 6-0 win over Raith Rovers at Stark's Park – and that set up a title party at Ibrox against Motherwell. All we had to do was win the game, but we flopped miserably. Owen Coyle scored twice to inflict upon us a 2-0 defeat. I think as a squad we thought it was a foregone conclusion we would beat them, but they were fighting for survival and were better than us on the day. They were more motivated and intent on spoiling the party and I could align myself with that. Back on the final day of 1988/89 I was part of the Aberdeen team that went to Ibrox a few weeks after Rangers had been crowned champions. Alex Smith made it clear to us that day that we were there to spoil the party and we did that by winning 3-0. I think Motherwell came with a similar attitude and, although we huffed and puffed, we couldn't find the goals we needed.

I remember coming in after the game and thinking we had blown it. Our last two games were away from home at two of the most difficult venues in Scotland, Tannadice and Tynecastle. I thought we were in trouble as outside Parkhead they are arguably the two toughest places to go and get a win.

But my concerns were allayed just two days later when we faced Dundee United and beat them 1-0. It was the win we needed to secure that ninth successive title and everyone remembers Charlie Miller's terrific cross with his left foot and Laudrup's bullet header for our goal that night. I played a vital part in the build-up for the goal too as it was my quick throw-in that released Charlie on the left wing.

That goal made life a lot easier for us. United were notoriously difficult to break down at home but after we got ourselves in front, I was pretty confident we wouldn't concede anything. When the referee blew his whistle at the end of the game there was an explosion of joy from the Rangers fans and the players were buzzing too. There was a slight tinge of disappointment that we didn't clinch it at Ibrox, but the boys enjoyed the bus journey back to Glasgow.

But I wasn't with them and looking back now that's one of the few regrets I have. After the game I elected to go home to

Newton Mearns with Kym, and I don't think I realised that there was going to be such a big party when the bus got back to Ibrox. And I was also conscious that I wouldn't be a Rangers player for much longer. I had pretty much agreed to sign for Leeds United and actually went to Leeds on the Saturday when Rangers played their last game of the season against Hearts. I had been given the chance to play at Tynecastle but decided not to and again I missed out as after the game the lads were flown back to Ibrox in a helicopter for another party with the fans. They were singing and dancing in the rain, but I was so wrapped up in my next move. I also think I was a bit naïve and didn't quite realise how significant an achievement winning nine successive titles was.

I had been part of six of those victories and had also added three Scottish Cups and three League Cups to my medal collection. But after 267 appearances in a Rangers jersey it was time to move on and embark on another challenge. Little did I know at the time that that next chapter would be the one that effectively brought an end to my playing career.

CHAPTER 7

SCUNNERED WITH SCOTLAND

I'M OFTEN asked about my Scotland career and what many see as a paltry return of just three full caps. After all, I was the first-choice left-back for the most successful team in the country so one would have expected my name would also have been first on the team sheet when Andy Roxburgh and then Craig Brown were selecting the starting XI. But that wasn't the case as the likes of Maurice Malpas, Tom Boyd and, latterly, Rob MacKinnon and Tosh McKinlay were chosen ahead of me.

My international career started back in 1983 when I was selected at under-14 level for a Boys' Clubs of Scotland fixture against Wales at Linksfield Park in Aberdeen. Indeed, the entire XI that day was made up of players from the Aberdeen Youth Service team. This was a Boys' Club select and I was joined by my Deeside team-mates Kevin Riddell and Martin Craig, with the rest of the squad comprising players from Sunnybank Athletic, Aberdeen Lads Club, King Street and Middlefield.

The game took place towards the end of my first season as an 'S' Form with Aberdeen and, although we trailed 1-0 at half-time, I equalised with a 20-yard 'daisy-cutter' eight minutes after the restart. And I was involved in what proved to be the winning goal a minute later. My cross into the box caused havoc and when the Welsh goalkeeper parried the ball, Andy Smith, who played for King Street, scored. This was the same Andy Smith who scored against Rangers for Airdrie in the Scottish Cup Final in 1992. We also played together in the Aberdeen Primary Schools select team.

That was a terrific experience but when it came to stepping up to the next level, I started to panic a bit as I didn't think I was good enough. To get picked for the under-15s you needed to go to regional trials and then a pool of 56 players would be selected to go to Inverclyde for three days. That 56 was to be whittled down to 32, each of whom would be back in Largs for a week before the final squad of 16 was selected for the schoolboy international against England.

That match was a huge deal. It had taken place every year since 1911, apart from during World War II and was televised live on TV. It drew huge crowds and one of the most famous encounters was in 1980 when 69,000 attended and watched my future team-mate, Paul Rideout, score a hat-trick as England won a gripping match 5-4. The likes of Paul McStay and John Robertson were in the Scotland team and I hoped to emulate them by making the squad.

I did well in the Aberdeen trials, scoring five goals, and my performances were good enough to ensure I was one of only three from the north-east to make it to Inverclyde. But although I made it to the last 32, when the letter from the SFA came in through the door it was a rejection, I hadn't made the squad. Scott Tait, who would be the best man at my wedding, was the only player from Aberdeen to make it and there were a few people surprised that I didn't join him.

I must admit I was disappointed not to make it and, if anything, the rejection fuelled the thought process I had that I wasn't quite good enough. But my determination to succeed won through and a year later I had trials at under-16 level. Before they took place, I decided to have a chat with Andy Roxburgh and Ross Mathie who were the coaching team. This was around the time I was being converted into a left-back by Aberdeen, so I wanted to know what position they wanted me to play. It was evident that Andy and Ross were aware of me and what I had to offer so I ended up playing as a left-winger and in central midfield.

Unlike a year earlier, I made the cut this time and my time at that level turned out to be the most enjoyable experience I had as a Scotland player. We had some really good players such as Billy McKinlay and Derek Whyte, and we did so well that I found myself representing Scotland at a major championship.

In May 1985 Hungary were hosting the European Under-16 Championship finals and the qualifying campaign for that was structured such that there were 12 groups, each comprising two teams. Scotland were drawn in Group 1 with Finland and the away match was played in Espoo, which is the second-largest city in the country. In addition to being my first appearance for the under-16s this was also my first experience of flying and I have to admit I was shitting myself. The safety briefing was frightening for a first-time flyer and at the end of a journey that lasted a total of ten hours we were shattered. And we must have still been suffering the effects of the travelling when we took on the Finns as we lost 3-1.

The home match was at Rugby Park two weeks later, and I started our comeback when I scored after just five minutes. I had the ball in the net just after the half-hour too, but the goal was ruled out for offside. My Aberdeen team-mate Alan Selbie then levelled things up at 3-3 11 minutes into the second half and two further goals from Terry Wilson of Nottingham Forest sealed our place in the finals.

Alan Selbie was a good lad, but he was terrible when it came to keeping secrets. He and I were part of an Aberdeen squad that travelled to Groningen in the Netherlands for a youth tournament and the last game was against Coventry City. In training, we had worked on a routine at a corner where one player would roll the ball out of the arc then walk away. Another of the lads would then collect the ball and dribble it into the box and try and create a scoring chance. When we won a corner against Coventry, we tried to work the routine but their defenders read it, cleared the ball and went up the other end and scored. We couldn't understand how they had known we were going to do that until it emerged Alan had divulged the plans to them. Both teams had snuck out of the hotel the night before the game and it transpired that during that time Alan had told the Coventry lads what we had been working on!

The squad for the finals was announced by the head coach, Ross Mathie, a few weeks later and I was one of four Aberdeen players named. Alan Selbie and I were joined by Scott Tait and Robert McRobb. Also in the pool were Gus McPherson of Rangers, Dundee United's Billy McKinlay and the goalkeeper, Les Fridge, who had recently signed for Chelsea.

When the draw was made for the tournament we were grouped with Greece, France and Iceland in Group C. We were staying in a hotel in Budapest – the Aberdonians, Tait, Selbie and Robertson shared a room – and our first game against Iceland was in Jászberény, which is about 37 miles outside the Hungarian capital. And it proved a memorable game for me as I scored both our goals in a 2-0 win. They came four minutes apart, late in the first half. The first was a header and shortly before the interval it was followed by a long-range effort.

We faced the Greeks next and they were joint top of the group with us having beaten France 2-0. This match was in Szolnok, but after East Fife's Paul Hunter equalised, Greece scored the winner six minutes from time to leave us up against it to qualify for the semi-finals. Only the group winners went through so, in addition to beating France, we had to hope Iceland, who had been hammered 4-0 by the French, beat Greece. In the end neither happened. Ross Mathie had to make five changes to the team that lost to Greece as some players were suffering due to the heat and humidity. The changes didn't make an impact as we lost 3-0 but the outcome was academic as Greece beat Iceland 4-0.

From a personal point of view the tournament was a great experience. I played in all three games and made a real impression, with media reports after the France game singling myself, Robert McRobb and Derek Whyte out as players who had 'tremendous potential'.

I moved on to the next rung on the international ladder after that and played in an under-17 tournament in Sweden – it was snowing so hard that all the games were played indoors – then on to under-18 level. And as I stepped up I was thrown into the heat of the qualifying campaign for the European Championship. That had begun back in November 1984, with

Scotland in Group 1 alongside the Republic of Ireland, England and Iceland. It all started with a 2-1 win over England at Craven Cottage before I made the bench when we drew 1-1 against the Irish four months later. I was absent from the starting XI again when we went to Reykjavík and beat Iceland 2-0 but made my first start at that level when goals from Scott Nisbet and Paul Wright earned a 2-0 win in the return fixture at Annfield, home of Stirling Albion.

We were now in pole position and a 1-0 win over the Republic of Ireland in January all but sealed our place in the finals in Yugoslavia. To be pipped at the post by the Irish, they had to beat England by three clear goals while we had to lose to England at Pittodrie. In the end we didn't need to beat England as they beat the Republic of Ireland 2-0 which meant the Auld Enemy clash was a formality. I was selected at left-back at my home ground and was involved in the move that created the first goal for our captain Gordon McLeod of Dundee United. Although England levelled the scores after I fouled Wayne Aspinall and gave away a penalty, further goals from Wright, Nisbet and Miller secured a 4-1 win. We were bound for the Balkans later that year.

However, I wasn't in the squad that was selected as by the time the tournament took place I was in the first team at Aberdeen and now had my sights set on playing for Scotland at under-21 level. And by February 1987 I had caught the eye of Craig Brown, manager of the Scotland under-21s, as he picked me in the squad to face the Republic of Ireland at Easter Road. This was the second of our qualifying games for the European Championships and we were joined in Group 7 by Belgium and the Republic of Ireland. Goals from Rab Shannon and Kevin Gallacher gave us an immediate advantage when we had beaten the Irish 2-1 in Dundalk back in October and we cemented our place at the top of Group 7 when we beat them again in Edinburgh.

I didn't start the match but was called upon at half-time to replace Derek Whyte. I took my place in a back four that included my team-mate Alex McLeish, who at the age of 28 was one of the over-age players in the team that night. That was permitted at under-21 level back then and, for a young lad like me, similarly to at Aberdeen, having that experience in the team was a huge benefit. In addition to Alex, Scotland included my future team-mates Ian Durrant, Gordon Durie and Ian Ferguson but the hero of the hour was Rangers' Robert Fleck. He had looked to be on the way out at Ibrox but had formed a lethal partnership with Ally McCoist and he carried that form into this fixture, scoring a hat-trick in a 4-1 win. Fergie got the other goal with Dumbarton's Owen Coyle on the scoresheet for the visitors. The Irish side that night included the likes of Dennis Irwin, John Sheridan and Steve Staunton, all of whom would play in the top flight in England. That showed just how good the result had been and with two fixtures to come against Belgium we were in the driving seat.

I also won a 'B' cap that year. These matches were designed to give games to players who were being considered for call-up to the full national squad, so it was another boost for me when I was selected as I was only 18 at the time. It was also the first match of that sort for 30 years and we faced France at Pittodrie. The French were able to call upon the likes of Franck Sauzée, Eric Cantona and Laurent Blanc, while I had four of my Aberdeen team-mates – Bryan Gunn, Stewart McKimmie, Alex McLeish and Neil Simpson – alongside me in a navy blue jersey.

On the night, Ian Wilson, an Aberdonian who was playing for Leicester City at the time, was the top man for Scotland but it was his Leicester team-mate Gary McAllister who got the Scotland goal. The French went ahead after 21 minutes when Bernard Ferrer of Auxerre scored but Gary equalised early in the second half when he headed the ball beyond the French goalkeeper from close range.

Back at under-21 level I missed the next qualifier, away to Belgium, as I had chickenpox and a fractured foot meant I was also missing for the return fixture six months later, a last-minute Andy Walker goal giving Scotland a 1-0 win at Brockville.

We ended up topping Group 7 which took us through to the quarter-final stage. Joining us there were France, Spain, Italy, Greece, Czechoslovakia, the Netherlands and England. Inevitably we drew England and the tie was played over two legs, with the first leg at Pittodrie on 16 February 1988 and the return at the City Ground in Nottingham a month later.

We had a fantastic squad of players at that time. Our over-age players were Bobby Geddes of Dundee and Paul Hegarty of Dundee United and in midfield we had the Rangers duo of Ian Durrant and Derek Ferguson. On the bench for the first leg too was Ian Ferguson who had just moved from St Mirren to Rangers for almost £1m. England, managed by the former Manchester United boss Dave Sexton, had a pool of quality players too as they were able to call upon the likes of Martin Keown, Des Walker, Nigel Clough and Tony Dorigo. But their talisman was a man I would share a dressing room with a few years later: Paul John Gascoigne.

The first match was a fairly even contest. Given the abundance of talent in that area, most of the play was in the middle of the park and it was two of our midfielders, Derek Ferguson and Durranty, who carved out our best chance on the night. Derek's through ball to release Ian was brilliant but Perry Suckling in the England goal was equal to his effort. And we paid for that when, after 85 minutes, an effort from Watford's Gary Porter gave England a crucial advantage in the battle for a place in the last four.

Craig Brown made three changes to the team for the return leg. Alan Main replaced Bobby Geddes in goal – Cammy Duncan of Motherwell was supposed to play but injured a finger in training – and Stuart McCall and John Collins came in for Durrant and Derek Ferguson in midfield. Stuart, another who I would have the pleasure of playing alongside at Rangers, had been on the verge of playing for England but had a last-minute change of heart. He was on the bench for their qualifying tie in Turkey and was called upon to take to the field in the final minute. But the wee man took his time getting ready as he felt he should have opted for Scotland and, when he didn't get on, it opened the door to the Scotland team. As a country we were lucky to have such a combative midfielder in our ranks and Stuart and his wife were neighbours and close friends when we both signed for Rangers in 1991.

We were met by lashing rain as we took to the field at the home of Nottingham Forest and the conditions may well have contributed when I almost scored the goal we craved. I made my way forward and shot for goal but, after initially spilling the ball, Suckling managed to snaffle it before any of our forwards could pounce. But that was as good as it got for Scotland and me, another late goal proving our undoing, with Manchester City's David White getting the decisive counter with eight minutes remaining.

Writing a couple of days later in the *Glasgow Herald*, Ian Paul noted that I had committed a couple of 'cardinal errors' but had 'contributed some fine play'. In his opinion the first cancelled out the last but I was still only 19 and this was only my third under-21 cap. I was still learning my trade, not just at international level but at club level too and I hoped to garner more experience with Scotland in the qualifying campaign for the Euros in 1990.

We were bracketed in Group 5 this time and ended up with one of the toughest sections possible. We were up against reigning champions France, Norway and Yugoslavia, with the latter able to call upon the rich talents of Alen Bokšić, Davor Šuker, Zvonimir Boban and Robert Prosinečki.

We faced the Norwegians first in Drammen in September 1988. I played in that one but after Joe Miller put us ahead from the penalty spot Norway equalised and earned a point. And our hopes of qualification were dealt a further blow when Šuker and Prosinečki were on the scoresheet when the Yugoslavs beat us 2-0 at Tynecastle. Injury counted me out of our third match against the French at Tannadice – they had Marcel Desailly and Didier Deschamps in their starting XI and Thierry Henry on the bench, and although Desailly was sent off they still won 3-2 – but I was back at left-back when we were taught a lesson against Yugoslavia in the Gradski Stadium in Podgorica.

Essentially, we couldn't get near them and were 2-0 down after only 32 minutes. A fine goal from Kevin Gallacher gave us hope but that proved to be false when further goals from Šuker and Prosinečki condemned us to a 4-1 defeat. And to compound our misery we went along to watch the senior team play 24 hours later and they too were outclassed, losing 3-1.

We finished the campaign with a 2-0 win over Norway in Perth – Mike Galloway and Billy McKinlay got the goals – and that would be it for me at international level until I won my first full cap against Northern Ireland at Hampden over two years later. There had been talk when I was at Aberdeen about myself and Stewart McKimmie being the regular full-backs for Scotland but that never materialised. And when I went to Rangers I remember a cartoon appearing in one of the newspapers that depicted me getting a trophy cabinet made to house all the Scotland caps I would be getting now I had moved to Glasgow. That too never materialised.

I hadn't been called up before the Northern Ireland game and the first I knew I was in the squad was via Teletext. We met up before the game and I shared a room with Keith Wright of Hibs who was also winning his first cap. Gordon Strachan, who in his mid-30s was at the heart of the midfield for a Leeds United side pushing for the English First Division title, was captain for the night and strangely I was picked alongside him in midfield as Maurice Malpas was at left-back, with Stewart McKimmie, Goughie and Dave McPherson completing the back four.

I should have been buzzing as in my mind playing for your country should be the highlight of your career – nothing would ever beat it – but I was pretty disappointed at the end of the night. Coisty scored the only goal of the game after 11 minutes but playing in the wide midfield role was a strange experience and I think I only touched the ball a couple of times in the opening half. I reverted to left-back in the second half – Gordon Durie came on for McKimmie and Malpas was moved to right-back – and played a lot better but I don't know if the initial selection in midfield, the fact it was a friendly, the weather wasn't great or that it was a pretty poor crowd, this one, after all the big games I had played with Aberdeen and Rangers, was a bit of a let-down.

That should have been the springboard for me, the first of many caps for my country. Indeed, I thought I had a chance of making the squad for the 1992 European Championships that summer in Sweden. Although there were very few places left up for grabs, many felt that getting selected for the next friendly against Finland a month after the Northern Ireland game would be an indication I was in with a shout of making the final squad. But I picked up an ankle injury playing for Rangers the weekend prior and that ruled me out.

I wasn't too disappointed to miss the Euros as I felt I was young enough that I still had a better chance of playing in at least three or four major tournaments in the years ahead. The first of those was the World Cup in the USA in 1994 but it wasn't difficult to start to read between the lines for my international fortunes as I didn't pull on a dark blue jersey again until September 1993, when we took on Switzerland at Pittodrie in a qualifier.

I made the 22-man squad for a few of the games prior to that but I always had a weird feeling that, although I was selected, I wasn't going to play. Maurice Malpas, who was coming to the end of his career and Tom Boyd were the chosen ones at left-back. Malpas was a bit of a 'steady Eddie' and a good defender, but I felt I offered a bit more going forward. Boyd offered a bit of versatility as he was a right-footed left-back. They were the two Andy Roxburgh favoured so for me that meant when the squad was whittled down to the matchday pool of 18, I was either in the stand or on the bench.

But the picture painted both before and after that Switzerland game was a better one. I hadn't made the original squad but Boyd was suspended and there were some injuries, so Walter phoned me on the Sunday prior to the game and said Andy wanted me to go and play. I joined up with the squad on the Monday then played really well on the Wednesday – it was from my through ball that John Collins scored our goal in a 1-1 draw – and I drew a huge amount of praise after the game. Archie was there and he told me afterwards that he thought I had been brilliant, so I genuinely thought that was it, I was going to be in with a shout of being Scotland's left-back.

But it didn't work out that way and I was soon back on the sidelines. I travelled with the squad to Malta for our last fixture in the group a couple of months later, but I was benched again. And to compound matters another left-back, Motherwell's Rab McKinnon, was chosen to start. This was Craig Brown's first official match in charge – he had been in a caretaker role since Andy Roxburgh resigned in September – so I was hoping that his appointment might effect a change in my international fortunes as I didn't really think Andy rated me. I had worked under Craig with the under-21s but it soon became evident that even though Walter felt I was the best left-back at his disposal, Craig clearly didn't agree.

For the most part I was picked as a sub and I knew that as a defender there was very little chance I would get on. And it would eventually get to the stage that I knew well in advance of the game that I wouldn't be in the starting XI. There was one match against Russia in the qualifiers for Euro '96 and they had Andrej Kanchelskis roaming down the right wing. But in the media Brown was talking about how Tom Boyd was going to stop him in his tracks so it was pretty obvious that unless Tom picked up an injury, I wouldn't be playing. That impacted my confidence and I used to go back to training with Rangers after being away and it would take me a wee while to get that confidence back.

No one ever spoke to me and explained why I was being left out, but the lack of dialogue was partly my fault too as I was so quiet. At Aberdeen and Rangers I had no need to go and speak to the manager as I was playing the majority of the time so perhaps my personality held me back from asking Andy and then Craig why I wasn't being picked for the team.

The next international was a friendly against the Netherlands at Hampden in March 1994. But prior to that there was a B international arranged against Wales at the Racecourse Ground in Wrexham. Craig was looking to use this game to blood some young players – Stephen Wright, who I had played with at Aberdeen, was selected – and get a look at some fringe players so, given that I was 25 and was picked, I clearly fell into the latter category.

Frustration was starting to creep in. Although I was an established Premier Division player with over eight years' experience in the top flight and had played in the Champions League, it was clear that Craig still needed convincing that I merited a place in the Scotland team. As it was, I was one of only a few to get a positive review in the press after the Wales game. It was a drab and dismal match that we lost 2-1 but the fact I had played well made me think I would be in with a shout of playing against the Dutch.

Craig must have been in agreement as he picked me to start the match and, in my opinion, this was my last chance to stake my claim for the number three jersey. But the match proved to be my last one for Scotland. Notable players in a world-class

Dutch XI that night were Dennis Bergkamp, Frank de Boer, Frank Rijkaard, my former Aberdeen team-mate Hans Gillhaus, and Brian Roy, who scored the only goal of the game after 23 minutes. But the main man for me was my direct opponent, Gaston Taument of Feyenoord.

Craig played three at the back that night – Craig Levein, Colin Hendry and Alan McLaren were the centre-backs – which meant myself and Stewart McKimmie were encouraged to push forward. At that stage of my career I hadn't played in that system a lot so there were a few times when Taument got in behind me and I had to cover a lot of ground to catch him. Eventually that took its toll and, just after half-time, I pulled my hamstring. I was eventually replaced by John Collins after 65 minutes and when that injury kept me out the Rangers team for a couple of games I decided enough was enough.

I was called up to a few squads after that but after we lost 1-0 against Greece in Athens in a qualifier for Euro '96, I elected to say that I didn't want to be considered again. By then I wasn't even making the bench so, while a few folk thought I was a bit arrogant when I said I wasn't going back to play for Scotland, it was for my own good to call time on my international career.

I spoke to Craig after the Greece match and told him that I didn't want to be involved if there was no real chance I was going to play. By then I was thinking he was only picking me in squads because the media were putting pressure on him to do so. Craig suggested that we keep it quiet and review things ahead of the next match but, when he spoke to Walter ahead of that one, Walter confirmed that I didn't want to be considered.

Things turned a bit sour after that. Craig and I had agreed to keep things between ourselves but when the media kept asking him why he wasn't picking me, he eventually succumbed and told them I didn't want to play. We both knew that wasn't the case. I wanted to play for Scotland, but it wasn't doing me any good travelling to games and sitting around hotels and in the stand when I could have been at home training with Rangers. I needed every bit of confidence to ensure I stayed in the Rangers team and by now going away with Scotland was becoming counter-productive.

Given what I achieved in my career, it is often a surprise to many that I didn't win over 50 caps for my country and get a place in the Hall of Fame. But when I'm asked if I would give up anything I achieved for more Scotland caps I say no. I have no regrets and hold no grudges. At the time I didn't realise how highly regarded I was by my peers and the coaching staff at Rangers but clearly the Scotland management team felt there were other left-backs who were better than me and I accept that. To be fair, there were times I pulled out of squads with niggly injuries that I would have played through for Rangers but, having taken the risk against the Netherlands, I wasn't prepared to do it again.

Irrespective of how it ended, I am immensely proud of the recognition I received at international level. From under-16 through to the full squad I consider myself fortunate to have played for my country. And when you consider that the likes of John Brown didn't win any full caps, I look back on what I achieved with a real sense of pride. I also have no hard feelings towards Craig Brown or Andy Roxburgh. Until Steven Clarke in 2020, they were the last two coaches to lead Scotland to a major championship and for that they deserve a huge amount of respect. It's just unfortunate that it had to end the way it did for me.

CHAPTER 8

THE END OF THE ROAD

I FIRST had an inkling that my future lay away from Ibrox in December 1996. I was offered a new deal to stay at Rangers for another three seasons, but we had reached an impasse in negotiations as I was looking for an extra year which would have secured me a testimonial. I then started to hear about interest in me from Italy, and my agent, Jim McArthur, was invited to go out and speak to clubs out there. The one club that stuck out for me, though, was Inter Milan who were managed by Roy Hodgson. Paul Ince was playing for them at that time too.

I spoke to Walter and Goughie and they said the interest from Inter was genuine. They had sold Roberto Carlos in the summer of 1996 and I think Roy saw me as being the long-term addition to his squad. Italian football was shown on Channel 4 back then and I remember being talked about on *Gazzetta Football Italia*, which James Richardson anchored. It looked as if I was going to be leaving sooner rather than later as Rangers were looking to do a deal that would see me leave before my contract ran out in the summer. Jim negotiated a contract for me with Inter and I believe terms were agreed between the clubs too. It was all good to go until Inter decided that they were going to put all new signings on hold and shortly afterwards Roy was no longer the manager, so the move was dead.

Around that time Jim was also talking to Valencia and Atlético Madrid and both clubs made offers. There was still interest from Italy too and one weekend when Rangers didn't have a game I went across and spoke to Torino and Lazio. I was also invited to the castle of the owner of Perugia to talk terms, but I was advised by a couple of people that that wouldn't have been the best move for me.

Surprisingly there wasn't much interest from clubs in England but eventually Leeds United got in touch. They were managed by George Graham and he was on the phone to Jim on a regular basis, so it was arranged for me to go and meet him. However, it had to be done discreetly so instead of flying to Leeds from Glasgow, I flew from Edinburgh. George picked Jim and me up at the airport and whisked us off to a restaurant and over the next couple of hours he pretty much sold playing for Leeds to me. And the deal was pretty much sealed when George told me that he had tried to sign me before when I was at Aberdeen and he was manager of Arsenal.

I had played at Elland Road before for Rangers, so I knew what the atmosphere was like and I was relishing the opportunity to play in the Premier League too. But perhaps a portent of things to come, the deal almost collapsed before I even played for the club as I failed my medical. I had not long returned from the surgery on my right knee, so I sought reassurance that all was okay with it by arranging a private scan. That came back with no issues, which was a relief, but when I was scanned as part of the medical, I was asked if I had a problem with my left knee.

When I said no the guy carrying out the medical was surprised as he told me I had no anterior cruciate ligament. It had basically snapped and withered away and there was nothing there.

I remember developing a limp as I walked out of the MRI unit and the next couple of days were a nightmare. Medical reports were going back and forth between Rangers and Leeds and it transpired that I had ruptured my ACL five years previously. I knew nothing about it and the physios told me the strength I had in my thighs had compensated and allowed me to play on.

We were staying in a lovely hotel called Oulton Hall and George came and told me not to worry, as they would make the deal work. But when you fail a medical it's only natural to worry. I knew that if the deal fell through I would be in limbo, without a club and perhaps unlikely to get one given what was happening with my knee. But Leeds stuck with it and, after making some adjustments to my contract, I signed.

It should have been the start of an exciting time for me and my family but the news about my knee clouded everything. I did enjoy pre-season – although I did have to get an injection in my knee to take the pain away – and I played in most of the games until the early months of 1998. But once I knew about the damage to my knee, it was always at the back of my mind. I was in pain most of the time and reckon I must have only been about 70 per cent fit for the games I played for Leeds.

After a couple of appearances on our three-match tour of Scandinavia and a few more in friendlies on home soil, I made my Premier League debut in a 1-1 draw against Arsenal at Elland Road. Jimmy Floyd Hasselbaink got our goal, and I was also part of the team that beat reigning champions Manchester United 1-0 at the end of September.

That result showed our capabilities, but we were really inconsistent. We lost three successive matches at the end of August against Crystal Palace, Liverpool and Aston Villa, all without scoring. Two of those were at Elland Road and we were beaten there again in September when Leicester City left with a 1-0 victory. In my time at Rangers, Ibrox was a fortress and I knew how important picking up points at home was if you wanted to mount a title challenge. Yet on our day we could turn on the style as witnessed by our 4-1 win over Newcastle United. They would end the season as runners-up and were an excellent side, but we showed that day that if we could rid ourselves of our inconsistency we too could compete at the top of the table.

I was settling in well, due to us having a great bunch of lads in the dressing room at Elland Road and also the great rapport I struck up with the other 'newbies' in the squad. George had brought in Hasselbaink from Boavista, Bruno Riberio from Vitória Setúbal, Alf-Inge Håland from Nottingham Forest and my fellow Scot David Hopkin from Crystal Palace. They all stayed at Oulton Hall. Kym and I didn't move into our house in Linton until a couple of months after I signed so it was good to have some familiar faces around the hotel.

Although I settled well off the park, I have to admit I struggled with the way Leeds played. At both Aberdeen and Rangers, I was encouraged to go forward but that was curbed by George Graham as he wanted us to sit in and defend and hit on the break. He also changed how I defended too. He wanted me to show players inside whereas I had always done the opposite. At the age I was then it was very difficult to make those changes.

My knee held out and I played in 24 of the first 25 league games. I missed our trip to face Arsenal in January and had

I was sent off after just six minutes of the Scottish Cup semi-final in 1992 for a robust challenge on Joe Miller. Fortunately, the lads battled to a 1-0 win.

I was part of a Rangers team that won 12 trophies in my six years there. This was after our first Scottish Cup win in 1992.

I won four Scottish Cup medals in my career. Above I am lifting the trophy after Rangers beat Hearts 5-1 in 1996, while, right, I am with Kym back at Ibrox after Rangers' win in 1993 clinched the domestic Treble.

Both pictures courtesy of Rangers FC

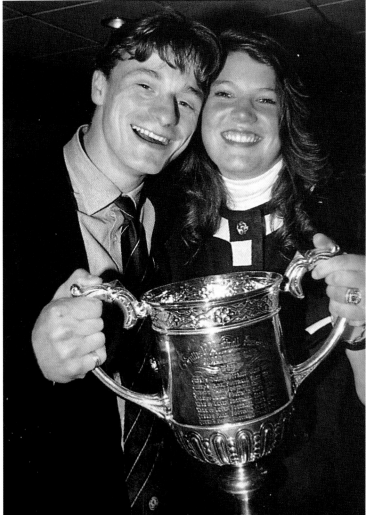

Celebrating with Paul Gascoigne after one of the goals he scored to help Rangers win their eighth successive league title.

BELL'S
PREMIER DIVISION

WINNERS
SEASON
96/97

The celebrations begin after we clinched nine-in-a-row at Tannadice in May 1997. One of the biggest regrets of my career is not going back to Ibrox with the rest of the lads on the team bus. (Picture courtesy of Rangers FC)

In action for Leeds United in July 1997. My dream move to England was wrecked by a knee injury that all but finished my playing career.

With Mason and Jordan ahead of one of my appearances for Montrose in 2002.

I am proud to have represented Scotland from U14 to full international level. This is me in Italy for a tournament with the U18 team.

With my 94BW Sereno Soccer Club team after we finished as runners-up in the National Finals in Massachusetts in 2009.

Addressing the media at the launch of Phoenix FC. Starting the club seemed a good idea at the time but the dream soon turned into a nightmare.

My assistant coach, Jimmy Lindsay, and I with the I-League 2 trophy in 2018. It was a remarkable achievement for Real Kashmir to win that in my first full season as manager.

A proud dad and coach moment. With Mason after he was voted man-of-the-match in Real Kashmir's 2-1 win over Mohun Bagan in their 80,000-capacity stadium.

I was shocked when the BBC documentary featuring my time at Real Kashmir picked up a BAFTA Scotland award in 2019. This is Kym and I with director Greg Clark, Sandeep Chattoo and members of the BBC team at the awards ceremony.

My family mean the world to me. The top picture was taken at our home in Linton, Yorkshire and the bottom one shows the kids all grown up. I'm proud of them all.

also been absent a week earlier when we started our FA Cup campaign with a 4-0 win over Oxford United. However, during that spell I was a frequent visitor to the medicine cabinet in the physio's room. I was taking three or four Voltarol tablets a day and I needed to take them not just to get me through games but also training too. The tablets played havoc with my stomach and I recall spending the bus journeys back from most away games in the toilet.

I also bought a machine that applied pressure to my knee after training in order to reduce the swelling. But even the pills and machinery couldn't help me on 7 February when my knee gave way when I landed after going up for a header in our game against Leicester City at Filbert Street. I completed the 90 minutes but when I got off the bus later that night I couldn't bend my leg. I was still taking anti-inflammatories but rather than the recommended dosage of one per day I was popping about three or four. That's not good for your stomach lining but even they couldn't shift the pain. The following Monday I could barely jog so I was taken to Sheffield to see a surgeon who operated and cleaned my knee up.

The recovery from that kept me out until I replaced Ian Harte two minutes from the end of a 3-3 draw against Coventry City at Elland Road on 25 April. I made one further substitute appearance when I replaced Harte again towards the end of our 3-0 defeat at Old Trafford. But even after brief appearances like those my knee would swell up. However, I was determined not to let the damage in my knee get me down and I resolved in that summer of 1998 that I was going to get myself super fit. I managed to do that and arrived for pre-season training in great shape.

We gathered at Roundhay Park and I managed to last about 20 minutes of the first 40-minute run before my knee started slipping. I could feel a lot of movement, so I went to see the physios and it was arranged for my knee to be reconstructed. That counted me out of all of 1998/99 and by the time I was fit I was working for a new manager.

George Graham had left to take over at Tottenham Hotspur and David O'Leary was the man who replaced him at Leeds. For me it wasn't an ideal appointment. I played three friendly games for the reserves ahead of 1999/2000 against Goole AFC, Harrogate Town and Selby Town – I scored our second goal in the latter match – but it eventually got to the point that even if I was fit, O'Leary wouldn't pick me for the reserve team. Eventually Roy Aitken, who was on the coaching staff, spoke to me and said the club were looking to get me off the wage bill. I couldn't understand how they could do that as I wasn't even playing for the reserves, and having been out for over a year with a serious injury, it was unlikely that any other club would take me on.

I eventually got back into the reserve team and then, out of the blue, my agent got a call from Dave Bassett who was manager at Barnsley. He wanted me to go down and train with them for a couple of days. I did that and really enjoyed it and Dave must have been happy with what I did as he picked me to play in a friendly against Sunderland. I was up against Kevin Kilbane and, although I hadn't played much football, I thought I had a decent game.

However, the next morning I was in the bath at home in Leeds and my left knee was massive as it had swollen up so much after the game. As I lay there looking at my knee my agent called and said that everything had been agreed between Leeds and Barnsley for me to go there on loan. I asked him when the next game was and he said it was something like three days later, with another a couple of days after that. At that point I had to be honest and say my knee couldn't cope with that kind of schedule, so I turned the move down.

By now the best I could hope for at Leeds was to play for the reserves. I wasn't able to train that often either. But there were still teams interested in me and Jocky Scott, who was manager of Dundee, and Ebbe Skovdahl, who was in charge at Aberdeen, came to watch one of the reserve games I played in. Both were keen to offer me a deal but, given the state my knee was in, I had to face facts: I couldn't play at that level anymore.

I went into the training ground at Leeds the next day and, with help from England's Professional Footballers' Association, who really looked after me throughout, I negotiated an early end to my contract and then travelled to Bradford for another clean-up operation. And after that the surgeon who carried out the operation told me what I already knew: I could no longer play football at the top level.

Although my playing career was pretty much over, I actually remember being relieved when he told me. I had soldiered on for a couple of years, barely training never mind playing, and I was picking up injuries in other parts of my body like my groin and my hamstrings as they were having to work harder to compensate for the state of my knee. I had also popped many pills and had even resorted to buying a cream from the USA to try and numb the pain. It was called Zostrix and when you applied it, it burned your knee so much that you couldn't feel it. I just wanted to keep playing but, in the end, it got so frustrating that it was best to stop.

I had already made plans for a career after football when I started a computer business with a friend in Wetherby. That filled the void for a while but come the start of the new season I was hankering after a return to the game. The lure of playing was too much to resist so I started playing charity matches. That gave me the buzz again and I had a four-week stint out in Thailand and Vietnam playing games as part of an initiative called Search for a Soccer Star.

Having thought I was completely finished, playing in those games convinced me that, while I couldn't train every day, I still had something to offer. I mentioned this to a friend, and he got me in touch with John Sheran who was the manager at Montrose. I spoke to John and we agreed that I would sign a two-year deal as player-assistant manager and to show you how much the football bug can bite you, I was only on about £60 a week and commuted from Leeds to Montrose a couple of times each week for training and games.

I joined up with the squad in July 2002, and I made my first appearance in a Montrose jersey against Aberdeen in a friendly at Links Park. We lost 2-0 but it felt great to be back out on the pitch again. The squad was a good blend of youth and experience, with the likes of Ray McKinnon, who had played for Dundee United, Nottingham Forest and Aberdeen, also part of the first-team picture.

Before my first month at the club was complete, I had added another medal to my collection. After playing against Inverness Caledonian Thistle and Plymouth Argyle, I was part of the XI that was picked to face Dundee United in the final of the Forfarshire Cup. The match was played at Links Park and United were managed by my old Aberdeen gaffer, Alex Smith.

And we pulled off a bit of a shock when, in front of a mere 250 folk, late goals from Keith Gibson and Ralph Brand gave Montrose a 2-0 victory.

That was a sweet way to start what I hoped would be a bit of an Indian summer for my career. A couple of years earlier I was done and dusted but those four pre-season games gave me a bit of hope that I had some game time left in me, albeit at a lower level. Alas, it wasn't to be.

A week after the win over Dundee United I made my league debut in a 1-1 draw against East Stirlingshire and three days later I played for the first time in the Bell's Challenge Cup. That ended in a 1-0 win over Albion Rovers and it was the same outcome when we faced Queen's Park at home in the league the following Saturday. I must admit I found it difficult playing in the Third Division and in the match against the Spiders I took a torrent of abuse from the 20-odd away fans who had travelled to Links Park. As I wasn't accustomed to playing at venues like this, I thought I would only have to withstand the barrage for the first half. But when we emerged after the interval the punters had walked round to the other side of the ground and I was pummelled for the second 45 minutes too.

I played a further seven games after that and scored one goal, a 30-yard free kick against Cowdenbeath in a 3-2 defeat in the opening round of the League Cup at Central Park. During that run of games, I got a sense of perspective on how lucky I had been earlier in my career to play with the likes of Brian Laudrup and Paul Gascoigne. I was a decent player, but I realised when I was at Montrose just how much playing with these guys made me a better player.

But I admired the dedication of the players at this level. They were working all day and training at night which, plus the games on a Saturday, meant they were spending a lot of time away from their families. There were some great characters in the squad too and it was a really enjoyable time for me.

The last of the fixtures in that sequence was on 21 September 2002. We played Morton at Links Park and I was playing left-back. I had never really had problems with my calves during my career, but I had started to notice them tightening up a lot. They were tight during the Morton game too and, when I stepped forward to clear a ball in the box, I felt like I had been struck by a baseball bat. My Achilles tendon had ruptured and, although I got surgery in Harrogate to repair the damage, this was definitely the end of the road for me.

Although I finished at a younger age than most players in that era, I still managed to make over 500 appearances in my career. I had been a first-team player since the age of 17 and had won all the major honours available in Scotland. I had played at the highest level with Rangers and impressed in the Champions League and, although I only won three caps, I had also played for my country. I could have no complaints.

However, if the experience at Montrose had taught me one thing it was that I had to stay in the game in some capacity. I had done some coaching with Montrose and really enjoyed it and that was where my next step would be in the wonderful world of football.

CHAPTER 9

MANAGING

MY FIRST opportunity to be a manager came at Elgin City. It wasn't long after I was off crutches – March 2003 if I recall correctly – when their chairman, Dennis Miller, who was on the board of directors when I was playing at Aberdeen, called me and offered me the chance to get into management. I wanted to stay in the game, so I met with him and the board members in a place called Fochabers. Typical of me, I didn't do any research about the club and when they agreed compensation with Montrose and offered me the job, I took it. I signed a one-year rolling contract, but I didn't realise that the club had been badly affected by flooding in the area and were still in the throes of recovery from that. The flood damage had been so severe in fact that the club almost went out of business.

I also didn't realise that the previous manager, Harry McFadden, had won just one of his 13 games in charge since his appointment in December 2002. Harry had been director of football when Alex Caldwell resigned following a 4-0 home defeat against Peterhead, Elgin's 13th league game without a win. The plan was for Harry to take the role on an interim basis until the end of the season, but the board must have changed their mind and I was appointed.

With form like that it was no surprise that Elgin were second-bottom in the table, although in their short time in the Scottish League they had never finished any higher than that. And of the seven league games I oversaw before the season ended, we lost four, including a 5-0 defeat against East Fife. We were still second-bottom at the end of the campaign, with just five wins from 36 league games, but I was never going to be judged on how we did in those seven matches. Instead I now had to rebuild the team. But I was 35 years old, lacking experience and had the dubious honour of being the youngest manager in the UK.

It was therefore going to be a real baptism of fire and if I needed that confirmed then I got it when I attended training for the first time. We trained two days a week – Tuesday and Thursday – on the pitch at the stadium, Borough Briggs, and for that first session, I was shocked when only eight players turned up. Three of the players in the squad were from Glasgow so they trained down there with the assistant manager, Willie Furphy. Kevin Steel was from Dundee, so he didn't come to training and neither did Davie Ross who lived on one of the islands off the coast near Brora. I didn't realise that the team never trained together before I took the job and that made it more difficult for me. This was the first time in my career I had experienced that as even at Montrose all the players trained together.

Usually the Tuesday session involved some fitness work while on the Thursday we would do some ball work. But most of the tactical discussion would take place before the game and you had to hope it all came together. Attacking and defending set-pieces were done on a board in the dressing room and the best I could do was keep the team changes to a minimum and try to have consistency when it came to selection. That helped build an understanding among the players and we got better as a result of that.

To give you an idea about a matchday experience, if we were playing Gretna away the bus would leave Elgin about 6am. Some of the players would have had to travel from Inverness to get there too. I would be picked up in Aberdeen then there would be numerous stops to pick up other players. We would have our pre-match meal in Moffat and then complete the journey to get to the game.

My first full season in charge, 2003/04, started inauspiciously when we travelled to Station Park and lost 4-0 to Forfar Athletic in the first round of the Challenge Cup. We had tremendous backing that night from a small band of travelling supporters – they actually accounted for half of the crowd that turned up – and I hoped to reward them with a good start to the league season. But it didn't work out like that and we started poorly, and we continued to ship goals at an alarming rate. We conceded five against Queen's Park at Hampden, three in a 3-2 loss to Peterhead, another three in a 3-3 draw at Montrose and then four when Brechin City dumped us out the League Cup at Borough Briggs.

We had to try and stem the tide, but I wasn't helped when in October I found myself in the midst of a goalkeeping crisis. We had two goalkeepers, Martin Pirrie and Peter Hamilton, but both of them ended up injured, leaving me without an experienced stopper. I think I might have had an under-16 player, but we were due to face Albion Rovers at Borough Briggs and I felt it wasn't right to pitch the young lad in.

I made some calls trying to get someone in as an emergency loan but drew a blank. But then I got a call about an upcoming Rangers function from a mate who was a Rangers supporter and he suggested Andy Goram. He had been out the game for ten months after leaving Queen of the South, but the chap told me he had seen him play in a charity game recently. I thought we had no chance of getting him, but I called him on the off chance. In those days you could play someone for three games as a trialist so that was my plan if Andy agreed to sign. After a bit of bartering over the financial aspects, he agreed so I approached Dennis Millar and after a bit of persuasion, we managed to broker a deal.

I met Andy when he got off the train a couple of days before the Albion Rovers game and he looked to be in good shape. The club had advertised that we had signed him too, hoping to put some more numbers on the gate but, if I'm honest, it was a disaster.

Ahead of Andy's debut we had the worst defensive record in the country. We had conceded 27 goals and it was only mid-October. Given his experience and pedigree I hoped Andy would help stem the tide, but his arrival didn't. He missed a couple of crosses in the first half and we were 2-0 down at the interval. By the end we had lost 5-1.

After the game I went into the boardroom and Dennis asked for my thoughts. With a mild hint of sarcasm, I told him I thought Andy's distribution had been good! I then asked how many more had come through the turnstiles as a result of Andy's arrival and, as deadpan as you like, Dennis said we had got 44 more in than we had had at our previous home game.

We extended Andy's contract until Christmas and he played a total of five games for Elgin before we had to let him go. In fairness, I don't think Andy at his peak could have saved us but there was a funny ending to the whole situation. I got a call from Dennis one day and he told me not to be getting any ideas. When I asked what he meant he told me that he had read in the newspaper that Paul Gascoigne was looking for a new club. I think it was clear from what Dennis was saying that Paul's next destination was not going to be Elgin!

At that time pretty much everything that could go wrong did got wrong. In February we faced Montrose away and lost 4-3. After the match two of my players were selected for a drugs test. The players were chosen randomly by the SFA but if I had been asked to pick a pair who would have failed the test, it would have been those two. When the results came back, one of the players failed.

We followed the Montrose defeat with another three losses – the last a 6-1 drubbing against Stirling Albion – and thereafter we won just three of our last 11 league games. With a mere six wins from 36 we finished ninth in a ten-team league. Our points total of 25 was 17 better than bottom side East Stirling but left us 15 adrift of Albion Rovers who finished eighth.

We didn't end the season empty-handed, though, as we won the North of Scotland Cup. Our road to the final started on 17 March when we beat Rothes 2-1 away from home. An emphatic 6-2 win over Lossiemouth took us through to the last four where a double from Alex Bone was enough to overcome Wick Academy.

Alex had joined earlier in the season from Peterhead and had a bit of a pedigree. He had played for the likes of St Mirren and Ayr United, but his most successful stint was with Ross County. He was a good goalscorer and, in addition to scoring four of the six against Lossiemouth, he would end the season with 15 league goals.

The final was played at Mosset Park in Forres and our opponents were Inverness Caledonian Thistle. Managed by the former Hearts striker John Robertson, they were on the verge of promotion to the Premier League and were at full strength. Twenty-four hours earlier they had beaten Raith Rovers 1-0 while we lost 1-0 at home to Stirling Albion. All the lads who used to travel from far and wide to play for us stayed the night in Elgin prior to the final. Needless to say, a night out was arranged, alcohol was consumed and I was met with a very hungover squad in the dressing room. But despite that we won 1-0 and it was nice to get a bit of silverware at the end of my first full season in charge.

However, despite the cup win our form otherwise had been poor and this wasn't what I had signed up for. I had hoped to get Elgin pushing for promotion, so something had to change. And that change for 2004/05 was the introduction of a Skill Seekers programme. In total 11 lads were taken on: Pat Vigurs, Anton Lennox, Darren Kelly, Stewart McKenzie, Martin Charlesworth, Fraser Bremnar, Calum Reid, Paul Napier, Gary Wood, Phillip Reid and Ian Vigurs. Ian, who later played for Inverness Caledonian Thistle, Ross County and Motherwell, made his first-team debut aged 15 and I also selected Gary, Phil and Paul for the first XI. A guy called Kenny Black, who initially made his money in painting and decorating before moving into nursery care provision, also came into the club and he gave us a bit of financial backing. That was welcome as all the YTS guys needed accommodation. In addition to attending classes to obtain their qualification, the lads would do ground staff duties and train full-time. Having these guys added a bit of depth to my squad and gave me a good balance between youth and experience and that helped us immensely. I also recruited a number of experienced Glasgow-based players such as Jamie McKenzie, John Allison and Willie Martin in a bid to add a bit more quality to the pool. Added to that, we managed to get three players who had just been released by Blackburn Rovers: Kieran Renton, Stuart Cumming and Adam Nelson.

The season started with defeat away to Alloa and after opening our league campaign with a 2-0 win against Stenhousemuir we travelled south to play Berwick Rangers in the League Cup. This would be the first of two ties against 'the wee Rangers' and on both occasions we found ourselves 2-0 up. But in the first of the games we were pegged back to 2-2 before Berwick edged it in extra time. And almost a year later we were at it again, blowing a two-goal lead to lose 4-2.

After that game I was raging. I came in and slammed the dressing room door closed. I told our fitness coach, Davie Johnston, that the players, pretty much the same ones who had played a year earlier, had embarrassed me and the supporters so he had to take them out and make them run. Davie went towards the dressing room door but as he pulled at the door handle, it came off. He had no idea what to do next. In my rage I had been kicking everything and anything around the dressing room, so I don't think he wanted to let me know what had happened. Instead he firstly tried to stick his finger in the hole left by the handle he had removed to try and prise the door open then I saw him bending down and whispering through the hole trying to get someone outside to open the door.

That spared the players their punishment run but that kind of thing summed up the frustrations I had at that level. I had an eclectic mix of good professionals who were too good to play in the Third Division, others who thought they were better than what they were, and some who just didn't give a fuck. The lack of professionalism in the latter two groups was something I found hard to deal with.

Despite that we recovered from the first of those Berwick defeats and had an excellent season in 2004/05. Gretna ran away with the title, finishing 20 points clear of runners-up Peterhead. We lost all four league games against them – including a 6-2 thrashing at home – but after two years of finishing in the lower reaches of the league, I had Elgin pushing hard for the play-offs. We still had some issues with training as some of the guys had to come in at night while others were still training in Glasgow, but it was a lot better than it had been up to that point. However, we just couldn't get over the line and two wins from our last six games ruled us out. We eventually finished sixth on 43 points, five behind Queen's Park who finished in the last play-off spot.

The 2005/06 season was all about building on what we had done, finding some consistency, pushing on and fighting it out at the top end of the table. But my journey with Elgin would end halfway through as I became embroiled in a bitter takeover bid. By this stage Kenny and I were paying some of the players' wages, so Kenny decided he was going to take over the club. He was willing to take on the debt – estimated at £180,000 – lay down an artificial pitch that could be used by the local community and develop a sports bar, restaurant and shop. I was following the dream and my heart was ruling my head as I tried to get Elgin promoted. Kenny was trying to buy shares and when Dennis Miller resigned he thought he was in a strong position. He managed to secure the shares he needed and there were rumours that my former boss Alex Smith, who had just left Ross County, would be coming in as director of football.

But all this needed to be ratified at an Extraordinary General Meeting. At that meeting one of the directors stood up and said that Billy Robertson had secured share capital. This was news to Kenny as he thought the shares had been frozen. Had he known about the shares Billy had procured, he would have made an offer for them. Something didn't add up and my response was immediate: in support of Kenny Black, I resigned as manager the next morning. I left Elgin in the play-off positions and my last game in charge was a 2-1 defeat against Stirling Albion in the Scottish Cup.

I have to admit that the experience at Elgin was a chastening one, but it didn't curb my enthusiasm to be a manager. Kenny was unperturbed too and moved on to become director of football at Montrose in July 2006. Eddie Wolecki was the manager of the club, but Kenny approached me about coming in as co-manager with Eddie. I had experienced the co-manager role as a player at Aberdeen and the success it had delivered so, as I was desperate to get back in the game, I accepted the offer.

I wasn't paid initially, and I felt for Eddie as it was apparent from day one that Kenny wanted me to have sole charge of the team. I felt very uncomfortable and awkward and Eddie wasn't too enamoured either. He ended up doing pretty well with Airdrie after he left Montrose and he had some really good ideas but, in my opinion, they weren't suited to part-time football.

Things didn't start well – we lost 5-0 at Stenhousemuir and Peterhead beat us 3-1 at Links Park in the League Cup – and within a couple of months Eddie reached an agreement with the club and left. I was now manager in my own right and my first match in sole control was a 1-0 win over East Fife at home. We were unbeaten for the next three games and I was voted as the winner of the manager of the month award. But after that there was a disastrous run that saw us lose six successive league games and exit the Scottish Cup at the hands of Highland League side Deveronvale.

It was pretty clear that things weren't working out. The compensation agreement with Eddie did little to get me a salary for being Montrose manager and, although he spent a bit of money, the players Kenny brought in didn't really fit into the team. We arrested the decline briefly when we beat East Stirling 3-0 away but after we lost 3-2 at home to Albion Rovers on 13 January – our fourth straight defeat – I tendered my resignation. I didn't feel as if I was in sole control of the team and, with my reputation on the line, I thought it best to leave the club.

It was time for a change after that. As a family we loved the USA and for most of the close-seasons when I was playing, Kym, the kids and I would spend about five weeks in Florida. After I finished up at Montrose we sat down and decided to move Stateside and see what opportunities were available over there. Another exciting and challenging episode in my football career was set to begin.

CHAPTER 10

STATESIDE

WHEN I left Montrose, I still had a hunger to stay in the game but I wanted to try something different. And that's why I decided to go to the USA to see if there were any opportunities for me over there.

Initially a chap called Derek Thom and I went over for a fortnight to suss things out. Derek and I had been friends for years as he stayed across the road from us after we moved from Garthdee to Peterculter around 1985. When we went out there, I spoke to a couple of people and the vibes were good. They said if I was looking to do some coaching there were some potential openings so I came back and spoke to Kym and she suggested I go out for a couple of months, do some work and see how it was.

I rented an apartment in Santa Monica, California, and secured some voluntary work with a club called Laguna Niguel. I also took the chance to go and visit Bobby Clark, who, if you recall, had been part of the coaching team in the youth system I had been part of at Aberdeen. Bobby had been in America for a while, coaching Stanford University for four years before taking charge of the University of Notre Dame's men's team in 2001. He would remain in charge there until 2017 and it was at Notre Dame that we met up. As luck would have it, when I visited Bobby, Lenny Taylor was also there. It was good to catch up with them both and talk over old times when I was starting out in the game and I stayed for about a week. Bobby knew I was interested in moving out to America to coach, so he put me in touch with Les Armstrong.

Although he was born in America, Les had spent most of his life in Aberdeen. Like me, he had been in the youth ranks with Aberdeen and I later found out that he was my cousin George Stephen's best friend. It transpired that the club Les was with, Sereno Soccer Club in Arizona, was on the lookout for coaches. Ally Maxwell, who had been a team-mate at Rangers, was working there too.

Founded in 1994, Sereno were recognised as having one of the most successful youth setups in the country. Their roll of honour included 125 state champions, nine regional champions, and one national champion. And by the time I arrived, 17 players who had played for Sereno had been capped for the US national team.

I was invited down to Phoenix and I was impressed. I thought the programme was as good as, if not better than, some of those in the Premier League and at the end of the week I spent there I was offered a job as coach for three of the youth teams. I went home after that and discussed it with Kym and, despite a bit of resistance from Chelsea, who didn't want to leave Scotland, we decided that we would go for it and move out to Arizona. It took a while to get all the paperwork completed and approved for our visas but in July 2008 we got the green light.

Although Chelsea had been reluctant initially, she thrived, and the boys loved life out there too. Mason, who was 13 when we moved, was in the Aberdeen youth system before we left and when we got to America he moved into the ranks at Sereno and impressed enough to earn a full athletic scholarship at the University of Washington. That was very rare, yet he was courted by numerous institutions such as Harvard, Stanford and the University of Notre Dame. I want to take the chance to go on record here and say Mason earned his scholarship; it didn't come about because I was his dad.

The coach at the University of Washington was Bobby Clark's son, Jamie. It cost between $30,000 and $50,000 a year plus accommodation to send someone to college then and most of the degree courses were four years. That made football at the level I was working at big business as a player like Mason that impressed coaches could secure a scholarship and in so doing save his or her parents in the region of $200,000.

At Sereno they had age groups from under-eight up to under-18 – boys and girls – and the setup was all based on trying to get kids into college soccer. It was a pay-to-play model too, so a significant part of my role was to deal with the parents. The cost for them was huge. Club fees were around $3,000 and that didn't include the purchase of home and away 'uniforms' and training kits which could amount to another $400. On top of that if we had to go to a tournament the parents didn't just pay to get their kid there, they also had to pay for the coach too. That meant if we were taking 18 players then each parent had to pay an 18th of the travelling and accommodation costs of the coach.

In addition, there were other challenges, particularly if kids weren't playing. I also had to deal with the fact that Mason was in one of the teams I coached which brought about accusations of favouritism. That was never the case – all the players were picked on merit – and my decisions were vindicated when that team won the State Cup, the regionals and came within an ace of winning the nationals only to be beaten in the final. Our State Cup triumph was even more remarkable when you consider that we did it without a recognised goalkeeper. Our stopper was ruled out with a broken hand, so I had to play Angel Rascon, our centre-forward, in goal for the entire tournament

At one point my team were ranked number one in the country but that success had to be maintained as if you weren't winning State Cups or regional competitions, the parents of the better players would simply move them to another club that was winning and there would then be a mass exodus as half the team followed suit. As you can imagine, it was pretty cut-throat and not for the first time in my coaching career I was a bit naïve. I thought I would be taking on a role that would be fun but pretty soon I realised there was a lot of politics involved.

The selection process for entry into the college system involved literally hundreds of college coaches like Bobby Clark coming along to the tournaments we played in to watch players. I would be asked for my opinion on players by them and that meant I built up a good working relationship with some of them. It was also my role to coach and guide the players in my teams, but it was hard as you always had parents breathing down your neck. In some instances you would have a kid who wasn't that good but his parents were paying a lot of money for him to play and there were others where parents would ask me why a certain youngster had got an offer from the University of Notre Dame but theirs hadn't. However, most of those parents hadn't played football and their lack of familiarity with the game was one of the reasons why they couldn't understand that their kid simply wasn't good enough.

Football was still an up-and-coming sport in America back when I arrived, although it was about to get a shot in the arm with the arrival of David Beckham at LA Galaxy. The most athletic children would still favour baseball, basketball or American football but I still got the chance to work with some smashing young players at Sereno. And as I did, I fairly rapidly ascended through the coaching ranks. Within a year of me arriving, Les Armstrong and Ally Maxwell left, and I became director of coaching and soon after that I became executive director. Once in that role, I wasn't just coaching, I was pretty much running the whole club.

I loved the job, but it was stressful and time-consuming. When I arrived at Sereno we were working with around 500 kids but by the time I left, that number had risen to over 3,000. They were working with 20 full-time coaches and the staff was swelled further by a number of part-time and volunteer coaches. In addition to keeping an eye on that I was also working with the board of directors, which had been voted in by the parents. I also had to try and ward off potential suitors for my coaching staff as it was inevitable if a coach left, the majority of the team he or she worked with would move on too. To put that into context, a team of 20 kids was worth around $40,000 to the club so losing them in one fell swoop would have a significant impact at that level.

But it was soon time for a change again. Around 2011 one of the coaches, a Portuguese chap called João Bento, and his brother Rui, had come up with the idea of putting together a United

Soccer Leagues (USL) football team in Phoenix, Arizona, as there wasn't a professional team there. He asked me if I wanted to get involved and the concept intrigued me, so I agreed. The big hitters in Phoenix were the basketball team, the Phoenix Suns, and the baseball team, the Arizona Diamondbacks, but this was an opportunity to throw a soccer team into the mix. It took a couple of years for it all to come to fruition as we had to buy the franchise, but Phoenix FC was born on 2 July 2012.

We were placed in the USL Professional Division, which is the third tier in the pyramid in America. But any hope of making a success of the venture was doomed to failure from the off. As the Suns and the Diamondbacks were playing in the 'big' leagues of their respective sports, the public viewed us as semi-professional or minor league even though the players were paid well, and we were full-time. That diluted interest straight away and on top of that things turned sour when we became embroiled in lawsuits, some of which are still going on today.

I invested some money in Phoenix FC so, alongside Rui, Shawn Diedtrich and Eric Cornwell, I was part-owner as well as head coach. We were all keen to get going and get our club established in the USL and it all started well. We had a squad that was a mixture of players from the US, Brazil and Mexico. We also had Anthony Obodai who had played for Ajax and been capped by Ghana, and two Scots – Darren Mackie, who had been at Aberdeen, and Scott Morrison who had played latterly for Ross County. Scott was excellent for us, only missing one league match, but it wasn't so good for Darren. He had struck up a promising partnership with Aaron King and we did really well in the pre-season games. But in the last training session before we were due to face Los Angeles Blues at the Titan Stadium, situated on the campus of California State University, Darren pulled his groin. He was out for several weeks and, as the season only runs from late March until mid-August, he only played in 12 of the 24 league games.

We lost that opening match 2-0 – Obodai was sent off – but a week later we won our first home fixture when we beat VSI Tampa Bay 1-0 thanks to a goal from our Brazilian midfielder Netinho. That match was a complete sell-out, with 4,198 turning up, but interest soon waned. We lost our next two matches 3-1, the first against an Orlando City side managed by former Everton player Adrian Heath, and with results being inconsistent the fans eventually started to stay away. On top of that, what was going on off the field took centre stage and eventually led to the club folding.

We were one of only two teams in the league without a shirt sponsor so we had been looking for someone to invest in the club and were introduced to an individual who was supposed to have a bit of money behind him. It didn't work out, though, and the upshot for us was that we soon started to run out of money. The deal that had been done to rent the stadium we used, the Sun Devil Soccer Stadium, from Arizona State University saw us paying an exorbitant amount of money – apparently around ten times more than other teams were paying – and it was a similar story for all the other agreements in place.

And it all came to a head one day when we were in Florida to play VSI Tampa Bay. Our form was poor going into this one – we had drawn two and lost five of our previous seven games – but in the second half Obodai went clean through on goal and rounded the goalkeeper, Alex Horwath, who proceeded to bring him down. Horwath was sent off and Darren Mackie, now fit and back in the side, stepped up to take the penalty. To allow you to picture the scene, there was a huge lake behind the goal at the Plant City Stadium and I think that's where Darren was aiming as he ballooned his kick over the bar. To rub salt into the wound, Chad Burt scored nine minutes later and that was enough to win the game. And when he did, I looked out across that lake and sure enough floating away in the distance was a ball! It was difficult to laugh given the predicament we were in, but you couldn't help it.

By now, Canadian Tim Donald, a diamond of a guy, had come in and started clearing debts. He did a stellar job and was paying players out of his own pocket. But there were hidden costs that we didn't know about and we were struggling to stem the tide. While all of this was going on, I had the challenge of keeping the players motivated and I succeeded as we only lost one of our next nine games after the Tampa defeat. Included in that run was a 4-0 win away from home against Charlotte Eagles and back-to-back victories against Antigua Barracuda. We ended with three successive defeats to finish in 12th place, but had we managed to win a couple more games we could have made the play-offs.

But by then we were no longer playing at our home ground. We couldn't afford the rent payments, so we played our last match at the Sun Devil Soccer Stadium on 19 July when we drew 2-2 with Richmond Kickers. Our last three home fixtures were played in a sports complex in northern Phoenix called Reach 11, pretty much akin to a public park. There were no changing rooms there, so we got ourselves ready for the games in portacabins in the car park. These games were played right in the heart of the red-hot summer in Arizona and the only way to cool the cabins was to use a generator, which unfortunately packed in, so it was boiling hot. And the solitary light that was in there also went out so eventually I was doing team talks in the dark.

We soldiered on and I think my management style helped keep the players, who were unhappy at having to play in unfamiliar surroundings, going. It was little things like stopping at a 7/11 and buying them a case of beer between games and that helped develop a bond between us.

But as hard as they battled, we ended up losing all three games at Reach 11, the last of which against Rochester Rhinos was a seven-goal thriller. Goals from Donny Toia and Travis Bowen had us 2-0 up after 21 minutes but our lead had been halved by half-time and we also had Thomas Ramos sent off. Just after the hour we had surrendered our lead, with former Hibs striker Tam McManus scoring to put the Rhinos 3-2 up. But to sum up the spirit in the team we didn't stop pushing for another goal and it looked like we had secured a draw when Josh Bento scored in the last minute. But wee Tam scored again to give the visitors the win in what would prove to be the last match played by Phoenix FC.

We tried to renew our franchise for the 2014 season but eventually got a letter from the USL which said it had been terminated. But Tim Donald had been promised the franchise, so all did not appear to be lost. We started to prepare for the new season, moved into new offices and Tim was invited along to a meeting with the USL. And that's where things started to go pear-shaped. Tim had to pay a league fee of $32,000 and he was prepared to do that by wire transfer. But the USL was happy for him to hold off until the meeting and, in the meantime, Tim was talking to Kyle Eng about coming on board and helping out with the club financially. I also introduced Berke Bakay, who was the president and CEO of Kona Grill, a restaurant company based in Scottsdale, Arizona.

But when the meeting took place Tim was served with a termination notice. The reason for the notice? Non-payment of the $32,000 league fee! The franchise instead went to Kyle Eng who formed Arizona United. But that didn't work out and, in August 2016, he sold his majority share to an investment group led by Berke who rebranded the club as Phoenix Rising FC and tempted Didier Drogba to join.

Our financial plight wasn't helped by the fees we had to pay for the ongoing lawsuits, which took a while to be resolved. I had heard what the legal system is like in America but once I was actually involved in litigation myself I soon realised I was out of my depth. It affected my family too as we didn't know how long the process would take and how much money we were going to lose. You fear the worst.

There were so many problems to deal with. They were almost exclusively off-field issues, and that was all compounded by the fact I was still in the executive director role with Sereno when all this was going on. Due to the heat in Arizona I would take training with Phoenix FC at 8am then go into the office to undertake my role with Sereno – this involved a range of things including sorting wages and insurance, arranging to meet with the coaches, attending board meetings – before rounding things off by taking three further training sessions in the evening for the youth teams I was looking after. They would end about 10pm and during that time I was maybe at home for an hour before the evening sessions to get something to eat. And my working day didn't end then as I would be sitting in bed catching up with e-mails.

That kind of working day takes its toll on you and so did the fact that my coaching commitments saw me hopping around the country to get to games. For example, there was one instance where I had to go between Arizona and Hawaii which meant numerous internal flights over a very short period of time. On the Saturday I was on the sidelines for the Phoenix game and when that finished I boarded a flight to Hawaii. The under-19 team that Mason played for had qualified for the regional finals which were being held there. The internal flight was five hours long and there was something like a two- or three-hour time difference. I coached the team for games on the Sunday, Monday and Tuesday but, while the players were enjoying their day off on the Wednesday, I was back in Arizona to take the Phoenix team for a midweek game. After that was done Kym drove me to Sky Harbor Airport to let me catch another flight back to Hawaii. I had been in Phoenix for less than 24 hours.

As much as I enjoyed the football, that kind of travelling is one of the downsides of playing and coaching in America. Indeed, there was one occasion when I coached three different teams in three different states all in the same day. There was an early game at 8am in Arizona and after that I was whisked away to the airport to fly to LA to take a team in Orange County. On arrival in LA I picked up a hire car, drove to the soccer field, took the team for a game at 2pm then headed back to drop the hire car off at the airport. The last stop was Portland where the kick-off was at 8pm. I was shattered by the end of it but, on reflection, this all stood me in good stead for my next adventure.

Phoenix FC was eventually dissolved in March 2014 which was a sad day for all of us that had been affiliated with the club. I was, however, still executive director with Sereno so the plan was to focus on that. But pretty soon that was a done deal too.

CHAPTER 11

FROM ARIZONA TO INDIA

ALTHOUGH YOUTH soccer in America is very much parent-driven, there were some great and supportive members of the board at Sereno. The likes of Darla Sipolt, Mike Lavelle and Yates Hudson backed me and believed in my strategies and how devoted I was to the club and kids. They were instrumental while they were on the board. But eventually some others with their own agendas came in and attempted to drive the club in a different direction. And although I had worked hard to build a good reputation for the club, for some it seemed no matter what I did, they would find fault.

For example, in 2010 I played a significant role in securing a partnership with Chelsea and Adidas. Chelsea were looking to expand their US youth team network and, in addition to wearing their kit for games, we would host training sessions and camps with their coaches and potentially take part in player exchange programmes. It was real kudos for the club to get this yet there were some on the board who felt it favoured the boys in the team more than the girls. Looking back now, I would have to say that the parents of the girls were actually more difficult to deal with than the boys. Things would get particularly political when it came to the AGM and the board members were up for re-election. A new president came in at Sereno after the Phoenix saga ended and I thought he was okay but, in the end, he blindsided me. I had hired a couple of guys from California as we needed experienced coaches. Their respective appointments were among the biggest mistakes I ever made during my time in the States. All of a sudden, the president had earmarked one of them for my role as executive director and I started to hear rumours that I was going to get fired.

My response was to call the president who informed me there was going to be an EGM that evening to discuss my future. When he called me after that meeting, he said he had put two votes forward for the board to consider. The first was to replace the executive director role with a director of coaching (DOC) – which was passed – and the second was that I would assume that new role. The latter one wasn't passed as enough support had been gathered from the board to oust me.

One of the lads I had recruited from California was now the DOC and, to compound matters, I was told my coaching commitments would also be reduced. Rather than coaching three teams I was now only to look after one and I think the powers that be were hoping I would tell him where to go. But I decided to dig my heels in. The under-eight team I had to coach were brilliant. The parents were great too and they were surprised I continued after the way I had been treated. I'll admit part of me wanted to quit, but Kym said the kids in the team needed me, so I stuck it out.

However, I was actually on a hiding to nothing. Essentially the more teams you look after, the more influence you have with the parents and some of them were on the board. Basically, by downsizing me they hoped to force me out of the club. But I kept it going, kept taking the team to places like California to play in tournaments, kept going to coaches meetings, all the while pissing the guys off who wanted me to go.

In the end they brought me in and said they wanted to offer me the role of regional director or to revert to coaching three teams as I had done previously. I told them I would think about it and I managed to spin things out for a couple of weeks before agreeing to take on that position. In the meantime, I was looking around for other opportunities and one that appealed to me was a role at a club called Lonestar in Austin, Texas. I think the title was technical academy director and I would be coaching two teams as well. That sealed the deal for me, and I negotiated an end to my time with Sereno and got set to move the family from Phoenix to Austin.

The club are now called Real Salt Lake Arizona but that, if anything, makes it easier for me as the organisation I spent a number of years with no longer exists. I have a lot of pride in what I achieved with Sereno. It was never about me, never about money – admittedly I dug my heels in at the end but that was to be awkward more than anything – but the guys who have come in since I left have all been focussed on money rather than what was best for the kids. My focus was on the kids and their welfare and having a successful product rather than having a fistful of dollars. In fact, when I was executive director, I was one of the lowest-paid full-time coaches at the club. The board eventually rewarded me with a more appropriate contract but like most of my decisions in my coaching career, it was never about the money, it was and is always about the players and the enjoyment I got coaching them. Football treated me well when I was a player, and I am fortunate to have a financially astute wife too. That has given me the platform to take up opportunities like this and I am eternally grateful to Kym for that.

Having said that, moving to Texas was a mistake. In hindsight I should have taken a break from football in general at that time, but the bug kept biting. However, while I still wanted to be involved in the game, after getting a taste of it again with Phoenix FC, I hankered after a return to full-time, professional football. Why then I moved from one youth football setup to another I'll never know!

It soon became apparent that Lonestar was just like Sereno although the quality of opposition we faced was of a higher standard. We were playing against the likes of Houston Dynamo but, while I enjoyed that part of it, it was still parent-driven. I was getting involved in things I felt were needless like countless meetings and coaching clinics and, for me, there was too much emphasis on off-the-field work. I was spending a significant amount of time with the coaches in the office doing things like depth charts and that made it hard going. I would have enjoyed it more if we were investing our time teaching the kids in their respective teams about football.

Although the American dream turned into something of a nightmare, there were some good times. For example, at Lonestar, the executive director and a fellow Scot, Don Cameron, and I took teams to tournaments in Germany and the Netherlands, which was good fun. And when we were there, we got the opportunity to visit the likes of Borussia Monchengladbach and PSV Eindhoven which was a really good learning experience. We went to The Amsterdam Arena, home of Ajax, too.

There are other things when I look back that make me smile too. The first happened not long after we moved to Arizona. I was coaching an under-eight team, but I wasn't fully conversant with the rules. In essence you were only allowed to bring on a substitute at a goal kick, prior to a kick-off or on your own throw-in. I didn't know this so during one game in the State League when it was unlimited substitutions, we won a corner and I decided I wanted to bring on one of the big lads I had on the bench. I signalled to the referee that I wanted to make the change and the big kid went on and made his way to the box for the corner. As he arrived the referee walked over to the corner flag, picked the ball up, walked to the six-yard line and placed it down for a goal kick. I shouted to him that I thought it was a corner kick only for him to retort, 'But coach you traded it in for a sub.'

And that wasn't the first time the rules and regulations in the USA took me by surprise. My first tournament with Sereno was in California and I had a team made up of two age groups. They were a great bunch of boys, but I soon found out they were nowhere near the calibre of the players we were up against. We were in a section with three other teams, with the team that finished top qualifying for the semi-finals. Somehow we managed to draw our first game 0-0 against a team ranked in the top ten in the USA, although admittedly we never had a shot on goal, never got out of our six-yard box and the ball was hitting the post, the bar and players on the line.

In the afternoon we played our second game against another top-ten team but this time we were 3-0 down fairly quickly. Under a bit of pressure, our defence cleared the ball and as we attacked one of my players was fouled and the referee awarded a penalty. As my player was about to step up to take the kick, the opposition coach started to have a go at the referee. This went on for about five minutes and ended when the referee blew his whistle. The parents of the kids in my team started jumping about and told me we had won the game! I couldn't understand as we were losing 3-0 but, due to the verbal abuse he had been subjected to, the referee called the game off which meant we got a 3-0 win.

I was even more confused when the parents told me we were now in with a shout of making the semi-finals. I went to the scoreboard to check the results and sure enough we were sitting top of our group on eight points. I was scratching my head now as I thought the draw in the opening game coupled with the 'win' in the second game would have given us four points. But the scoring system is different in the States. In addition to getting three points for a win and one point for a draw, you also got a point for a clean sheet and a point for every goal scored up to six goals. In the end all the hype died, and we didn't make it through as we got battered in our third game but it was cool to live the dream for a wee while.

On another occasion I had an under-15 team playing a team called San Tan in the State League in an 8am game at a place called Westside. The pitches there were a bit smaller than the ones at Reach 11 so the San Tan coach came up to me prior to the game and said, 'Coach, I hope you don't mind but I am only going to play with ten players today.' I told him I didn't have an issue but asked him if he was short of players. His response blew me away; his rationale for playing with one fewer was that it would give his team more space! It didn't work. We beat them 4-0 and, having had a full substitutes' bench, the coach now had to contend with a bunch of unhappy parents who were paying top dollar for their kids to play football.

But by the end of 2016 I was starting to look for other openings, although my next venture almost cost me my marriage. I was contacted by an agent who told me there was an opportunity to coach a relatively new club called Real Kashmir. I had had a couple of opportunities to move before this. There was an offer from Uganda and one from China but if I took the latter one the whole family would have had to move as we were all on visas at the time. But there was something drawing me to India, and Kashmir in particular.

I would later find out that the region had witnessed three major wars between India and Pakistan since 1947, with more than one and a half million people losing their life. But thanks to two friends – Shamim Meraj, who owned the local newspaper, *Kashmir Monitor*, and Sandeep Chattoo, who was in the hotel business, football was back at the forefront. They formed Real Kashmir and the Kashmiris took great comfort from the game in the midst of ongoing strikes, curfews, armed conflicts and heavy military patrolling. However, not for the first time in my career I didn't do any research into the role or what I was getting myself into.

It was at Christmas when I first got wind of the chance to coach in Kashmir. As there was no academy football in January, I had a bit of a break in my schedule in Texas so the plan was to go back to Phoenix and spend some time with Kym and the kids. But then I got the call from Shamim who invited me out to India to coach Real Kashmir for six games. The timing was perfect as the games would be in January so I spoke to Don Cameron at Lonestar and he agreed that I could go. It's fair to say Kym wasn't quite as understanding as Don – you'll find out exactly how she felt later in the book – and she was so annoyed that she didn't even take me to the airport.

With the benefit of hindsight, I can understand why she was so pissed off. I was going to another country to coach a new club in a war zone while we were in the throes of packing up and moving from Phoenix to Texas. But even though it might have been perceived as the last job in the world that anyone would have wanted, such was my desire to get back into the professional game, I jumped at it.

But once again thanks to my blasé attitude I didn't do any due diligence. In the batch of six fixtures Real Kashmir were due to face a team called Lonestar and at one point I actually thought that was the team I was going to. I naively thought there would be some tie-up between my team in Texas and this team in India so that was my first mistake. I also went by what I had seen on Karl Pilkington's *An Idiot Abroad* TV show, so I was drawn by the fact that India was a beautiful country and that it was hot too. Kashmir, surrounded by mountains in the Himalayas, seemed attractive too. It is often referred to as 'Heaven on Earth' but when the aircraft touched down at Srinagar airport it was as if I had entered another world.

Leaving behind a very annoyed wife, I secured a visa to travel to India and embarked on an arduous journey that started on a Friday and ended the following Monday. The first leg was a five-hour flight from Phoenix to Philadelphia and, following an eight-hour layover, I flew to Doha which took 12 hours. Thereafter I had a 14-hour wait which meant sleeping in the airport as the world welcomed in 2017. The penultimate leg was a five-hour flight to Delhi and when I arrived there I thought things weren't too bad. Delhi is very cosmopolitan, and the airport was very plush so after another layover – eight hours this time – I was full of hope as the journey was completed with a two-hour flight to Srinagar.

Although mentally and physically drained, I had been buoyed by my experience in Delhi but, when I arrived in Srinagar, it was like walking through the gates of hell, albeit it was freezing as it was snowing. That put my notion of it being hot to bed fairly quickly and when I got into the terminal building there were members of the Indian Army with guns everywhere.

This wasn't exactly the first impression that I had been hoping to get but I kept an open mind as I was met by a chap called Showkat Akhter at the airport. He escorted me to a car which took me to the hotel I was staying at, the Comrade Inn. Located at Rajbagh in the heart of the city, the hotel is now marketed online as 'your home away from home' and an 'opulent boutique property' but it most certainly wasn't like that when I stayed there. I've been in some bad hotels in my career but this one was the worst ever, a real shithole. There wasn't even any WiFi so folk were running around trying to use hotspots from mobile phones. That meant calling home, where things were still fraught and tense, was a nightmare for me.

The journey to the hotel was a real eye-opener too. There were cows and donkeys in the road and there was a constant din from the loudspeakers as people were praying in the mosques. After three days of travelling I was knackered, and it was as if life was passing me by. For the first time I asked myself what the hell I was doing, which I would do numerous times over the next few days.

As bad as the hotel was, I had to make do but just as I got into my bed to sleep there was a knock at the door and the coaches I would be working with were there. There was Iftikar, who coached the goalkeepers; Ajaz, the youth coach; and Satpal Singh, who was the assistant manager. Although Satpal spoke English I couldn't understand him, and it was even worse when he started to write down the names of the players. His writing was illegible, so we were struggling to communicate on a basic level already.

I thought at that stage that it couldn't get any worse, but it did when the power went down. I thought it was simply a power cut due to the adverse weather, but I was informed that this happened three times every day for two hours in the winter. Essentially demand outstripped supply and I now had a real sinking feeling. To get myself back into football at the top level I had left domestic turmoil behind in Arizona and now I couldn't call home to see if everything was okay, I had to contend with no power for a large part of the day and I couldn't communicate effectively with my coaching staff.

I did manage to get out the hotel room to take training but that too was a chastening experience. When I arrived at the training ground, I found out that the players had to bring their own balls and there was no training kit. The guys who turned up did so in their own gear, with some sporting Manchester United and Chelsea kits. Others turned up for training wearing leather jackets.

By now I had had enough. I went out for a traditional Kashmiri dinner with Shamim and told him everything. I was adamant I was leaving but he asked me to at least stay and take the team for the first of the six matches I had signed up for. He invited me to stay in his house too. That at least got me out of the hotel, so I agreed.

I packed the bags I had, checked out of the hotel and headed to Shamim's house and was met by this palatial building. It was beautiful and once I got inside I found Shamim's family and friends dressed in traditional attire, sitting on the floor eating with their hands. This was another part of life in India that I wasn't aware of and something even now I find difficult to adjust to.

I also met Shamim's housekeeper, Fayaz. He was a solid, tough-looking bloke but a really nice guy. He took me up to the bedroom I would be sleeping in and asked if I wanted a bottle. I thought he was offering me a bottle of wine or beer, but he actually meant a hot water bottle for my bed. And as for the bed, it was massive. I reckon it could have slept eight comfortably. It was a far cry from the hotel bed I had slept in, so I got in and was looking forward to a good night's sleep. But as I got into bed Fayaz literally tucked me in and pulled the sheets so tight that I couldn't move. It was so tight in fact that I couldn't get up for a pee during the night!

I awoke the next morning all set to take training but when I looked out the window I saw at least two feet of snow on the ground. Although the training pitch was Astroturf there was no way it would be playable and when Iftikar picked me up and took me to the pitch there was no way we could train. The session was cancelled and the next day while the police cleared the pitch, we were taken to an indoor facility. I was expecting a school gym hall, but we were met with a room that was 20ft by 8ft with a couple of ceiling fans. It was chaos, with balls hitting the fans and the windows. It later transpired that we were training in a space in someone's front room. I found that out after we trained there for a second time. My driver was late picking me up and, as I waited for him, people were moving furniture back in.

Incidentally, in the short time I was there I was always late for training. That wasn't my doing, though. Iftikar had this strange habit of stopping every day en route to the ground to buy a cigarette – not a packet, only one. I didn't know you could buy single cigarettes and Iftikar never did explain to me why he did it.

The day after we trained indoors, we got the chance to go and see what had been done to clear the snow off the pitch. But when I arrived, I was met by big mounds of snow and only small areas of maybe ten square feet that had been cleared for us to train on. It must have been like a scene from a comedy movie as the players jockeyed their way around the piles of snow that looked, from a distance, like snowmen.

This was hardly ideal preparation for my first game which was against Dehli United at the Dr Ambedkar Stadium in New Delhi at the end of January. One of the coaches, Intikab, and I took a flight to get to that one, but the team had to go by road and that set in motion a chain of events that meant I was in Dehli for four days before my players arrived.

The road between Kashmir and Delhi is narrow and at that time of year with all the snow that was falling it was even narrower. As a result, you can only go one way for two days then the opposite way for another two days and so on. On top of that there's a tunnel on the route and as the lads made their way through it there was a landslide of snow that trapped them inside. There was no way of communicating with us as there was no internet and their phone batteries were dying as they had no way of charging them. We simply had to wait until they got there, and, in the meantime, I had all the money I had on me stolen from the safe in my hotel room. Under the circumstances we asked for the match to be postponed but our request was refused. By the time my players arrived we had 15 minutes to warm up before kick-off and, not surprisingly, we lost, 2-0.

My second match in charge was also in New Delhi. It took place a week later against Sudeva Moonlight and, not surprisingly, this also showed me what life was like as a coach in India. It ended in another defeat, 4-3 this time, but my abiding memory is having my half-time team talk interrupted. It is custom for dignitaries to be invited to games and introduced to the players. But on this occasion they were running late so, rather than the ceremony taking place prior to the match, it took place when they arrived, which was right in the middle of the half-time interval.

After that match we made our way back to Srinagar. I took training a few times and eventually managed to sort out a flight back to the States. But I almost didn't make the flight. A couple of days before my return I went back to Shamim's house after training and was met by a woman and two children who I didn't recognise. It turned out to be Fayaz's wife and kids and I was told later that Fayaz had gone into town to get his phone fixed. It soon transpired that they didn't speak any English, so we sat in silence. Although they were watching me, I didn't want to do likewise so I pretended to watch the TV. Given this was a period of the day when there was no power, it wasn't even on, but I felt more comfortable staring at a blank screen than I did making eye contact with complete strangers.

Eventually I couldn't take it anymore and, after I had dinner, I made a signal to show them I was going to bed. I remember lying down on my cavernous bed and thinking about the fact that I was due to head back home in a couple of days. As my mind drifted towards Texas there was a knock at the bedroom door and in came the woman and two kids. Once in the room they stationed themselves at the bottom of the bed and started to stare at me. I started to panic. I genuinely thought they were going to kidnap me and, given the poor communications, I had no idea how I was going to raise the alarm. I started planning an escape route with my laptop, with the intention of finding somewhere with internet access to allow me to book a flight home. But I didn't know my way around, so I was mightily relieved when Shamim arrived back although it took a while for my heart rate to return to normal.

In the end I only coached two of the six games I had originally signed up for. The adverse weather meant that there were a number of postponements and I hung on as long as I could as I had promised the owners I would coach the team in the first home game. But I had also told Don Cameron I would be back in Texas in time for the games resuming there and on top of that I had to get back and see Kym and try and patch things up with her.

I arrived back in Texas and sorted things out with Kym, but I ended up leaving Lonestar. I probably took the piss a bit by staying in Kashmir for longer than I had agreed with Don so, when he called me in for a chat, I expected to be told my services were no longer required. He said that after being away for so long he could not keep me on as the other coaches were asking where I was. He felt that if I continued in my role, it could cause problems. We agreed to part ways and, to be honest, I was glad to get out.

Yet the experiences in both Arizona and Texas shaped me as a coach. I had nine great years in America, on and off the park. I met some great people who I'm still in contact with today and each team I looked after were successful. Kids from those teams went on to play soccer at college but, by the end, I was tired and needing a new challenge. And for all that the experience in Kashmir had been an eye-opener, it served its purpose. It confirmed that I wanted back into professional football and within a few months I was back in India and back in the firing line.

CHAPTER 12

KASHMIR

AFTER I left Kashmir in February, Shamim and Sandeep were in regular contact with me. Although we had lost the two games I had taken charge of, they made it clear they wanted me back and, after a bit of deliberation, I decided to go. By now the family were in the process of moving back to Scotland so I flew back to India in June for around six weeks to try and get the team fit.

The squad weren't the most technically gifted players in the world so I knew they would have to have a good level of fitness. But my return to Kashmir coincided with Ramadan so I was trying to do pre-season training while the players were fasting during daylight hours. In order to embrace the culture, I took part in it too but I didn't realise that they couldn't even drink water. That made it even tougher to get them fit and after the first few days they were pulling up with a number of different injuries.

I came home after that but only to make the final arrangements for one of my first tasks, to organise a tour of Scotland for the team. I arranged for the team to stay in a halls of residence in Partick and sorted out some games too. We would play Albion Rovers, Forth Wanderers, Partick Thistle under-20s and Stenhousemuir, although the trip didn't get off to the best of starts as we became embroiled in red tape when the players were initially refused visas to travel.

After a lot of hard work, we managed to get things sorted but time was tight as the visas were only approved the Sunday before the Albion Rovers game, which was scheduled for the Thursday. The squad flew to London on the Tuesday then caught a coach up to Scotland and they arrived at 2am on the day of the game. It was no surprise therefore that my sleep-deprived players were 4-0 down at half-time. The game ended 5-1 and we followed that with a 6-0 loss to Stenny and 2-2 draws against Forth Wanderers and Thistle's under-20s.

In total, the team were in Scotland for five days. As well as the games I took the squad for a tour of Ibrox and Rangers' training centre at Auchenhowie and, overall, it was a worthwhile exercise. Of the players who embarked on the tour, only one, Danish Farooq, remains with the club today.

When the team travelled back to India I stayed in Scotland. The plan was for the lads to go back via London but en route they were going to stay with Shamim's cousin in Gillingham. But the journey home was again fraught with challenges and I was soon called upon to help when two of the players found themselves caught in a delicate situation. I was playing badminton with Mason when I was called on my mobile by Ajaz, the youth coach. He gave me a number to call and said the police wanted to talk to me. When I asked what had happened, Ajaz told me that two of the players, Amir Renan and Isfaq Hussain, had been held on the street by the police.

I started to panic a little, but I called the number I was given and, essentially, I was asked to vouch for them both. The policeman I spoke to asked if I was the coach of Real Kashmir and when I confirmed I was he told me that Amir and Isfaq had been seen on London Bridge talking to a Caucasian gentleman with a suspicious package. The gentleman was in fact one of our players, Danish Farooq.

Senses had been heightened by an incident on the bridge a few weeks earlier, but it turned out the 'package' was a pair of trainers that had been bought at Lilywhites. However, even after they found that out the police then thought the lads were selling stuff on the street, something you needed a licence for. In the end it all blew over but dealing with the call was a bit of a reality check for me that something so innocent could be perceived as something more sinister.

I went back to India soon after that to get set for the new season. We arranged to play a game in a village called Bandipore and it was a big deal as this was the first floodlit match to be played there. It took about two or three hours to get there but when we arrived. I noticed that other than the stand the only thing that separated the supporters from the pitch was a rope. The dressing rooms were a bit different to what I had been used to as well. They were made out of corrugated iron and not long after the players and I had gone in to get ready for the game there was a huge bang. We all shit ourselves and some of the lads dived on the floor. To be honest it sounded like a gunshot, but it turned out that the noise had been created by a kid kicking a ball against the iron.

Despite this being the first floodlit match, the lights were pretty poor so when the game started it was pretty dark. And sure enough, after only five minutes they failed. A crowd of about four or five thousand was expected but, in reality, there were around 20,000 people there by the time the match kicked off. When the lights went out, they all breached the rope barrier and flooded on to the playing surface.

After a delay of around 15 minutes the game restarted but the rope was now gone and everyone watching the game was now pretty much on the touchline. As the crowd were on the lines there were no throw-ins as the ball was simply hitting them and coming back into play.

At one point I had a guy next to me who kept saying 'match, match'. As he didn't speak English, I thought he was saying it was a good match and I nodded in agreement. But he kept on saying 'match' until he eventually took out a cigarette, put it in his mouth and pointed at it and said 'match'. Here I was coaching a game of football and one of the supporters was asking me to help him light his cigarette!

We were ahead at half-time – our goal prompted another invasion of the pitch – and the size of the crowd meant we couldn't get back to the dressing rooms. I had to do my team talk with throngs of people round about me and the players and I were getting pushed and jostled as I passed on my instructions. It was pretty scary but nothing in comparison to what happened when the home side equalised with ten minutes to go. There was yet another pitch invasion and during this one of our players was struck with a fence post. All hell broke loose after that and I can remember being grabbed by one of Shamim's security staff and getting bundled into a car. We left at speed, travelling down dark alleys to get away before we eventually went back after it had all calmed down.

Our game against J&K Bank was another experience I'll never forget. Their team was made up of employees of the

Jammu and Kashmir Bank. Essentially the players joined the bank when they left school and became professional footballers. When they finished their playing career, they got a job with the business which gave them both security and a pension.

J&K Bank were the best team in the state – they rarely lost – so we weren't expected to win but, despite having no strikers to pick, that's exactly what we did. I played a Brazilian box formation and we won 1-0 and, for the second successive match, it all kicked off at the end. And I have to hold my hands up, I was complicit in the incident that started it all off. Towards the end I sent on a sub and basically told him to sort a few of their players out. He took me a little too literally though, and ended up breaking one of their player's legs.

But that, for me, was a watershed moment. No one thought I had a chance of doing anything with this team so to beat one of the top teams in the country gave us a huge lift. I also felt I had the backing of the owners too; they now felt I had what it took to deliver what they wanted, promotion to the I-League.

My squad was still a bit threadbare, though. From our trip to Scotland only Danish and Hamad remained, and we were only allowed two foreign players in the team. I signed a Nigerian defender, Loveday Enyinnaya, and a 6ft 5in striker called Bernard Yao from the Ivory Coast, but I felt I needed more bodies so ahead of the league season starting I arranged a trial in Kolkata, the capital of the state of West Bengal.

We arrived late at night to find that our hotel rooms had been given away so I ended up in a hotel that was on a par with the Comrade Hotel I had stayed in during my initial stint in Kashmir. The room allocated only had a single bed and I had to share this with our technical director, who I didn't really get on with. There were wires hanging out the lights and the toilet was disgusting but we made do and got up the next morning ready to select players from the trial matches.

Players were invited to attend through agents and I expected it would be the same as it was in Scotland or indeed America in that around 30 players would turn up. Imagine my surprise then when I arrived at the ground where the trials were taking place and there were about 200 players present. It was like the cast from *Ben Hur* were there! Matters were made even worse when it transpired that the bibs and balls we had brought with us had been left back at the hotel.

We were only there for two days and the trials ran from 10am to around 5pm. On day one, when I managed to sort the trialists into their preferred positions, I found out there were 17 goalkeepers. I had been concerned that I would struggle to get any more than a couple of keepers so I was pleasantly surprised. However, I had to hastily plan to whittle the numbers down such that we only had 30 players turning up on the second day.

But it soon became political. Each agent was there pushing their own players and, when it came to the final match being played on the last day, there were players playing who I had said didn't make the cut the day before. But despite all that the trial was a success as I managed to recruit five players to join the quest for promotion.

It was now late November and it was around then that my bed went on fire. Kym loves a warm bed but I don't so to regulate the heat in our bed at home, we invested in a dual-control electric blanket. But I thought I had found her an even better one out in India. I was still staying at Shamim's house and, given the frequency of the power outages and the lack of heaters there, each bed had an electric blanket. The way it worked was that you would be really cold when the power was out then there would be a surge and the blanket would come on and it was soon roasting hot. I was so taken by the heat that I called Kym and said I was going to bring a couple back for her.

But a few nights later it was so hot that I couldn't even put my toe on the blanket. I could smell burning but I thought it must have been someone setting a fire outside, until I turned the light on and there was smoke and my bed was burning! Before I knew it there were flames so, in a panic, I called Kym. It must have been about 3am and I was yelling at her that my bed was burning, there was smoke everywhere and I wanted her to tell me what to do. I eventually managed to put water on the bed and, as it was smouldering, I threw it out an open window. But as soon as it hit the fresh air, it burst into flames again. Suffice to say I didn't have any of those blankets in my luggage the next time I returned home.

The league campaign kicked off on 21 March. There were 18 teams in what was referred to as the I-League Second Division and they were split into three groups of six. Real Kashmir were in Group A alongside Delhi United, Hindustan, Lonestar Kashmir and the reserve teams of Pune City and Delhi Dynamos. Pune and the Dynamos were two of the seven Indian Super League reserve sides playing in the second tier. There was no reserve league in India and the setup was similar to what happens in Spain with Real Madrid and Barcelona fielding their respective B teams in the lower leagues.

There was a condition, though; these teams couldn't qualify for the play-offs to decide the league champions. The play-offs, which were to be staged at the FSV Arena in Bengaluru in late

May, were contested between the three teams that topped their section and the best runner-up. To get there we had to play each team in our group home and away and, at the end of those ten games, the line-up would be decided.

We started our campaign in Group A with a 0-0 draw at home to Pune City reserves and followed that with wins over Delhi Dynamos (2-0) and Lonestar Kashmir (2-1). We then drew three of the next four fixtures. After drawing 1-1 against Delhi United away from home and playing out a 0-0 draw with Hindustan, we beat Delhi United 1-0 before blowing a 3-0 lead to draw 3-3 at home against Hindustan.

The victory over United was hard-earned – Atinder Mani scored the only goal four minutes before half-time – which made the eventful scouting mission I had gone on five days earlier worthwhile. The games in League 2 were not televised so I decided I would go and get the lowdown on United. I flew to Delhi and then arranged to get an Uber from the hotel to the ground. I had given myself plenty of time to make it for kick-off but about halfway there the driver slammed on the brakes and the car screeched to a halt in the middle of nowhere. He told me to get out as he had to get home as his grandmother had suffered a heart attack. While I understood he needed to go I requested that he sort me out with another driver as I couldn't call for one as I had no idea where I was. He didn't, and no matter how loudly I shouted at him, it made no difference.

I got out and the guy drove away at pace. I was raging but, as I was shouting at the car driving away, a guy emerged from a hut. He sold tobacco and, when he asked me what was wrong, I explained my predicament. He guided me into a forest and in among the trees we happened upon a white bedsheet drying out. In behind it, fast asleep on a hammock, was Seikh, who just happened to be a taxi driver. He was persuaded to take me to the stadium, and he did so in a presidential car. I made the game with time to spare too and watched as Delhi drew 0-0 against the Dynamos.

That wasn't the only time that a scouting trip turned into an adventure. In 2019/20 we were due to play Gokulam, so after we drew 1-1 with East Bengal in Kolkata, I decided to go and watch them play Indian Arrows in Goa. The club organised a couple of flights to get me there and I watched the game and wrote my report.

After the game I went to the airport and caught a flight to Delhi and when I got there I checked into a hotel for the night before my early flight to Srinagar the next day. After I checked in for that flight and went through security, I boarded the aircraft only to find out that the flight was cancelled due to poor visibility in Srinagar. After disembarking and getting out of the airport, I went back and checked into a hotel.

I booked on another flight for the following day, but the same thing happened, so I was back in the hotel again. When I got there, I found out that Sandeep's son, Samarth, was travelling to their home in Jammu from their family home in Delhi so it was decided that we would both fly to Jammu and I could either fly to Srinagar from there or complete the journey by road. Throughout my time in India, Sandeep's family have made me feel so welcome. They are an amazing family, and I am thankful for the support they have given me through this journey. As far as owners and chairmen are concerned, Sandeep is the best in the business.

If the airport in Srinagar is closed, the only way to get there from Jammu is by road. And it's arguably the worst road in the world; in fact, it's more like a farm track than a road. After a gruelling 12-hour road trip I eventually returned to Srinagar almost a week after I had attended the game. And after all of that, our home match against Gokulam was postponed!

We followed the 3-3 draw against Hindustan with wins over Lonestar (2-1) and the Dynamos (3-2). In the latter game we almost contrived to surrender another three-goal lead. My team were really good at getting their noses in front, but we had a bad habit of not being able to defend that lead. And that almost cost us a couple of vital points against the Dynamos. Atinder Mani, Danish and Ritwik Kumar Das put us 3-0 up before half-time but two goals from our hosts in the last 12 minutes made for a nervy ending. We clung on, though, and the win gave us an opportunity to make the play-offs going into our last fixture, against Pune in a place called Pirangut.

The win over the Dynamos had taken place in New Dehli, six days before we were due to play Pune. I was advised that we should travel to Pirangut by sleeper train and that it would take 12 hours. It turned out the chap who had told me the journey time had been a wee bit economical with the truth. In total we were on the train for 30 hours and the beds were essentially benches that you lay on. It wasn't the smoothest of rides either. We were thrown around due to the momentum of the train and when we got off it felt as if we had been hit by a bus. Here we were, a matter of days before arguably the biggest match in Real Kashmir's history and my players were battered, bruised and limping along the platform.

We had two days to train ahead of the game, but we didn't have anywhere to go. I spoke to the manager of the hotel we were staying in and explained that all we needed was an area of grass to train on. He took me and members of the coaching staff in his car and we eventually found somewhere suitable. When we arrived back at the hotel we asked the manager about hiring a bus to get us back to our 'training ground' but he told us there were none and on top of that the only car the hotel had use of was the manager's one. I was now stuck as I had a squad of players that I needed to keep ticking over before the game but having found somewhere to facilitate that I now had no way of getting them there.

The problem was solved by the hotel manager. He was expecting a delivery of vegetables and said we could use the vegetable truck to get us to our training facility. I followed on behind the truck in the manager's car and watched the heads of my players bobbing up and down as they sat among the turnips, carrots and potatoes. The journey was about 20 minutes long and when we got to our patch of grass my players emerged brushing soil from their clothes and removing carrot stocks from their hair. Fortunately, this happened only once as we trained at the stadium for the next two days before we faced Pune.

Ahead of our game with Pune, one of the play-off spots had already been taken but we went in tied with Hindustan on 19 points. Both sides were yet to be beaten but across the three groups there were four teams in a position to claim the available play-off places. A draw could have been enough for us but we had no phone contact or internet reception so we had no idea what was going on elsewhere. Pune were a very technical team but our big Ivorian striker, Bernard Yao, scored against the run of play after 21 minutes.

I knew we would have to defend for our lives after that but we held our lead when we got to half-time. A few minutes before the interval the weather took a turn for the worse and the rain came down in torrents. It was so heavy that it caused a power cut so during the half-time interval we were in the dressing room in complete darkness. There was, however, some light in the corridor outside the dressing room so I hoisted the tactics board up on top of a chest freezer that was located there. I then detailed what my team had to do to defend the narrow lead we had.

Our right-back was Nachiket Palav but I couldn't pronounce his name, so I referred to him as Tony. He was up against a lad called Chesterpoul Lyngdoh, who now plays for Real Kashmir, and I pointed out to Tony that Paul kept running inside but I instructed him not to track his run and go with him. That would have pulled him out of position, but Tony was one of these lads who liked to argue back. Voices started to get raised but as I had been a full-back throughout my playing career, I implored him to trust me as I knew what I was talking about. But he kept coming back at me so eventually I snapped and told him in no uncertain terms that if he followed Paul inside even once I was going to put him in the freezer that the tactics board was sitting on and leave him there.

By the time we came out for the second half the rain had given way to hailstones the size of golf balls and the two canopies that covered the dugouts had blown away. It was freezing cold – I'm from the north-east of Scotland but I don't think I've ever been so cold in my life – and we hung on to win 1-0. When the game ended the ground was enveloped in glorious sunshine and that reflected our mood as we found out that Hindustan had drawn 0-0 against Delhi United, so we topped Group A and made the play-offs.

Although they had slipped up in their last game, Hindustan joined us in the play-offs. TRAU, who won Group C, and Ozone, who had been runners-up to the Kerala Blasters reserves in Group B, made up the quartet that would fight it out for the single promotion place.

The play-offs took place at the FSV Arena in Chagalatti, Bangalore. As you might have gathered by now, we didn't travel there in the lap of luxury. We went by bus, but it wasn't the type of luxury coach I had been accustomed to when I travelled to games with Rangers. The bus we were in didn't have any toilet facilities or air conditioning, so we had to stop every 50 miles for comfort breaks. Given that the distance between Pune and Bangalore is over 500 miles, it took us 24 hours to reach our destination.

We were now in a mini-league and we kicked off with a match against Ozone on 24 May, 11 days after our win over Pune. Ozone were coached by an Englishman, Dave Booth, and we went 1-0 down after 26 minutes but were level at half-time after Nadong Bhutia equalised. But we conceded a second goal after 67 minutes and going into the dying embers we looked down and out. I made a couple of attacking changes to try and force a draw and they worked as we equalised in the last minute. I was quite content to have rescued a draw, but my players weren't prepared to settle for a point and five minutes into injury time Bernard scored to give us a 3-2 win.

Three days later we were trailing going into injury time again, this time against TRAU. They had lost 1-0 to Hindustan in the first round of fixtures and, as Hindustan had drawn 2-2 against Ozone before we faced TRAU, I knew a scoring draw would leave my team just needing a draw in the last match to secure promotion. And we snatched that draw with an own goal a minute into injury time. In the dressing room afterwards, the players were dejected but I explained that even winning the game would still have left us only needing a draw against Hindustan. I hadn't wanted to tell them that as it might have messed with their heads.

One of the lads who was particularly down was our midfielder, Farhan Ganie. He was moping about the hotel the next day and I couldn't understand why as I had told him that he had been our best player on the park. I asked one of the players what was up with him and it turned out that he thought I was having a go at him. In typical Robertson style I had hollered at Farhan, who doesn't speak English, that he had been fucking brilliant, but he had taken my shouting and swearing to mean he had had a bad game. It all got sorted out, though, and we were now all set for a showdown against Hindustan.

And that inability to hold on to a lead that I mentioned earlier almost came back to bite us against Hindustan. We led 2-1 at half-time and when Bhutia scored our third after 67 minutes, we were coasting. But Hindustan pulled one back with ten minutes to go and we were hanging on in the end.

But we resisted everything that was thrown at us and remarkably I had guided Real Kashmir to promotion with a record of eight wins and five draws in the 13 games we played. History was made that day – 30 May 2018 – as for the first time, a team from the state of Jammu and Kashmir would be playing in the top flight in India.

We returned to the hotel and Sandeep laid on a slap-up meal and a free bar. But with the exception of about five or six players, the team was made up of Kashmiris and devout Muslims. They therefore didn't drink alcohol and after the meal they all retired to their rooms. Here I was in a hotel lounge with my assistant manager, Jimmy Lindsay, at about 9pm on the day of one of the greatest achievements in my career, watching an Indian soap opera on TV.

I think the muted celebrations were down to the fact that our achievement had been so unexpected. But over the next few days folk in the region began to realise just how significant an achievement it had been, and we were afforded a hero's reception when we landed at the airport in Srinagar. I was taking calls from media outlets all over the world and, all of a sudden, the Real Kashmir story was the one that everyone wanted to know about. And the story spawned not just one but two BBC documentaries, the first of which won a BAFTA Scotland Award in 2019.

After the season was finished, Kym and I went to Dubai for a break and to spend time together. While we were there, I got a message from a guy called Greg Clark from BBC. He said he wanted to do a documentary on a Scottish guy working in bizarre places and having read about Real Kashmir's success in winning the league, he thought our story would make good viewing. We spent a few hours on the phone, and I told him some of the bizarre things that had happened to me in my time so far in Kashmir.

Before it went any further, Greg wanted to make sure I would be good and natural on camera, so he came to my house to do an interview. As you know by now, I've always been quiet and shy so there was a chance it wouldn't work out. But as soon as the BBC saw my interview telling tales from Kashmir, laced I must say with a few F-words, the deal was done and the first of the documentaries, *Real Kashmir FC*, was commissioned.

When Greg came over to Kashmir to start filming, I had a microphone on 24/7 but I soon became oblivious to having cameras focussed on me all the time. That meant I would blow up and swear a lot without thinking as I assumed that Greg would cut all that out. However, when I spoke to him, he said that it would stay in as it made compelling viewing. He assured me that we would get to view it to make any changes before it aired, but due to another documentary getting pulled the week before airing, the rush was on to get it finished. As a result, we only got to see it a few days before, by which time it was impossible to change anything.

I felt with all the swear words the public perception wouldn't be good. The programme was edited and, although I know I swear a lot, I didn't think there would be as much included as there was. But my concerns were unfounded as the reaction was very positive, and the viewers thought it was good entertainment. Indeed, it was so successful that the BBC immediately started talking about a second documentary.

When it came to the BAFTA award, I was shocked when Greg called to tell me. The documentary earned nominations in two categories, Director-Factual and Single Documentary. And it was, the latter category that we were successful. The production company and the BBC had a table at the ceremony in Glasgow and Kym and I were invited as guests. We had a great evening, rubbing shoulders with the cast of *Still Game*, *Chernobyl*, *Outlander* and *Derry Girls* among many others.

I'm just a wee boy who grew up on a council estate yet here I was picking up a BAFTA. I was blown away when we won as I never expected to as we were up against such tough opposition. Sandeep had travelled across to be there too, and I think he was just as proud as I was when we won.

A Bollywood series on the club has also been agreed and work on that will start soon. But although that kind of recognition is nice, my focus is always on my team. I was hopeful therefore that our triumphant first season was just the beginning for us. We had put our heart and soul in to get the club established and continue to do so on a daily basis. When we started on the journey, I couldn't have imagined the success that was to come. The first chapter of the tale had ended happily, and I hoped that the next ones would reach a similar conclusion.

CHAPTER 13

IN THE I-LEAGUE

THE I-LEAGUE in India had first been played back in 2007. Real Kashmir were one of 11 teams in the top flight in 2018/19 and the first of what should have been 20 league matches was played at the end of October.

While I didn't need to run trials like I had done the year previously, my squad did need an overhaul. We were inundated with calls from agents before the season started but one of the biggest challenges for my coaching staff and me was that we had no experience of playing at this level in India so didn't know what level of player we needed. Our budget was also a lot lower than that of other teams in the league so we took a bit of a gamble with the players we brought in.

My first priority was a goalkeeper as the guy who had been between the sticks in League 2, Sukhwinder Singh, was approaching his 40th birthday. Getting a good goalkeeper in India is tough but I managed to get Bilal Khan from Pune City and he proved to be a great acquisition as by the end of the season the nine clean sheets he kept was the best in the league.

I was also able to add more foreign players to my squad as the I-League allowed six rather than the two we had been permitted in League 2. I was on the lookout for a big striker as Bernard, who had done so well for us in League 2, had an issue with his visa. I ended up replacing him with one of his best buddies, another Ivorian called Gnohere Krizo, who at 6ft 7in tall fitted the bill for me perfectly. I was also able to procure the experienced midfield player Armand Bazie, who had been part of the Minerva Punjab team that had won the title the previous season. Zambian international Aaron Katebe also came in from a club in Vietnam called Nkang.

I hadn't seen these guys in the flesh – I relied on reports from agents and videos of them in action – but I go with my gut feeling when signing players and thus far I have been spot on. But I didn't have to rely on my gut when it came to the last of our foreign recruits, Mason Robertson. It was actually Shamim and Sandeep who persuaded me to go and sign my son as Shamim had been impressed by his professionalism when they met him during the tour of Scotland the previous year.

I had also shown them footage of Mason in action during his spells at University of Washington, Stenhousemuir and Peterhead, and he offered a bit of versatility as he could play at the heart of the defence or up front. Kym was a bit apprehensive about Mason coming out to Kashmir but, although he had verbally agreed to stay with Peterhead for 2018/19, the move to India gave him the opportunity to go full-time. That was what he wanted, and the club really pushed the boat out to get him over. That and the fact he would be staying with me in the guest house at Shamim's sealed the deal for his mum.

There was no pressure for Mason or indeed Jordan to go into football, but Mason took to the game as soon as he could walk. Similar to me, he's a quiet kid and of the three kids, Mason was the easiest when he was a baby. We learnt from the mistakes we made with Chelsea and he used to sleep for ages. On one occasion when we came back from a holiday in Orlando, he slept for about 25 hours!

He's a talented player and there are times that I regret moving to America when we did as I feel it impacted Mason's career. I feel he's good enough to play in the Scottish Premier League but playing soccer in America seems to carry a bit of a stigma. But he's done well, and his long-term goal is to move back to the States where he has a fiancée called Paloma.

Of the three kids, Jordan is the most streetwise. Rather than listen to advice he needs to go through things in order to learn. But in contrast to Mason, Jordan wasn't really interested in football. When he was with a boys' club team in Leeds with his brother, there were plenty of times he would do the warm-up then decide he didn't want to play. It wasn't until after we moved back to Aberdeen, following the end of my time at Leeds, that he really got into playing on a regular basis.

He's actually a very good player. Both he and Mason are aggressive, but Jordan has got a bit more pace. But although he played for Sereno and college soccer at St Mary's in San Antonio and Waldorf University in Iowa, he drifted out the game. He played for Culter Juniors when we came back home but, due to work commitments at that time, he couldn't make training which meant he couldn't play at the weekend. As a result, he was away from the game for a while but he's back now playing for Banchory St Ternan. One of my old Skillseekers, Anton

Lennox, got him back in the game and its good to see him playing again.

I took the players to Mumbai for pre-season training and that gave Mason and the rest of the new recruits a chance to get to know the rest of the squad. Integration was also helped by the fact that the players all stayed in Sandeep's luxury five-star hotel in the centre of Srinigar. And when we got back from Mumbai, that's where Mason ended up too as he got on so well with the other lads that they invited him to move in.

Real Kashmir were scheduled to make their I-League debut on 31 October but prior to that I got a chance to assess my newly assembled squad when we took part in the Kashmir Invitational Cup. The tournament was organised by the Jammu and Kashmir FA and the Jammu and Kashmir State Sports Council, with eight teams taking part. This would be a good gut check for my squad as the reigning I-League champions, Minerva Punjab, were involved and they would be the first team we would be facing when the league action got under way.

Not surprisingly, given the tension in the valley, the tournament was fraught from start to finish. We kicked off with a 7-0 win over Delhi United on 18 October, a day later than planned. That was due to a strike call by the Joint Resistance Leadership (JRL) in the aftermath of the Fateh Kadal gunfight. And a couple of days later three militants were killed in the Kulgam district and six civilians also lost their lives in a blast following a gunfight.

In such circumstances, football seemed irrelevant but the organisers decided to adjust the schedule so that two matches were played each day. We managed to reach the final after we defeated Bengaluru after extra time. Mason scored in the 120th minute to give us a 3-2 win and a shot at the champions. Or so we thought! Due to the ongoing situation in Kulgam, the organisers decided to cancel the final and declare ourselves and Minerva Punjab joint winners.

Political angst aside, the matches were ideal preparation for the season for my players and ironically our next match was against Minerva Punjab at the Tau Devi Lal Stadium in Gurgaon. It was a great day for two debutants as our goalkeeper, Bilal, was the man of the match while Krizo scored the only goal with 16 minutes to go. I admit I was nervous before the game. Although we had done well pre-season, I didn't know if the squad we had pulled together would be able to compete, but this performance showed we could mix it with the best of them.

But trouble never seemed to be too far away and within a few weeks there were rumours going around that I was going to be sacked. We followed the win over Minerva with a goalless draw at home against Churchill Brothers who had their goalkeeper sent off just before half-time. This was the start of a run of six successive home games, but our next two outings brought back-to-back defeats against Neroca (2-0) and Mohun Bagan (1-0).

We deserved to get something out of both games but, all of a sudden, individuals from within the club started to question my team selection and our style of play. Jimmy Lindsay, who had been my assistant in League 2, was no longer around so I felt a bit isolated and that was made harder when it became clear that a couple of members of the coaching team were trying to undermine me.

Football is a fickle business, but I stood my ground. At the start of the season my main objective was to survive in the top division and, as we had a pretty low budget compared to the other teams in the league, we had to play to our strengths. And although there were some people within the club who were against me, never at any point did I lose the dressing room. You'll have seen from the BBC documentaries that I'm not slow in venting my fury, using some rather colourful language in the process. But that's never directed at the players as I want what is best for them. My players respect me, and I respect them. We are very close and have a great rapport. I look after them and the upshot of that is we trust each other and get results. In fact, players who have left the club are still in contact with me.

That relationship reaped a rich reward as we followed those two defeats with an unbeaten run of 13 games. We started by beating Indian Arrows (2-0) and Aizawl (1-0) before ending the run of home matches with a spectacular 6-1 win over Shillong Lajong.

Mason scored his first goal for the club in that match, and I have to admit I was glad he was there as we followed that emphatic victory with a run of six away games that saw us on the road for 45 days. My team did well on the field in that spell. We were the first team to defeat the league leaders, Chennai City, and Mason bagged a double when we beat Mohun Bagan 2-1. The latter result against a real giant of the game in India sent shockwaves around the country but during that time I became more and more isolated. I spent the majority of the time in my hotel room on my own and I missed having Jimmy Lindsay as my right-hand man.

I felt that there were some who were trying to influence my decisions and there was a lot of friction, but I put my personal circumstances to one side as we were building up a head of steam in the race for the title. We won three and drew three of those six away matches and on 10 February we were scheduled to play our crucial home match against East Bengal.

We were on 32 points after 16 matches, while our opponents were on 28 points having played two games fewer. Four days earlier in wintry conditions we had beaten Gokulam Kerala 1-0 to move to the top of the league. The players had struggled as the ground was very heavy, but the narrow win meant, with just four games to go, we were sitting two points behind the leaders, so back-to-back titles was a realistic possibility. However, the snow got worse over the next few days and the East Bengal game was postponed. The match was rearranged for 28 February but by then Srinagar was in turmoil following a terror attack, the consequences of which arguably cost my team the league title.

On 14 February, a matter of days after we were due to face East Bengal, the Pulwama attack took place. Forty Central Reserve Police Force (CRPF) personnel were killed just 20km away from the airport in Srinagar. A convoy of vehicles had been targeted by a suicide bomber and the attack was regarded by some as the deadliest terrorist strike in Jammu and Kashmir for 30 years.

Our next league match, against Minerva Punjab, was due to be played just four days later but, in the wake of the attack, our opponents refused to travel to Srinagar. My players and I were there at the designated kick-off time so there was an argument that Minerva had forfeited. As per FIFA rules, we should have been awarded three points and a 3-0 win. However, Minerva's counter-argument was that their team had not travelled to Srinagar as they had security concerns. They were looking for the match to be moved to a neutral venue or to obtain written assurances with regards safety from either the Indian Army, the Indian government or the Home Ministry. But when they weren't forthcoming, they simply didn't turn up.

But we were never awarded the victory. Although the club put out a message of 'let's play to heal', Minerva's stance was that they hadn't forfeited the match and if that was the decision taken then they would appeal and take the matter to court if necessary. Within a couple of weeks, the All-India Football Federation (AIFF) decided that a rematch would take place. But even that didn't come to pass and eventually, when any result declared would have no impact on who won the title, both teams ended the campaign having fulfilled only 19 of the scheduled 20 league fixtures.

As a coach this kind of situation is really frustrating. Looking back now, I can fully understand the concerns that Minerva had but I have been in Srinagar for a couple of years now and I know we are safe. You expect to take the flak when your team loses or doesn't play well but when you are in with a realistic chance of winning the league and something like this happens, circumstances you have no control over, it makes my job even more difficult.

We should have won the league in our debut season but were denied that opportunity, not just by matters off the field but on it too. We played three league matches after the attack. We drew 2-2 with Indian Arrows before our unbeaten run was ended when we lost the rearranged match against East Bengal. And that defeat cost us our shot at glory.

With tensions still high in Srinagar, the match took place in New Delhi which meant we lost home advantage and our chances were dealt a further blow when we had our Ghanaian forward, Abednego Tetteh, sent off before half an hour had elapsed. He was stupid. The referee had yellow-carded him after a clash with one of their defenders and he decided to voice his displeasure, which earned him a second caution. It was another of those situations that, as a manager, you have no control over. You can tell your players to keep their discipline and outline the impact losing a player can have but you can't legislate for things like that.

I was less than pleased with Tetteh as we were 1-0 behind at that stage and when we conceded another goal just before the interval, I was raging. Although a penalty from Aaron Katebe midway through the second half halved the deficit, we couldn't find another goal. The defeat ended our title hopes and, after beating Neroca 3-2 in our last match in Imphal, we eventually finished third. The 36 points accumulated from our 19 games left us six adrift of runners-up East Bengal and a further point behind the champions, Chennai City, a team we had beaten twice over the course of the season.

Although there were frustrations throughout our debut campaign there was plenty to be pleased about. My team had shown they could compete against and match the best teams in the country, and we had the best defensive record in the league. We had really captured the attention of the public too. When I first came to India, crowds of around 200 were attending our home matches but over the course of the season that had grown to over 20,000 and the atmosphere for the matches was among the best I've experienced in my career.

At the end of the season, Kym, and Mason's fiancée Paloma arrived for a visit and we decided to go and visit the Taj Mahal while we were in Delhi before spending a couple of weeks on the beach in Goa. But we had a bit of a disaster in Delhi. We went to a shopping mall and on the way back to our hotel in an Uber we heard a noise and the car stopped in the middle of a busy motorway flyover. We sat in the car but were soon told by the driver to get out as he had a flat tyre. We asked him to get another driver but in broken English he told us we would have to call and book another car ourselves. However, we had no idea where we were so we could not tell another taxi driver where to pick us up. We ended up walking for a mile or so to exit the motorway in the midst of the busy Delhi traffic, which was pretty scary with cars and trucks speeding past us.

I was hopeful that that and our performances on the pitch would continue in 2019/20. But once again the political situation in Jammu and Kashmir would have a bearing on the outcome, as would the small matter of a global pandemic.

CHAPTER 14

ARTICLE 370 AND COVID-19

LEAGUE FOOTBALL eventually returned to Srinigar on Boxing Day 2019. It had been 323 days since our last action at our home ground and, after drawing our first two matches against East Bengal and TRAU, the 2-1 win over reigning champions Chennai City was our first win of the season. It was great to be back in front of our own fans and while I felt the previous season was tough I was convinced this one would go like clockwork. But the landscape had changed considerably in the region since the last time we had played there.

Every time I go back home after a spell in Kashmir, I always think things are improving and when I go back there will be fewer hurdles to overcome. But when I arrived back in August it was pandemonium after a landmark decision was taken to revoke Article 370 of the Constitution of India. Alongside Article 35A, Article 370 permitted residents in Jammu and Kashmir to live under a separate set of laws from residents of other Indian states. Given the volatility of the region, many feared more unrest so tens of thousands of troops were deployed, schools and colleges were shut, and the meagre telephone and internet services were suspended.

On the day Article 370 was revoked, I arrived in Kolkata as we were scheduled to play in the Durand Cup. When the news broke, we didn't know if the Kashmiri players or staff would arrive as there was no way to communicate due to the suspension of phone and internet services. It wasn't just the players and staff coming from the region either; they were bringing the kit and training equipment too. They did arrive but they couldn't contact family to see if they were safe.

The plan was that we would play in the tournament and head back to Kashmir afterwards. There were 16 teams competing, five from the ISL, six from the I-League, one from the Second Division and four teams from the armed forces. We were placed in Group C alongside Goa, Chennai City and Army Green. The games were in Kalyani, which is roughly 30 miles outside Kolkata, and before our opening match against Chennai City, we had only trained for two days. That was the first time we had done so for five months but a late goal from Danish got us off to a winning start and a further win and a draw saw us top our group.

That took us through to a semi-final against Mohun Bagan. Unlike ourselves, they had been training and playing for several months and in the end that was decisive, as despite an injury-time goal from Krizo that took the match to extra time, we conceded two goals in the extra half-hour to go out. However, I had nothing but admiration for my players afterwards. They performed so well despite the uncertainty in Kashmir so I hoped we could get them back there as soon as possible. But we found out that wasn't possible as there was a complete shutdown. As a result, we stayed on the road for five weeks and became like the Harlem Globetrotters, playing games against a host of ISL clubs.

Our travels took us to Mumbai, Jamshedpur, Kerala, Goa and Chennai and I met some familiar faces along the way. The former Hull City manager Phil Brown was in charge of Hyderabad and John Gregory, who had been Aston Villa manager when I was playing for Leeds United, was at the helm at Chennaiyin.

When we eventually got back to Kashmir there was still a lockdown, which meant no internet and no phone lines. That meant I couldn't contact Kym for a long time which was really hard. I also couldn't tell her I couldn't communicate with her and that made me concerned and worried that all was okay at home. The TVs in our hotel didn't have the cable service activated either as there were no phone lines open to pay and all the programmes that were available weren't in English. We also had to train at 6am to stay out of the eye of the public, so we came back for breakfast at 8am and had a full day to fill in, which was tough.

But we got on with it and, although we failed to win the next three matches after beating Chennai City, three successive away victories kept us in the hunt for the title. Results after that were mixed but, despite losing 1-0 at home to East Bengal on 9 March, my team were sitting fourth in the table on 22 points. With six games to go our hopes of winning the championship looked to be forlorn – Mohun Bagan were the runaway leaders and were 17 points ahead of us – but we were only a point adrift of second-placed East Bengal with a game in hand.

Our next three league matches were due to be played at our home ground and, although our form at the TRC hadn't been great, there was no reason to believe that we couldn't do better than we had done in the previous season. But within a matter of weeks, football was the last thing on everyone's mind as the world found itself in the throes of a global pandemic.

Our next match was scheduled for 14 March when we were due to face TRAU. They had taken two flights to get to Srinagar and both teams were stripped and ready to play. All we were waiting on was clearance from league officials as they said they would allow the game to be played before they suspended the competition the following Monday. But after a two-hour delay the match was postponed.

Shortly afterwards, a statement was made that all I-League matches were to be suspended until 31 March due to the coronavirus pandemic. But that date was extended when, on 24 March, India was in lockdown after the Prime Minister Narendra Modi decreed that he was limiting movement of the population for 21 days as a preventive measure. Domestic and international flights were also suspended, leaving me in limbo.

By now I had joined the players and was living in Sandeep's hotel. In fairness, being stranded in the hotel wasn't a new thing. Given the volatility in the region, shutdowns had been commonplace but this wasn't localised, it was global. And Kym, who had come out to Kashmir just as the season was suspended, was stranded too. It was a worrying time. Although we had Mason with us, Chelsea was back at home in Aberdeen as was Jordan who was one of the lucky ones. He had been in Mexico but had managed to get on one of the last flights out of the country. Kym and I were concerned about our elderly parents too and I was particularly keen to get home as my mum was undergoing chemotherapy.

We were, like thousands of stranded Brits, trying to find a way home, so we found ourselves pretty much isolated in the hotel. Most of the local lads had gone home but our foreign players and Jimmy Lindsay, back as my assistant coach, and Jonathan Craig, our goalkeeping coach, were in the same situation – but as Srinagar airport was closed, the only way in or out of the valley was on a single-track road. I had been on that road once in my time in Kashmir and with large swathes of it being on a cliff edge with no barriers and a part called The Bloody Gutter – that's where some cars had ended up after being struck by rocks that hurtled down the hillside and knocked them over the cliff – I was adamant I would never be on it again. But needs must.

The British government were arranging charter flights to get UK citizens out of India but they were only flying from Goa, Mumbai and New Delhi, so when just over a month later we were contacted by the British High Commission and placed on standby for a flight, it looked the only way to guarantee getting home was to hit that road again.

We were told that the BHC were trying to arrange a transit permit for us to take us to Amritsar, which is about 250 miles from Kashmir. Charter flights to the UK were operating from Sri Guru Ram Dass Jee International Airport in Amritsar and the plan was to get there and then fly back home. The permit was granted in early May and with Jimmy, Jonathan, Kym, Mason and one of the players, Kallum Higginbotham, in tow, our journey home started at 5am with a bus ride to Jammu. It turned out it was good we left when we did. As we were making our way along the road I have mentioned – well, when I say road it was more like a bumpy dirt track that was often shared with horses and goats – it transpired that two militants had been shot and everything had been shut down. Had we left Srinagar any later we wouldn't have got out of India.

By the time we got on the aircraft, there was a sense of relief that we were going home. Although we were surrounded by staff wearing white protective suits and were handed a meal in a plastic bag – this constituted a cheese sandwich and some chocolate buttons – after weeks confined to the hotel with limited contact with my family, I was just glad that there was light at the end of the tunnel.

At the time of writing I am due to head back to India for the 2020/21 season and will be walking into the unknown yet again as the league setup has changed and all the matches will be played in Kolkata. The latter, in my mind, is a disadvantage for us. Although crowds were small to begin with, the TRC was bursting at the seams on plenty of occasions – often we would get in excess of 20,000 at our 14,000-seater stadium – and that made for a raucous and intimidating atmosphere. The fact that the TRC sits 6,000ft above sea level and there are harsh winters in the region also worked in our favour.

The season has also been shortened as each team will only play each other once. Thereafter the league will be split, with the top six playing each other once to see who wins the title and the bottom five fighting it out to see who is relegated. If my experiences in India to date are anything to go by, there will no doubt be twists and turns and hurdles and problems to negotiate and overcome.

But although my players hadn't played competitively for eight months, my coaching staff and I worked hard to get them fit for the season ahead of them. To help with that we were one of 12 teams who took part in the prestigious IFA Shield in December. Ourselves, Mohammedan Sporting, Gokulam Kerala and Indian Arrows from the I-League sides were joined by eight teams from the Calcutta Premier League, and it was one of the latter, George Telegraph, we faced in the final. Our Nigerian forward, Lukman Adefemi, who had scored a hat-trick in the semi-final, put us in front from the penalty spot before Mason netted what proved to be the winner with a header on the hour mark.

Winning the tournament meant a first national title for a team from the region of Jammu and Kashmir and it has been a real shot in the arm for the squad. Confidence ahead of the first league game is high and I feel I have assembled a group capable of winning the championship. That would probably trump everything else I have achieved in the game and if we were to achieve that you'll hear a roar from this quiet man that will reverberate around the world.

EPILOGUE

AS A PLAYER, manager, son, husband, father and friend, David Robertson has made an impression on plenty of people. Here a selection of those people share their memories and stories of David.

LESLIE ROBERTSON

Father and son. There's no better way to start off this part of David's story than to get an insight from his dad.

Although I had a couple of years playing amateur football, it was mostly rugby I played but I was a big Aberdeen fan. Eventually, after a lot of coaxing, I got David interested in the Dons and he started to play football at his primary school. I would go to as many games as I could but, if work commitments meant I couldn't go, my wife and sister would often go instead.

I was involved with the boys' club David played with, helping them raise funds and looking after the financial side of things. Through that I met Alex Ferguson a few times and he would often tell me how much he admired David as a player. But he was honest enough to say that he didn't see David as a left-winger and thankfully Lenny Taylor shifted him to left-back, which helped him get taken on as a professional by Aberdeen.

That was a very proud day for me, and I was over the moon when he made his debut for the first team. He did really well and soon the phone was ringing in the house, with both Fergie and Kenny Dalglish keen to take David to England. I didn't advise David against going – it was up to him if he wanted to go – but in the end I think he made the right decision to stay with Aberdeen. He could have gone down to England and disappeared as so many young players did back then. But instead he improved as a player over the next few seasons playing alongside the likes of McLeish, Miller and McKimmie.

When David decided to join Rangers, he made the right move for himself but, as a red-hot Aberdeen fan, I was disappointed the club didn't go out of their way to keep him. If I'm honest it spoiled my enjoyment of football. I went to watch him at Rangers but only because David was playing there and when he left to go to Leeds I didn't go back to following Aberdeen. Instead I went to watch my youngest son, Michael, playing and I eventually started to watch Culter Juniors.

David's move to Leeds was a disaster – I still don't know how he got through the medical when he signed – but his love for football meant he wouldn't be out the game long. Having said that, when he told me he was going to Kashmir I couldn't believe it! He admits himself that he didn't do his research before going there but he didn't seem to be getting a chance in Scotland. He's done really well and I'm just happy that he's happy.

When I speak to folk about David, as his dad, it is lovely to hear them say he's a nice guy. Although he comes across in the BBC documentaries as being angry at times, he's very even-tempered. I'm proud of what he has done with his life but if I was asked to sum my son up then for me he will always be just David.

SUSAN ROBERTSON

Sibling rivalry is rife in all families so what was it like chez Robertson? David's older sister, Susan, tells her side of her brother's story.

My dad would take David and me to Duthie Park on a Sunday afternoon when we were younger. We would play on the swings and the chute before Dad would take us up the 'big green' to kick a football around. David wasn't really that interested to begin with, but he soon became hooked and it cost me my swing in the back garden! He hooked a net up over the frame and that was it commandeered for football practice. To be honest I didn't feel too bad about it as I used to use it too when we had a kick-about.

Although there are three years between us we spent a lot of time together. We would often take our bikes along the old railway line and in July, when Wimbledon was on, David would be Bjorn Borg and I would be Virginia Wade when we played tennis in the garden.

When David joined Aberdeen I was really proud but, although I went along to a lot of his games when he played for the school and Deeside, I wasn't able to go to as many with the Dons as I was often away at the weekends because I played in a pipe band. But my friends would always ask how he was getting on and, while his move to Rangers in 1991 might not have gone down too well with the Aberdeen fans, as a family we were really pleased for him.

His career has now taken him to India, and I found out about the move on New Year's Eve. We were over at my mum's house and she told us that he was at the airport ready to fly out to Kashmir. To be honest, I was stunned as I knew what things were like out there. I thought that he must have done some research and that this was the right move for him, but it turned out he hadn't!

People who know David have been surprised with what they have seen in the BBC documentaries and I was no different. As a young boy he was very quiet and shy and, although he knows his job and is a good coach, I was a bit taken aback at how forthright he was. I think, however, he does come up against a lot of frustrations because of the different culture and mentality in India. He must feel at times that he is being held back due to circumstances that are outside of his control.

If I was asked to sum David up, I would say he is loyal and has a good sense of humour. I am very proud of what he has achieved in football but, for me, he'll always just be my wee brother.

MICHAEL ROBERTSON

When Michael Robertson was born in 1981, David was already starting to make an impression on the football field. Like all wee brothers, Mike aspired to be just like his older sibling and here he shares his memories of growing up with him.

Although I'm 12 years younger than David, we shared a bedroom in the houses in Garthdee and Peterculter. Those were great times and I have to admit I idolised my big brother. Although I was never any good at football, when I did play, I always tried to copy what David did.

Like David, I didn't really like going to football matches when I was younger. I always remember being bored and I cried during the first game I went to as I was so cold. One abiding memory I have is of a match at Pittodrie when David wasn't playing. He came and sat with my dad and me in the main stand and I got more enjoyment out of talking to my brother than I did out of watching the match.

But that all changed when I went along to the 1990 Scottish Cup Final against Celtic. I fell in love with the game after that. But earlier in the season, not long after I had watched on TV my brother help the Dons beat Rangers to win the League Cup, David took me along to Pittodrie for a look around. We went into the boardroom and the manager, Alex Smith, was there and he let me hold up the League Cup trophy. David also took me into the room where Teddy Scott used to keep the kit and it was the most fascinating place I had ever seen. On the walls there were pennants from many of the memorable matches my team had played over the years and there were shirts from the opposition teams up there too. We would sometimes go out on the pitch for a kick-about and on a couple of occasions David would hoof the ball over the main stand and into the car park. We would then retrieve it on our way out and take it home with us!

I was still at school when David moved to Rangers and I admit I took a bit of flak from my classmates, especially on a Monday morning if the Dons had lost to Rangers. I was still an Aberdeen fan but because David was a Rangers player I got called all the names under the sun and I used to dread going in on days like that. And on one occasion it was worse than ever as not only did Aberdeen lose, but David also scored one of the goals!

He had managed to get my dad and me complimentary tickets for the game, but this was the first time I can remember us ending up sitting with the Rangers fans in the South Stand. Aunty Betty was also with us and as we made our way to our seats we found that there was someone sitting in them. They weren't there for long, though, as Aunty Betty grabbed the guy by the lapels and lifted him out of the way.

Although I get a great buzz when I'm watching Aberdeen, I always got a similar feeling no matter where David was. When he was at the likes of Montrose and Elgin I would go along and watch games and, even when he was at Rangers, I would go along and support my big brother. I was never a Rangers fan, but I was always a David Robertson fan.

We didn't see each other for a few years after David took the family to America. I was living and working on the Isle of Mull at that time but we kept in touch and I remember him calling me up and saying that he was going to join this new team called Real Kashmir. He told me not to tell anyone and I have to admit I was really excited for him. But I didn't realise just how bad things were out there. When he told me, I thought he was exaggerating but when I watched the documentaries I soon realised how difficult things were for him. But unlike me and many others, watching the game isn't enough for my brother, he needs to be involved, even under the circumstances he finds himself in out in Kashmir.

Even though my brother has achieved all that he has in the game, he's never been big-headed and boastful. He remained the same modest guy he had always been, and he doesn't seek recognition for what he has done either. Had I been in his position I would have been the complete opposite, bragging about it to anyone who would listen. But David has never done that. He's just an ordinary guy who loves his football.

CHELSEA ROBERTSON

Born in the summer of 1992, Chelsea Robertson was the first of David's three children to arrive. Since then she has moved from Glasgow to Leeds, Leeds to Aberdeen and then Aberdeen to the USA as her dad finished his playing career and moved into management. Here she shares her memories of growing up as a footballer's daughter.

My dad is a huge inspiration. He is so passionate about football and that's why he gets so animated and angry at times. Mason, Jordan and I never really saw that side of him, though, and on the rare occasions when he got really mad at us, we knew we had done something wrong.

My dad is a loving family guy who loves family time, and he would do anything for us. He always puts us first no matter what and is always there for us when we need him. He would always make the time to take me to my dance classes, swimming lessons, and would always make sure he attended any shows or events that my brothers and I were in. He even took me to an S Club 7 and Spice Girls concert. I think he deserves a medal for that! There is also nobody better to cheer you up when you are having a bad day. We are really close and, although I am 28 years old, I will always be a daddy's girl.

As the daughter of a footballer, you expect to move around a bit. I was born when my dad was at Rangers, but it wasn't too hard when he moved to Leeds as, although I had friends in Glasgow, I was still quite young. It was the same when we moved from Leeds back to Aberdeen. But when we moved to Phoenix, it was different. By that time, I was out with my friends all the time so when Mum and Dad told me we were going to the States I was devastated to leave them behind.

Although it was awful to begin with – I think it took about a year before I started enjoying being in America – Dad was doing well and was happy. That made it easier and I ended up spending nine years over there and made friends who I am still in contact with.

My dad has supported me throughout my life, including through high school and college, and for that I am so grateful. He helped me move several times over the years and would even drive for hours from Phoenix to Tucson when I was in college just so we could spend a few hours together. He has always been supportive of my decisions and I couldn't ask for a better father.

By the time Mum and Dad were moving from Phoenix to Texas, I was back in the UK and when I first heard that Dad was taking a job in Kashmir I didn't know what to think. It was only when I went out there to visit him that I realised what he has to go through on a daily basis when he's working there. I miss him so much when he is away and just hope that he stays safe. We make sure to FaceTime all the time, or at least when the internet is working! I honestly don't know how he does it with no complaints, but I am so proud of him for doing it.

To sum my dad up, I would say he's simply a funny, passionate family guy. He is so genuine and everyone who meets him loves him. I am very lucky to call him my dad and I aspire to be just like him.

MASON ROBERTSON

Inspired and encouraged by his dad, Mason Robertson wanted to play football from a young age. He has achieved that goal, and after earning a scholarship in the USA, he is currently enjoying a successful stint under his dad's tutelage at Real Kashmir. Here he tells us about what it was like growing up with a famous footballer for a father.

My dad is an unbelievable, generous guy who has always been there for his family. But I have never seen him as David Robertson the professional footballer; to me he's always just been my dad. Our garden at home in Aberdeen was seven acres and my dad could always be found playing football with us, jumping on the trampoline, hitting a few balls on the par three golf hole or just joking around with us all.

Family always comes first and, whenever he didn't have his own playing or coaching commitments, he would always make the time to take me to my football training with the Leeds United youth programme and then Aberdeen's youth system. Hey, on occasion he would even take my sister to her dance competitions. Now that's dedication!

He's a very emotional guy too. When he first got the job in Phoenix, we were still in Scotland for a while and he really missed his family. He would often be crying on the phone, sending us nice messages and things through the post. We eventually moved out there and I remember being really upset to leave Scotland. But I really enjoyed it in the States making memories with my dad, my mum, brother and sister.

I was 13 when I joined a team at Sereno Soccer Club, where my dad was coaching and in my second year there I was fortunate enough to have him coach our team. There was no favouritism, I can assure you! I never called him 'dad' when we were training or playing matches, I always called him 'coach'. And there would be some sessions where he would tell me beforehand that he was going to yell at me. I probably wouldn't have done anything wrong, but this was my dad's way of showing the other players that I was no different to them.

The boys loved him. He was fair and, despite the team never having won the State Championship before, in his first year with the team they won every competition they entered and even got to the national finals, playing teams across the US. We were ranked number one in the whole of the US and we were on a high! Everything I have learnt in football I owe to my dad and for that I will be forever grateful.

One of the many things I admire about my dad is that it's never about him, it's always about what's best for his players. He never stands in anybody's way if the move they are making is the right one for them. He's a really nice guy although he can get a wee bit of a spark when things aren't going well but that's part of him.

Dad was instrumental in getting me out to Kashmir. I was with Peterhead and the manager, Jim McInally, had offered me a new contract while I was on holiday in America. But Dad wanted me to join Real Kashmir in the I-League and go full-time and that sealed the deal for me. He was adamant that I wasn't to come out to India just because he was there, I had to consider everything about the area too, although he did assure me that I would be safe. I had never been to Kashmir before, but the lure of full-time football was what convinced me to go. And my dad has been proven correct. We have spoken about my career several times and he wants me to do the best that I can. I have had several offers to go to the Indian Super League and that's all thanks to him.

But for the moment I'm happy at Real Kashmir. I have just signed a new contract and I'm enjoying my football. But the best thing about playing for Real Kashmir is getting the opportunity to work with my dad and spend quality time with the guy who will ALWAYS be my hero.

JORDAN ROBERTSON

The youngest of the Robertson children, Jordan currently plies his trade as a plumber while turning out for a local junior football side in Aberdeen. A talented player in the opinion of his dad, he explains here what it was like growing up and being coached by his famous father.

My dad is probably the most motivated person I know and, although I didn't start playing football until I was about eight or nine years old, it was my dad who got me interested in the game. He coached both me and my brother and I would never have achieved what I did in football if it wasn't for my dad. He had so much knowledge and experience having played the game and been successful at such a high level.

I only played for one club before we moved to America. I found out we were going when we were all sitting around the dinner table one night after school. When we were all summoned to the table the automatic reaction was that one of us was in trouble! But my dad told us he had been offered a job and we were moving to Arizona. I loved Scotland and loved the lifestyle we had so I wasn't sure how different it would be in the States. When you watch movies, America looks fantastic but at the age of 12 I didn't really have a clue what to expect and I was a bit sceptical about going.

But we enjoyed our time there. Unlike in Scotland, no one really knew who my dad was when we first went out as the main sports in the area were American football and baseball. I joined him at Sereno Soccer Club and, although the other players in the team didn't admit it to my face, you knew they felt I was only in the team because my dad was the coach. But that was never the case and my dad treated Mason and me exactly the same as he did any other player on the pitch. And he did that because he is a very caring person. It's never about my dad when it comes to football, he really cares about all his players.

Although he would give us pointers outside of training, being the coach's son didn't spare me or my brother from a bollocking. That happened a few times and it's only on those occasions that I remember being really scared of my dad. But unlike now when you see him on the BBC documentaries, he never used bad language to get his point across.

When Mason and I left Sereno I think that was the catalyst for my dad to return to full-time football. He realised that he didn't want to coach at youth level, and I think India has been a great move for him as he's now back on the football map.

I'm playing junior football just now, but I know Dad has been keen to get me to join him and my brother in Kashmir. But although it would be a good experience, I don't think I could adapt to the lifestyle and I'm also not too fond of the spicy food!

BOBBY CLARK

After starting his career at Queen's Park, Bobby moved to Aberdeen in 1965. He made 594 appearances for the Dons, winning all three domestic honours during his time there. He also won 17 caps for Scotland. After a season coaching Highlanders in the Zimbabwe Super League, Bobby moved to the USA and earned the nickname 'Boss' during successful spells in charge of Dartmouth College, Stanford University and the University of Notre Dame. He also had a two-year stint as manager of the New Zealand national team. He knew of David from an early age and coached him in the fledgling days of his playing career.

When I was at Aberdeen, I was also a part-time physical education teacher. I would train in the morning with Aberdeen and then teach PE at Harlaw Academy in the afternoon. And that was where I first met David Robertson. He was a quiet, polite and well-mannered young man and you could see during the lessons that he was among the best footballers in the class.

At that time, I was working with Lenny Taylor taking the youth team at Pittodrie and also the Aberdeen Secondary Schools select side. I did this in my last five years with Aberdeen before I left to go to coach in Zimbabwe in 1983. That meant I only coached David for a year or so at under-14 level but you could see even in that short period of time how good a player he was. He was a very good winger but the biggest thing for him was making the change from an attacker to a defender.

We wanted our full-backs to be strong attacking players and that made David ideal for the role. I had left Aberdeen by the time David moved to left-back so I wasn't part of the decision, but it was something I had always thought about when I watched him play. We had done something similar with a couple of other boys – Graeme Hogg, who ended up at Manchester United, was one – and I did so again when I coached in America. One of those lads was Justin Morrow and he was a centre-forward or left-winger. Initially he didn't want to move to full-back, but it worked out for him as he had a long career in the MLS with Toronto FC and was also capped by the US national team in that position.

Justin and David had similar attributes in the respect that they had pace and liked to get forward, and that's something I always wanted my full-backs to do. I had first experienced overlapping full-backs back in the early days of my playing career under Eddie Turnbull at Queen's Park and he continued with that style of play when he went to Aberdeen. I adopted that in my teams too as I felt it got the full-backs involved in large parts of the game as they were part of the build-up and then you would be encouraged to get forward and cross the ball into the box. And following David's career from afar, I could clearly see he was the perfect fit for the position.

The next time David and I met up was when he came out to the US. It was obvious he was keen to further his coaching career in America, so I gave him some advice. As he hadn't gone to college, he wasn't able to coach at that level but there were opportunities for him at club level. I put him in touch with Les Armstrong, who also had been a very good player in the Aberdeen youth academies, and that kicked off the American part of David's career.

I also told David that coaching in America wasn't like what he had experienced with Montrose or Elgin City. At that level the guys were coming in for training a couple of nights a week but at club level in America, you were looking after several teams so you would be coaching seven days a week. But David loved that, and he built very successful teams in Phoenix. He made a good impression too as he was eventually made director of coaching there.

I have watched with great interest David's career developing even further in Kashmir. It was a bold move to make and is proving to be a great experience for him. Although nothing like the situation in Kashmir, when I went to Zimbabwe it was three years after they had become independent and there was still a fair bit of unrest. But despite all that I loved coaching out there and it looks like it's similar for David in India.

He has done really well but it must be hard for him not having his family with him. When I travelled abroad in my career, my wife and kids came with me so although Mason is now playing for Real Kashmir, it must be challenging for David to be away from his family for long periods.

Although he has achieved great things in the game, David has never forgotten his roots and the last time I saw him was at one of our gatherings of the old youth team players we coached at Aberdeen. We met up in a pub in Northfield and David was the same quiet, humble and unassuming chap I had met all those years earlier at Harlaw Academy. I will continue to follow his career with great interest and I wish him all the very best.

LENNY TAYLOR

One of the most renowned youth development coaches in Scotland, Lenny, alongside former Aberdeen goalkeeper Bobby Clark, and Teddy Scott, produced some of the finest young talent in the Scottish game. David was one of the best players to graduate from that youth system and he regards Lenny as being instrumental in the fledgling days of his career.

Bobby Clark, Teddy Scott and I started the youth system at Aberdeen in 1975. Bobby and I were both school teachers and as I was in charge of the secondary schools football setup in Aberdeen, we knew all the youngsters from the area. We ended up with a very productive system and, when he became manager in 1978, Alex Ferguson became heavily involved. He was very pro-youth and a couple of days after he arrived at the club we were playing the final of the Scottish Under-15 Cup in Ayrshire. We were preparing the boys for the game when Fergie walked into the dressing room and that was an amazing boost for them before kick-off.

David didn't arrive at the club until a few years later but there is no doubt he is one of the best young players the club has developed. He was originally a left-winger and I have to say that he was good in that position. He loved motoring up and down the wing, but it was only after we moved him to left-back that he became a more confident player. He would sometimes get a bit frustrated on the wing when he didn't have the ball but as a left-back he could position himself to take the ball from the goalkeeper and we knew when he had the ball he could use it well. He could play a one-two and use his pace to get forward. He was a great crosser of the ball with his left foot and an excellent finisher as well.

David was very quiet and not really sure of himself in the beginning. There are a lot of players like that and those are the ones you can't be shouting at. They need to be taken aside and encouraged and I always felt strongly that you should praise a player three times more than you criticise them. As coaches we had to be honest with him and tell him what his strengths were but also highlight the areas he needed to work on. We never used to word 'weaknesses'. That encouragement was really important for David's development. You could see he had ability, but it was our job to give him the self-belief to unlock that. It took a wee while but, because David trusted us, within a few weeks of getting reassurances from us he started to believe in himself a bit more.

I thoroughly enjoyed working with David and allowing his talent to express itself. Early on he was susceptible to getting wound up and letting that get to him but, with our guidance, he realised that he could get his own back on those players by focusing on his own qualities and beating them with the ability he had.

He was a pupil at Harlaw Academy when he first came to the club. I had begun my teaching career there and Bobby was their PE teacher, but we were aware of David as he had been part of the primary school select teams. We would keep an eye on all those youngsters and eventually invite some of them in for training at under-14 level. David was in the group that was invited in and by the time he reached under-16 level he was training twice a week and playing games Saturday and Sunday. Those games would be against the second teams from some of the Highland League clubs, which was tough. That meant the kids like David had to grow up fast as they were up against semi-professional players who wouldn't be afraid to have a dig or two at them during the games.

We would also play games on a Thursday night on the red blaze surface that was part of the car park at Pittodrie. If you went to ground on that surface, you felt it. We deliberately invited local teams that were two years older than David's age group as that would be more of a challenge and, more often than not, Fergie would be in attendance. He was brilliant and Teddy, Bobby and I would meet with him every couple of days and he was always asking how the young lads were developing. If there was a player who caught his eye, he would come down to the game to watch them. That's what happened with David and he was eventually signed on schoolboy forms. And a few years later Fergie decided to offer him his first professional contract.

Once he was part of the first team, as youth coaches we almost left them to it but we would always be available if they needed advice. David remained the same nice, humble guy as he established himself as a first-team regular and we would talk regularly. And while I can't recall him speaking to me when he decided to go to Rangers, if it wasn't working out at Aberdeen then he had every right to take his considerable talent somewhere else. He had a career to make and, as disappointing as it was to lose him to Rangers, it gave David the opportunity to be more successful.

I still see David from time to time and it's nice to meet up with him and the other lads for a beer or two. Three years ago, we formed the Aberdeen Youth Development Veterans Club and when we arrange social gatherings it's great to see all the boys. And it's a real family affair too as David's son, Mason, also comes along.

He's doing very well for himself in Kashmir but after watching the first of the BBC documentaries I felt I had to give David some advice. I told him he needed to curb his swearing a fair bit. Bobby and I never swore at the boys so I told him he could still come across as passionate even if he wasn't swearing. He agreed, so when I watched the second one I expected to hear fewer swear words. But it was actually worse than the first one. You had to laugh, after years of listening to me when I coached him, he now wasn't taking heed of anything I said!

I can't speak highly enough of David, though. He's a great guy and I am privileged to have played some part in the fantastic career he has enjoyed.

ALEX SMITH

One of the most respected managers in the Scottish game, Alex Smith won the Scottish Cup with St Mirren in 1987 before becoming co-manager at Aberdeen. He had a big influence on David's career at a time when he was establishing himself in the first XI. After leaving Aberdeen Alex managed Clyde, Dundee United and Ross County and, on an interim basis, Falkirk. He also held the role of technical director with Falkirk.

The initial plan when I came to Aberdeen was that I was going to be going in to work alongside Ian Porterfield, but Ian resigned so I became the manager. Before that happened, in fact on my first morning, I was asked to take the youth squad to the university for training and, although he was part of the first-team squad at that time, David was in the group I took. This was the end of May 1988 and the youth team were due to go to a tournament in Switzerland and David was to be the captain.

Given he had played for the first team under Alex Ferguson and Ian Porterfield, David brought with him plenty of experience. Along with Eoin Jess, Stephen Wright and Scott

Booth he was a stand-out in what was a really good squad. As the new manager it was a great introduction to the club as it showed me the calibre of young players we had at Aberdeen at that time. And I knew from that first session that I would have no concerns about the left-back position.

David was a strong runner; aggressive, a good tackler and defensively minded. He could go forward too but in those days he didn't do it to the extent that he did when he went to Rangers. He had pace as well. But a lot players have pace and can't read the game. David wasn't like that. He would always get himself into a position where he could get where he needed to get to in behind the centre-backs to cover them.

In my second season – 1989/90 – there was bad weather round about Christmas, and we played a practice game at Pittodrie. David was running forward and got to the byline but went over on his ankle and broke a bone in his foot. He eventually came back for the Scottish Cup semi-final against Dundee United who were doing well under Jim McLean. But by picking David I got one over on Jim.

When David had been out, a lad called Ian Robertson had played at left-back. In the week leading up the semi-final David had trained hard, so I decided to pick him. But when the teams were submitted Jim thought I had still picked Ian Robertson as it was only surnames on the team sheet. He was planning to expose young Ian as he wasn't really a left-back – although he had done superbly well in David's absence, Ian was more of a midfielder than a full-back – but David came in and was outstanding. Although he had been out for so long it never crossed my mind to take him off as he was such a fit and strong boy.

We won both cups that season and, ahead of the penalty shoot-out in the Scottish Cup Final, Jocky Scott, who was co-manager with me, Drew Jarvie and I had decided not to pick the first five; we wanted to leave it up to the players. I was confident all of them would score apart from Brian Grant. I had managed Brian at Stirling Albion and knew he wasn't as self-confident as he was making out to be.

Both teams missed a penalty and that meant Charlie Nicholas, who was taking Aberdeen's fifth kick, had to score. I was banned from the dugout at the time and during extra time I had phoned down to suggest to Jocky and Drew that we took Charlie off and brought Eoin Jess on. But both of them suggested we keep Charlie on as his experience would be key if the match went to penalties. I'm glad I listened to them as Charlie confidently scored his penalty and took the shoot-out to sudden death.

Charlie was followed by Alex McLeish and Stewart McKimmie who both scored. After that the next in line in terms of experience was David. Apart from the two that were missed, all the penalties up to that point were great, either into the left or right corner of the net. But David's went straight down the middle and he just got enough power in his strike to score.

David won six league titles at Rangers, but he should have won one before he left Aberdeen. That was in 1990/91 but as late as March we looked to be out of the running. We were seven points behind Rangers when they came to Pittodrie and it was a tough, tight game. But David was involved in the winning goal. Jim Bett was fouled just in front of the dugouts, but he got up and took a quick free kick. He transferred to ball to David and he scampered up the park and played a great pass to Hans

Guillhaus who blasted the ball into the net. We won 1-0 and after that Rangers wobbled. They lost to Celtic at Parkhead in the Scottish Cup and the league and, when they lost 3-0 to Motherwell, Aberdeen were in the driving seat.

In hindsight it would have been better if that game had ended 2-0 as that would have meant Aberdeen would have had to go to Ibrox and win. That altered the psychology, but I still felt we were in control of the game until we lost a goal just before half-time. I felt if we scored first Rangers would have collapsed and we would have won the league. But we made a mistake for the second goal early in the second half and, with the crowd behind Rangers, we were never coming back after that.

That was David's last game for Aberdeen. For a few weeks before the game I had been trying to get him to sign a new contract, but I could sense that he was looking for a change. He wanted to go to a bigger club so I resigned myself to the fact that he would be leaving Aberdeen. There were a couple of clubs in England that were interested and, as I had a close relationship with Walter Smith and Archie Knox, I knew Rangers wanted David too.

I set up a schedule for him that would see him go and talk to the two English clubs before talking to Rangers. But he never went to the English clubs. I was working at a coaching course in Largs with Archie when he got a phone call asking him to go back to Glasgow. It transpired that Rangers had contacted David and got him into Ibrox to complete the signing. But there was never any animosity between David and me. I told him all along that he had to pick the right club and get the right deal for him.

David was one of Aberdeen's biggest assets, so he was a big loss. We didn't have another natural left-back in the squad and

I felt the young lads in that position weren't ready for the first team. But I had worked with David Winnie when I was at St Mirren and I knew he had the temperament to handle playing for Aberdeen. Although not as quick as Robertson, Winnie still had a bit of pace. He did a good job for Aberdeen but losing Robertson was a massive blow for the club. The timing wasn't ideal either as Willie Miller hadn't long retired and Alex McLeish only played once for Aberdeen during 1991/92 so I had pretty much lost three of my first-choice back four. Theo Snelders also missed a number of games through injury.

Given he played the number of games he did for Aberdeen and Rangers, playing as consistently as he did at the highest level, it surprised me that David didn't get the number of caps for Scotland he deserved. Scotland had good left-backs like Malpas, Boyd and the current national team manager, Stevie Clarke, but for me David should have ended up with 80 or 90 caps, that's how good he was. I knew the managers of Scotland at that time very well and they loved David. He was just unfortunate that Scotland had such a high standard of player in that position.

If I was asked to highlight what David's main attributes were then I would go for his power and his strength. The stamina he had to get up and down the field was tremendous. He was super fit and, although he didn't use his right foot very often, he was two-footed. He very rarely gave the ball way too as his passing was so good. At Aberdeen we didn't use him in an attacking sense as much as Rangers did. Allowing him to attack let him show other skills like dribbling and he could run for long distances with the ball at his feet. David's temperament was also very good.

Overall, he was a pleasure to work with. His attitude in training was first-class. He was mentally strong and he had to be given he was playing alongside Miller, McLeish, McKimmie, Jim Leighton and latterly Theo Snelders. He had experienced players in front of him too like Jim Bett, and Robert Connor who wanted the ball played to him a certain way so you had to be able to play the game. You couldn't get away with being ordinary and David Robertson was far from ordinary.

ARCHIE KNOX

After spells as manager at Forfar Athletic and Dundee, Archie Knox joined Aberdeen as assistant manager in 1986 just before David made his debut for the first team. Archie left Aberdeen along with Alex Ferguson to move to Manchester United but was reunited with David when he became Walter Smith's assistant at Rangers in 1991.

When I arrived at Aberdeen, David was still coming in and training with the other youngsters in the evening. I got involved with that and what struck me about David was how smartly he dressed as he always arrived in his school blazer and tie. You could see he had potential but so many lads do at that age. In my time in the game I have seen plenty of players who play their best football at a young age but then lose their way. But David was always a determined character, very quiet and you could tell he wanted to be a footballer. He was also a youngster playing in a star-studded, experienced team which was a huge help for him. The likes of Willie Miller and Alex McLeish would give him good advice and he learned a lot from them.

You could see immediately he had pace and a good left foot. But although he predominantly used his left, he was strong on his right-hand side too. He was good in the air and these were the qualities that attracted Walter and me when we took him to Ibrox in 1991.

There was no such thing as a day off for youngsters like David back then. They trained twice a day if they were good enough to be considered for the first team and David was one that was in that bracket. Although he had experienced players ahead of him in the left-back position he developed quickly and grew into the role. He didn't have the finesse to be a left-winger, but he certainly had the power, pace and recovery to excel as a full-back. Nobody would outrun him. If any player went beyond him, he had a real determination to get back and catch them. He was also capable of spotting the danger. He was a very good reader of the game.

There was no doubt that Walter and I thought he was good enough to play for Rangers. If we didn't, we wouldn't have signed him. The only difference between the David I saw at Aberdeen and the David I saw at Rangers was that he had developed into a top player. And initially when Alexei Mikhailichenko was playing in front of him, Walter and I would tell David to give the ball to Chenks and run. He was a very powerful runner with great stamina and, whether it was a through ball or a pass over the defender's head, Chenks would usually find him. Playing with guys like Chenks and, a few years later, Brian Laudrup also gave David more opportunities to go forward than he probably had when he was at Aberdeen.

We decided to alter the defensive system at Rangers around 1995 but we had no doubt that David would cope with the change from a flat back four to three centre-backs and two wing-backs. And that's because he had the ability to sit in and use the ball but also to run beyond people then slot back into position. He had great awareness of the game no matter what system you played. David was also very tuned in and knew everything he needed to about his direct opponent in every game.

Perhaps David should have had more caps for Scotland, but I think he was just unlucky that Tom Boyd and, initially, Maurice Malpas were in front of him. The national team management must have felt that those two didn't let them down, so they kept their place in the team.

To be honest, back then I didn't see David as managerial material. He always gave his all in training and games but in terms of speaking to people and organising people, that's something he must have picked up as he's gone along. I've watched the BBC documentaries about him out in India and how he manages to cope with the challenges he faces out there I don't know.

If I had to sum David up then I would use just four words, 'Top player for Rangers.'

BRIAN IRVINE

A long serving centre-back with Aberdeen, Brian was often part of the back four that included David, particularly towards the end of David's time in the north-east. After leaving Aberdeen, Brian had spells with Dundee and Ross County before retiring at the age of 39. Capped nine times for Scotland, he is now a police officer.

I knew about David before he made the first XI. We played together in a youth tournament in Viareggio and on numerous occasions for the reserve team. He was more often than not at left-back but would play on the left wing sometimes too. He had a great left foot and a powerful shot too. And although he was very quiet in the dressing room, he was a silent assassin. He would have an opinion and, when he did talk, he was as capable as anyone at making a cutting remark.

When David made his Aberdeen debut, I was up against Willie Miller and Alex McLeish for a place at centre-back. The competition couldn't have been tougher but when I did play it was tremendous to have David and Stewart McKimmie as the full-backs. Both were very quick so you knew that cover was there when required and you could also hold a higher line.

We were part of a team that were the main challengers to Rangers for the major honours. Rangers had the clout to get the best players – that's why they signed David in 1991 – but we still competed with them. We won a couple of trophies and probably should have won the league too.

In the Scottish Cup Final penalty shoot-out in 1990 I don't think David or I expected to take a penalty. But our circumstances were different. When it went to sudden death it wasn't that you didn't want to take one, you just didn't want to miss. Celtic had the advantage of going first so our guys had to score. I remember David was quite nonchalant for his – he only took a couple of steps for his run-up – but by the time it came to me, I felt the pressure was off a bit. Because Anton Rogan had missed there was less pressure on me than had been on the other Aberdeen players as they had to score, or we would have lost the cup.

There were a lot of similarities between my playing career and David's and after he stopped playing his coaching mirrored mine too. I managed Elgin and did some work in America and had some time in Korea. The love of the game is what drives you to take on what some would think are obscure roles so I can understand why he went to Kashmir. Once you've been in football living the quiet life, sitting at home isn't easy and the challenge he faces out there is one that any footballer would relish. But the one big difference between us was I stayed with Aberdeen for 12 years whereas David had a great opportunity to join Rangers that was probably too good to turn down.

Summing up, David was a great team-mate. He had lots of pace and a great left foot. He had a rocket shot and could ping a pass. And as a centre-back I liked his awareness too. That made a huge difference to me as I knew that he could get me out of trouble if a player got in behind us. He was one of the best players I played with.

PAUL MASON

Although coveted by Ajax and Feyenoord, Paul signed for Aberdeen from FC Groningen in 1988. He soon developed a bond with David both on and off the pitch and was part of a successful era for the club, scoring twice in the 1989 League Cup Final win over Rangers. After leaving Aberdeen, Paul played for Ipswich Town before announcing his retirement in 1999.

David was a good mate when I played at Aberdeen. We had the same sense of humour, so we got on really well. Unless you spoke to David, he didn't say much in the dressing room but his nickname was 'Psycho' as he could get angry from time to time. But he was a good lad and an excellent team-mate.

My first impressions of him were that he was big, strong, quick, powerful and very difficult to get past. When I joined Aberdeen, he was part of a really solid back four alongside McLeish, Miller and McKimmie that was pretty much set in stone.

We were both part of the team that won the League Cup in 1989. It was a memorable day, not just for me personally, but for the whole club. Aberdeen had lost the previous two finals against Rangers, so this was third time lucky. And it was from one of things that David was renowned for – his long throw – that I scored my second goal.

In the Scottish Cup Final, I was taken off at half-time in extra time. After the first five penalties are taken I have to admit you're not confident that anyone will score but I hoped when Robbo took his he would hit it as hard as he could as he had a powerful shot. It didn't quite work out like that, but it went in and that's all that mattered.

When I found out David was leaving to go to Rangers it was a bit demoralising to be honest. We were losing one of our best players to our main rivals and, although I was happy for Robbo as he was a mate, I wasn't happy as it made the Aberdeen team weaker. It was a big blow and, although the club got big money for him, it was always going to be difficult to replace him.

We hooked up again after we finished playing when Robbo was out in Arizona. I lived with him for a few months and I saw a different side to him. He was more intense and was working all day long, taking phone calls from parents and coaches. It was hard work, and he was under a lot of stress. But I could see he was well-respected and he coped very well with the pressure he was under.

My abiding memory of Robbo is that he was a strong and powerful player who gave his all on the pitch. He was undoubtedly one of the best players I played with.

ROBERT CONNOR

After starting his career at Ayr United and Dundee, Robert signed for Aberdeen in 1986. He was a team-mate of David's for five seasons and played in front of him on the left-hand side of midfield. Capped four times for Scotland, Bobby, as he was better known, also played for Kilmarnock, Partick Thistle and Queen of the South and had a spell as manager at Ayr United.

When I signed for Aberdeen, David was just a young boy and, as a lot of the young lads were at that time, he was very quiet. But I got to know him pretty quickly because we changed next to each other. Although David was quiet, he liked a laugh and a joke as I did so it wasn't long before he came out of his shell.

I think playing alongside Willie Miller and Alex McLeish helped him in terms of learning the game and he developed very quickly as a result. But, for me, David's main attribute was his pace. He was like lightning. When it came to training you didn't want to be up against him when it came to the short runs.

However, on the flip side, David was never keen on the long runs. He was also solid defensively and again a lot of that had to do with his pace. On the occasions that a player did get past him he could recover and get a tackle in. And when he went to Rangers, he could use his pace to great effect too as he had a guy like Brian Laudrup who had the ability to place the ball in front of him to run on to.

I won my first medals with Aberdeen in 1989/90 but David was out for a long spell that season when he hurt his foot. He had quite a few foot injuries and that might have been because he had a habit of kicking the ground quite often. I remember one game against Dundee United at Tannadice when he went to clear the ball but succeeded only in taking a big divot out the pitch. I think the ball only travelled about two yards! At the time his face was a picture but after the game he'd have a laugh about it.

In the Scottish Cup Final against Celtic, I took the second penalty. We only decided who was taking the penalties after the final whistle when Jocky Scott came up with a pen and paper and started jotting down names. David wasn't among the first five, but I remember his penalty. It trundled into the net – maybe he kicked the ground again – but it counted and that was all that mattered.

At the time David left for Rangers in 1991 we were their main competition. A lot of that had to do with the success that Alex Smith had in the transfer market, bringing in guys from the Netherlands and down south.

But when Rangers came in with the offer they did, you could understand why he left and also why the club sold him. We couldn't compete financially with them as there was such a big gap in the budgets.

I haven't seen David for a few years but watching him on the BBC documentary about Real Kashmir, he hasn't changed much. He might be a bit louder than he was when we played together but his sense of humour is exactly the same.

THEO SNELDERS

Signed for Aberdeen as a replacement for the legendary Jim Leighton in 1988, Theo Snelders was a solid, dependable goalkeeper and the last line of defence in an era when the Pittodrie side were pushing for domestic honours. A team-mate of David's at Aberdeen for three years, the pair also shared a dressing room at Ibrox after Theo signed for Rangers in 1996.

My first impressions of David Robertson were very good. He was a strong, powerful athlete who was good going forward and when I first came to Aberdeen I was very lucky as in front of me I had Stewart McKimmie at right-back, McLeish and Miller at centre-half and David at left-back.

David was only around 19 at that time but we got to know each other quite well as we bought a house in Broomhill Avenue, the same street that the parents of David's girlfriend, Kym, stayed. My wife Mirjam and Kym would travel together to watch our games too.

My second season was memorable as we won the cup double but David and I were also out injured for a while. I hurt my knee and then came back six weeks later and injured my other knee. I thought my season was over but both David and I came back for the semi-final of the Scottish Cup against Dundee United. I played two or three reserve games before I came back but David's comeback came from nowhere. There were still a few games to play after that, which gave us a chance to get minutes in our legs and a bit of rhythm again before we played Celtic in the final.

We were favourites to win the cup, which was unusual when you faced either Rangers or Celtic. It was strange also as Celtic had won the last two Scottish Cups, but we had beaten them 3-1 in the last league game and finished higher than them in the league so perhaps that's why. We also had a lot of quality in our squad. David was one of our top players, but we had Paul Mason, Jim Bett, Robert Connor, Hans Gillhaus and Charlie Nicholas too.

The season after that, we should have won the league. We were chasing Rangers for a while but all of a sudden it turned round, and we were ahead. Unfortunately, it wasn't to be and that was David's last game for Aberdeen. Because of his qualities I was disappointed to lose him, but I could understand why he left. At that time Rangers were at a higher level than Aberdeen and they had more money to spend. They were also in the Champions League every year. Also, as he had come through as a young player I don't think David got the same recognition that someone who had been brought in from outside the club may have got.

A few years later I joined Rangers and I could see that there were certain aspects of David's game, like his stamina, that had improved since we had last played together. The more games you play, the better you get, and David was still going forward and using his pace and putting good crosses into the box. Yet with the qualities he had David only has a small number of caps for Scotland and I find that hard to understand.

In the dressing room there wasn't much of a change, though; David was still the same quiet guy he was at Aberdeen. He was still very much a family man away from the pitch too. I was surprised therefore when I watched his documentary about Real Kashmir and saw him shouting so much. I thought it must have been his twin brother!

To sum David up he was excellent going forward, was very powerful and had great stamina. He could do what he did for the whole 90 minutes, no problem. He was one of the best players I played with.

WILLIE MILLER

Captain of Aberdeen during the most successful era in the club's history and when David made the first team, Willie Miller is one of the most respected figures in Scottish football. He played over 600 times for Aberdeen and after injury forced him to retire as a player he returned to Pittodrie as manager. Capped 65 times by Scotland, he now works with the BBC as a media pundit.

Although David started at the club as a forward, I can only recall him playing at left-back. He came into the side at the tail-end of my career and he was part of a crop of young players that were chapping at the door to get into the first team.

In my 20 years at Aberdeen there were several batches of young players who came in. I was one of them myself and we all had drilled into us the good habits that were taught at the club. David was part of the youth team that was looked after by Lenny Taylor and Bobby Clark and when you look back at the players brought through as part of that setup – the likes of John Hewitt, Neale Cooper, Joe Miller and Paul Wright – it shows just how good our development programme was.

When David came in, he was a very quiet individual. He was one of these guys who sat and listened to the senior players and the manager, and took in everything they said but was never very vocal. But on the park, he showed a lot of determination and a lot of grit. He was a very direct player who wanted to get forward and was very strong in terms of his physical attributes and that was something I liked.

My abiding memories of David, however, aren't for his defensive attributes; instead I recall how good he was going forward. I played with several good full-backs and I would compare David with Stuart Kennedy. Neither had any great frills when it came to getting forward, but both were willing to get forward and use their pace to great effect.

But David very rarely got stranded up the park. If the move broke down, he was quick to get back and fulfil his defensive duties. Any back four I played in the mantra was that you didn't lose goals so, first and foremost, as a defender you had to protect your goal. David, like any of his fellow defenders, would get a blast in his ear from me if he wasn't fully focussed or was caught upfield but I don't recall that happening too often. He was a joy to play beside.

When David made the breakthrough in the first team he did so on merit. In my time as captain, I was used to young players like David coming into the team, but they weren't treated any differently. There was no mollycoddling – they were there to do a man's job so were treated like men – and it was a game of hard knocks but David realised he had the chance to be part of a successful Aberdeen team. You could see he was strong enough to survive and meet the standards that we set.

Our attitude may have been perceived as being hard, but it was a realistic one and it was clear that David was going to embrace the challenge and not fall by the wayside. As a player you are judged by how you perform on the pitch and David's performances were of a very high level. And he also showed he was able to handle the pressure on big occasions, none more so than when he found the back of the net with his spot kick in the penalty shoot-out at the end of the 1990 Scottish Cup Final.

Playing well in the cup finals we played against Rangers and Celtic at that time attracted the interest of the Old Firm so it was inevitable that one of them would come calling for David at some point. When Rangers did there was no doubt, he deserved his move. I was disappointed that he left Aberdeen, of course, as he made a Rangers side that were flying high at the time even stronger. When I became manager of Aberdeen, I would have loved to have David back at the club. We were second to Rangers in all three major competitions in my first year and having someone like David playing for us might have made a difference.

David took his opportunity at Rangers with both hands and ended up with more medals than I won in my career. But the grounding and good habits he picked up from his time at Aberdeen, working with Sir Alex Ferguson, Alex Smith and Jocky Scott, being developed by two of the leading development coaches in the country and playing alongside the likes of myself and Alex McLeish was quite a potent formula for the development of a young player. There is no doubt that that stood him in good stead, but you needed talent, ability and mental strength too and David had all of those. For that reason, a lot of the credit for the success he had at Ibrox must go to him.

I'll always remember David as the quiet man in the dressing room but on the field, where it's more about actions rather than words, his actions were certainly good enough for me, good enough for Aberdeen and good enough for the best team in Scotland at that time.

ALEX McLEISH

One of the finest centre-backs produced by Scotland, Alex McLeish was at the heart of the Aberdeen defence when David made his senior debut in 1985. Alongside Willie Miller he was one of the pillars of success in that era for Aberdeen. He subsequently took on the role of player-manager at Motherwell and managed, among others, Hibernian, Rangers, Birmingham City and Aston Villa. Capped 77 times by his country, he also enjoyed two spells as manager of the national team.

The first thing we noticed about David when he started training with the first team was his pace and power. He was natural for the left-back position and you just knew when he got himself in the team it was going to be difficult for anyone to take his place.

I always had time for the apprentices like David as I had been afforded the same time by the senior pros when I had been in that position. I felt it was important they felt part of the team and pretty soon David was catching the eye of everyone.

David was an extremely quiet lad; a shy, unassuming kid. We did communicate on the park but most of the time we didn't need to. That was largely because of David's speed and acceleration. We were blessed with two quick full-backs in that era as Stewart McKimmie also had great pace. But David wasn't just a runner, he had game intelligence too. He had a lovely left foot and natural ability. He wasn't one, for example, just to hoof the ball forward.

Neither Willie Miller nor I had great pace so having these boys alongside us was great. We had the wise, old heads but we knew if someone got into the hole in behind us, we had pace on both sides to recover most situations. With David playing alongside me, I was always confident if a centre-forward escaped me that I had a speed merchant to go and pick up the pieces.

I was more often than not the left-sided centre-back as I was more adept than Willie with my left foot. The way we worked the 4-4-2 was that Willie would take on more of a sweeper role while it would be down to me to receive the ball from either the right-back or the left-back. From 1986 onwards the left-back, for the most part, was David and having him in the team was a big benefit for me.

I would always tell him when a high ball came forward, he would hear me before he saw me. He knew if I shouted, I was going for the ball, and if I didn't, it was up to him to go and try and win it. Although I was confident of winning high balls I knew that if I missed one and got beaten by the flick-on, David's pace was such that he would tuck in and would be quick enough to mop up in behind me.

Although David was very humble and quiet for the most part, he was a different animal when we had a night out. On those occasions it's fair to say he became a wee bit more vociferous. That was, I guess, a precursor to his days in charge in Kashmir as there was the odd expletive here and there! Yet the next day at training he could barely look you in the eye and was back to being that introverted lad again.

Players with pace are always a target for top clubs and pretty soon David was attracting interest. When it became apparent that Rangers were courting him, Alex Smith asked me, as captain, to have a word with David to try and convince him to stay at Aberdeen. We went for a walk around Duthie

Park but it became clear very early in our discussion that he was tempted by Rangers' offer. That made my task even harder, but we walked around for a couple of hours and I tried to put across all the manager had said to me to turn David's head back towards Aberdeen. Alex had briefed me to say that he was looking to take Aberdeen back to the glory days of the early 1980s and that David was going to play a big part in that era. David was very respectful and listened to everything I had to say but, in the end, he elected to leave Aberdeen and go to Rangers.

There was no doubt that David's departure weakened Aberdeen as we were losing a top performer. It's not easy when you lose someone of David's calibre and although Aberdeen got close to £1m for him that didn't guarantee we would recruit a ready-made replacement.

When David went to Ibrox he simply kicked on. As part of a team that was winning games most weeks, he became a better, more confident player. He got a bit of stick from the Aberdeen fans and, any time he was up against us after he left us, we wanted to win against him. But there was no animosity, and I was delighted he ended up winning six league titles and having so much success with Rangers.

When asked to sum up my recollections of David Robertson I remember a player with pace who was quick into a tackle to rattle his opponent; a very, very capable footballer. He was an all-rounder, not just good going forward but he would often crunch into tackles and was also good in the air for his height. A very underrated player and the fact he didn't play more often for Scotland just showed the quality we had in that position at that time.

EPILOGUE

ALLY McCOIST

Rangers' record goalscorer with 355 goals in 581 appearances, Ally has fond memories of playing against and alongside David. After 15 trophy-laden seasons at Ibrox, Ally enjoyed three seasons with Kilmarnock before retiring in 2001. Part of Walter Smith's coaching team with Scotland and Rangers, he took over the managerial reins at Ibrox in 2011 and was a figurehead for the supporters during one of the most turbulent times in the club's history.

What a boy David is! I played against him when he was at Aberdeen and he was one of our toughest opponents. He was good going forward and his pace was a real asset. I don't think he had blistering pace but he had a strength of pace. He was a physically strong runner and unlike some who were quick over five or ten yards, David could run the full side of the pitch.

You always knew you were in a game when you were up against David. He was more than capable of looking after himself and we would usually have a wee nibble at each other. But one day it got a bit out of hand and I want to take this opportunity to apologise to David. It was the penultimate match of 1986/87 – the season in which Rangers clinched the league title for the first time in nine years – and about half an hour in I sought retribution after David had had a wee go at me a few minutes earlier. I left one on him and I'll hold my hands up and say that I meant to leave one on him. But I knew straight away that I had hurt him and overstepped the mark and was out of order.

I was absolutely delighted when Rangers signed him, although I'll admit I expected him to smash me back in training to get his own back for that day. He never did, though, and there's no doubt David was an asset for us defensively. But from a selfish point of view, he was a dream to play with as he could get forward and put quality deliveries into the box for the likes of myself and Mark Hateley. He also had a good shot on him with both feet and I remember scoring in the Scottish Cup semi-final against Celtic after David's shot had been parried by Gordon Marshall.

He developed a brilliant relationship with Brian Laudrup too. Both were really clever football players and they very quickly established what they were both good at. David knew his main job was to stop teams attacking us but, when he did that, he would get the ball to Laudrup and move forward. Like all of us, David knew the quality that Laudrup had and that, if he made a run, Brian would see it and find him. After that he would whip the ball into the box, creating chances for myself and the other strikers.

In the dressing room he was very quiet – you could hardly get two words out of him – but you knew he was happy and content at his work. He was super-efficient and the best way to describe David would be that his rating was between seven and nine out of ten every week. He was consistent and very rarely missed games. When I went into coaching you look at a player's talent and ability, but I also looked to see if he turned up for his work. By that I mean how many games does he play? How many games does he miss through injury? How many does he miss through suspension? Particularly at a club like Rangers, you need guys that are going to be available to play a huge amount of games every season and David was one player that fitted into that category.

But as good as his overall fitness was, he was hopeless when it came to long-distance running. I wasn't the best at it either and neither was Laudrup but I remember Walter saying to me that Robbo could run at 40mph all day and Brian could do magic with the ball. But as I couldn't do either of them, he said I had best get better at the long-distance running!

David was a machine, though. He was very similar to Gary Stevens in the respect that they both owned the stretch of ground in front of them. If you were a winger up against David and you beat him then you had to get that half-yard and get the ball in the box pretty quickly as he would get back at you otherwise. And if David ever thought he didn't belong at Rangers then he was wrong. He was more than good enough to play at that level with us.

The BBC documentaries about his time in Kashmir were captivating. I had a good blether with David recently about his time there and we were laughing at some of the madness that goes on round about him. The story of his time in Kashmir is remarkable and the courage he has shown to make the move out there is unbelievable.

Although like me David loves his football, the setup would have been unknown to him, and added to that he has gone into an area that's full of uncertainty. He must wonder what is going to happen daily and in my book that takes enormous courage. When I became manager of Rangers it was familiar territory for me and, although it was a gamble, it is nothing like the one David took.

It surprises me that he hasn't been offered a job closer to home. I think it will only be a matter of time and if I was a club owner and looking at managerial credentials then David ticks every box. I'll remember him as a great player but in addition to that he's a great man.

MARK HATELEY

Signed for Rangers from Monaco in 1990, Mark Hateley forged a formidable striking partnership with Ally McCoist in the midst of one of the most successful eras in the club's history. Between them they scored over 300 goals and many of them were created by the forward runs David made from the full-back position. Mark left Rangers in 1995 to join QPR and after a brief return to Ibrox in 1997 he became player-manager of Hull City. After working in the media, Mark has now returned to Rangers as a club ambassador.

David would fit the model of the modern-day wing-back perfectly in the respect that he could get up and down the park for the whole game, defend well and be a threat in attack. Those were the things that brought him to my attention when he was at Aberdeen and when Rangers bought him I saw all those things first-hand.

When a club I played with brought in new players I looked at them and asked myself if they would make me a better player. David was one of the players who did enhance my game as I knew straight away that having him in the team would mean I would score more goals. He would raid up and down the left-hand side of the pitch non-stop and by doing that it provided myself and Alistair with another source of goalscoring opportunities. I scored so many goals at the near post from crosses from David after he had driven forward and delivered the ball into the box. In addition, he was a fearsome tackler and excellent in a defensive role.

Rangers paid just short of £1m for him, which was big money at the time, but he was well worth it because of what he brought to the team. He could play as part of a back four or as a wing-back and the simple reason for that is that he was a top player and top players can play in any system. He was quick and aggressive and could have played as a left-sided centre-back or as a holding midfield player too. He would flourish in any era because he was such a high-quality player. In today's game he'd be worth a fortune, probably north of £50m.

I take my hat off to him taking the role in Kashmir. I didn't see him as a manager when we played together but, to be fair, I didn't see myself or any of the other lads doing that either. When we were playing back then you were just focussed on playing, winning games, going out to celebrate winning things and mixing with the fans. Footballers then just lived in the moment. It's different now where things are a bit more regimented, but we just focussed on doing our job which was playing football.

I tried management myself for just over 18 months at Hull City and really enjoyed it. That was enough for me – it scratched the itch – but David has been in management a lot longer and done really well. The situation he finds himself in out in Kashmir must be incredibly difficult and I have so much respect for him. He has to make some huge sacrifices in terms of being away from his family for long periods to go out and prove to himself and everyone else that he is an excellent football manager. He has the admiration of his chairman and he has in his team one of his sons, Mason, who must have so much admiration and respect for his dad given he is also experiencing life out there too.

There have been some who have watched the BBC documentaries on Real Kashmir and made reference to the amount of swearing David does. But that wasn't a surprise to me. He was a man of few words in the Rangers dressing room but, when he did speak, the majority of the time he used only two words, 'fuck' and 'off'!

David Robertson is a really good guy and has deserved everything he has achieved and continues to achieve in the game. He is up there alongside the best left-backs I've played with; the likes of Paolo Maldini at Milan, Luc Sonor at Monaco and Kenny Sansom with England. They were all great players and, in my eyes, David belongs in that circle.

STEPHEN WRIGHT

Another in the long line of players produced by the youth system at Aberdeen, Stephen broke into the first team towards the end of David's time at Pittodrie. They linked up again when Stephen joined Rangers in 1995. Similar to David, Stephen was an attack-minded full-back but his career was badly compromised when he damaged his cruciate ligament in a Champions League match against Juventus in 1995. He left Rangers in 1998 and had spells at Bradford City, Dundee United and Scunthorpe United. Capped twice for Scotland, Stephen is currently head of academy at Dundee.

My first impressions of David were that he was solid and compared to the rest of us he looked like a man. When I went up to Aberdeen to train during the school holidays, I always looked at him and aspired to get to the level he was playing at. He was fast, powerful and strong and he was an inspiration. He still played for the youth team after he made the first team so for young players like me who were only a couple of years younger than David it was brilliant to get the opportunity to play alongside him.

One of the first times I did was at a tournament in Switzerland not long after Alex Smith took over as manager. David was captain of the team and I was lucky enough to be his room-mate. Although he was the senior player in the squad, he was a down-to-earth guy who loved a bit of banter. I think Alex played David in a few positions in the games over there and, for me, he had everything.

We had a good laugh on that trip and one night he led me astray. Alex had imposed a curfew and David and I were in our room when David told me we were going out for a walk. We sneaked out and managed to have a couple of drinks before sneaking back to the hotel without any of the coaching staff noticing we were gone.

I eventually established myself in the first team in what was David's last season at Aberdeen, 1990/91. I came into the team as Stewart McKimmie was out injured and I modelled my game on those of Stewart and David. I was similar to David in that I was fast and liked to get forward and I was on the crest of a wave playing alongside David, Alex McLeish and Brian Irvine. Brian didn't get the plaudits he deserved, and I also got the opportunity to play beside Stewart as Alex Smith brought him in at centre-back after he returned from injury.

Alex encouraged David and myself to get forward, to go on overlapping runs and get crosses into the box. It was a good partnership and it almost helped Aberdeen win the league that year. Unfortunately, when we met Rangers on the last day of the season everything went right for them and they almost had a siege mentality that helped them get over the line.

That was David's last game for Aberdeen. When I heard he was leaving my first thoughts were that it was a massive loss for Aberdeen. And that was proven as over the next few seasons that I was there the club really struggled to replace David. In that time, although we had some good players who played at left-back, none were as consistent as David. I don't think the club realised the value of David until after he had gone to Rangers.

Four years later it was me signing for Rangers. I was brought up a Rangers fan, so it was a great move for me. Although Aberdeen had become embroiled in a relegation battle, I was happy at the club but when Walter Smith spoke to me about going to Ibrox it was too good an opportunity to turn down.

Going to Rangers saw me team up with David again. I hadn't spoken to him before I moved to the club but it was back to the good old days when we went to Il Ciocco for pre-season training as Walter decided David and I would be sharing a room. It was good fun but we had both grown up since Switzerland so there was no sneaking out this time around!

Just like when we were at Aberdeen, I looked up to Robbo when I started at Rangers. We were both played as wing-backs and I initially struggled with the role. At Aberdeen we played a back four and, as a full-back, you didn't have the same freedom to go forward. But David was tailor-made for the position. After I injured my knee against Juventus I used to go and watch the games and I would watch David a lot, and doing that showed me how to play as a wing-back. David would just start running and maybe two or three passes were exchanged before he got the ball. But invariably Laudrup or Gascoigne would find Robbo with the final pass and he would be in on goal. Nobody could stop him either because of his pace and his power. However, although he enjoyed running during games, the same can't be said for training. He was one of the worst when it came to the long runs.

To sum David up as a player he was strong, powerful and aggressive. That must have come naturally to him as I never once saw him in the gym or doing any press-ups. David was pacy and an excellent defender. You would have hated to play against him as he would always let his opponent know they were in a game. He was a huge influence on my career and one of the best players I played with.

PIETER HUISTRA

A left-winger, Pieter arrived at Rangers from FC Twente Enschede a year before David. Over the course of three seasons they struck up an extremely productive partnership on the left-hand side and often shared a room together on away trips. Pieter left Rangers to move to Japan in 1995 and is now assistant manager to Shota Arveladze at Pakhtor in Uzbekistan.

I knew of David before he came to Rangers as he had played so well against us for Aberdeen. Left-back had been a position where we had used a lot of players in the season before David signed, and before he left, Graeme Souness was looking to improve that area. Stuart Munro played there, and we used some young players too. John Brown also played left-back but I think Walter Smith wanted to play him as a centre-back.

Between us we soon developed a good understanding. We didn't have to do much extra work in training as we worked on instinct. I knew when David had the urge to attack so I would try to make room for him to do so. But David also had to learn that if there was no room then he had to stay put. I had a good understanding with all the full-backs I played with and David was no different.

That understanding was helped by the fact we shared a room when we went to Il Ciocco for pre-season training. As long as I was at Rangers that was where we went for pre-season. It was tough – almost always running – and I hated it! I think for David it was the same and we spent a lot of the resting time between sessions together. We would talk and watch television and maybe also take a dip in the pool. We spent a lot of time in our rooms, so it was important that you hit it off and I got on really well with David. I think that was really clever from Walter, putting us in together like that.

David and I also lived near each other and there were some nights out when I would be responsible for making sure David got home okay. In fact, I think there were a few nights when I don't think David knew how he got home! But that was a great thing about that team, we looked after each other. We worked very hard during the week, never gave up and went into every game looking to win it. And at certain times we would all go out together and have a good time with some alcohol. However, the next day we would recover and work hard in training. You had to do that. There was a lot of camaraderie in that team but also a lot of competition for places, so you had to be sharp.

As a winger myself I wouldn't have relished playing against David, and I would have relied on my full-back to follow him when he moved forward. David's strengths were his stamina, his timing and also his crossing. Defensively he was very good, but he knew when to time his runs forward and any opponent that played against him had a hard time. And when he had to be, he was ruthless when he was tackling which was also a good quality he had.

Our game didn't change in the Champions League, and David would still be attacking. When that team were on their game, we were difficult to face for any club. The only time I can remember us changing the tactics was before David arrived. We played Red Star Belgrade in the second round of the European Cup and Souness played with a sweeper and played five at the back. You could see pretty quickly that nobody felt at ease in that system and we lost 3-0. However, in 1992/93 a lot of credit has to go to Walter as he didn't change the system. It didn't matter whether we were playing Marseille or Leeds United, we always used the same formation. The players may have changed but the tactics didn't.

Of all the full-backs I have played with, David is the best. Like the others he became an international player and our communication on the park was key. We had an understanding, an intuitive connection and we worked together to make space for each other. We both knew when the right moment was to pass, when the right moment was to attack or defend.

IAN FERGUSON

One of only three players to play a part in each of the seasons that made up Rangers' nine titles in a row, Ian Ferguson was a tough, no-nonsense midfielder in one of the greatest-ever Rangers teams. Ian played alongside David in each of the six seasons that David was at Ibrox. He left Rangers in 2000 and, after a spell with Dunfermline Athletic, he moved to Australia where he had coached and managed at the highest level.

Before he came to Rangers, David stood out as a young, up-and-coming player. Both himself and Stephen Wright caught the eye and, when it came to getting up and down the park, David was relentless.

He was very quiet in the dressing room, in fact you only used to get a word out of him when he was out with the boys having a few drinks! But although he was quiet, he took in everything. He didn't try to be a big shot, but he was a big part of that dressing room.

You get players who come to Rangers and can't handle the pressure, but David wasn't in that category. There was a lot of pressure on him when he came in because of the transfer fee and the rivalry between Aberdeen and Rangers but he showed great strength of character to deal with that.

On the pitch he gave everything and that's what I loved about him. For me, he was a seven or eight out of ten every week and I liked that about players, that consistency. And because of that, when David left in 1997 it was always going to be difficult to replace him. That was one of the reasons I think that we didn't do ten in a row. We brought in Ståle Stensaas and he did a good job but he wasn't the same calibre as David.

The opposition didn't get much joy down our left-hand side over the years and that's largely because of how good a defender David was. He would win the majority of his battles and was disciplined. He would get up and down the line, was a good passer of the ball and he could also pop up with the odd goal and created a number of goals for us too. I thought he was different class for Rangers.

BRIAN LAUDRUP

Arguably the finest foreign player ever to grace Scottish football, Brian Laudrup was a team-mate of David's for three seasons. They developed an almost telepathic relationship in the midst of one of the most successful eras in Rangers' history. A European Championship winner with Denmark in 1992, Laudrup also played for Bayer Uerdigen, Bayern Munich, Fiorentina, AC Milan, Chelsea and Ajax.

Although he had been capped for Scotland and had been a regular in the Rangers first team for three seasons, I honestly didn't really know much about David when I joined Rangers. But when we went to Italy for pre-season training, David instantly caught my eye. Like me, he wasn't a fan of the long running sessions and he would often be alongside me at the back of the group. However, when the ball came out and we played five-a-side games I soon understood what he was all about.

David was strong in a one on one defensively and incredibly fast with a good left peg. Initially, however, we didn't understand each other at all. He would ask for a pass into his feet which I thought was too predictable. I wanted David to use his incredible pace and time his runs into the space behind the back four. It was difficult for us at the beginning, but we soon sorted things out. In fact, pretty soon we didn't have to talk to each other on the pitch as we knew instinctively what we wanted to do.

One game I remember playing alongside David in was the 3-3 draw against Celtic in 1995. It was one of the most exciting games I was ever involved in as it had everything. Six goals, end-to-end action and, of course, the stunning Andy Goram save from Van Hooijdonk. I scored our first goal that day although that honour should have fallen to David. He scored a peach of a goal when he ran on to my through ball and beat the goalkeeper. The goal was ruled out for offside but, in my humble opinion, it should have stood.

There in that moment he showed all of us exactly what he was all about. He combined pace with intelligence and timing and that is a dangerous weapon in football. And the finish from a very difficult angle was perfect. It was a moment of beauty!

Walter gave me a free role in the Rangers team and David's strengths made it very easy for me to operate. He would single-handedly take care of the left side as he was a warrior who would take on every challenge. It didn't matter if the task was to keep the opposition's attacking players quiet by doing the rough stuff or make life difficult for them when he set off as a brilliant counter-attacking option, he was excellent at everything he was asked to do.

David was a quiet character, and, like most Scots, he had a good sense of humour. I was quiet too and, in that respect, I think we had more in common. We both preferred to do the talking on the pitch!

I'm often asked what the highlight of my time at Rangers was. I always answer the same: winning nine in a row. For myself, David and the other players it was the Holy Grail. He was a very important player during that era, and, for me, he was one of the unsung heroes. And if I am asked to name my all-time Rangers XI, David will always have a place in it.

YATES AND MICHELLE HUDSON

Part of the Robertsons' 'American family', Yates and Michelle Hudson met David when he was coaching at Sereno Soccer Club. Yates, a successful businessman, was a board member and Michelle was the club's registrar.

We first met David Robertson in the summer of 2008. We never could have anticipated the impact he would have on our lives. He was assigned to be the new coach for our son Zach's team, but little did we know that he was going to be much more than that.

David was taking over a team of talented boys whose biggest achievement was placing second in the State Cup competition the previous season. He went to work getting to know the boys and dedicating himself to figuring out how to develop each player to the strongest of their abilities. He would get to know each player both as a player and a person. He would then put all of those pieces together to make them a team and applied his magical coaching formula to create success. Truly this season played out like a movie and, under David's direction, it was only the beginning of a long successful ride. They took first place in the State Cup, then first place in the regionals and were finalists in the nationals. Though they did not make it to the nationals again, they would end up earning six State Cup championships in total.

Naturally, David eventually became our club's director of coaching. His approachable demeanour and easy-going attitude as an administrative leader were a breath of fresh air to our club. Sereno was one of the top clubs in the country and therefore it attracted a lot of type-A parents who could make things difficult. But David remained steadfast in his focus to develop the players and make the club even greater. He hated the politics and wished that didn't come with the job.

One of the many things that stand out regarding David is the fact that he was always the coach who was willing to take on the unsuccessful teams. And then he would somehow pull that team together and bring them to the next level. It is easy for a coach to take on a team that is already successful and ride that out. David was always up for the challenge of turning a struggling team into a successful team. And that shows what he is made of as a leader and coach.

David is the biggest mixture of toughness and softness in the same person. He is truly an oxymoron. He is super funny, and we have laughed and cried with him. He loves deeply, works hard and is loyal to the end. He is so much more than a coach. He is an amazing father, husband, son, brother and friend too. He puts as much into vacuuming and doing dishes as he does coaching. If only everyone could be as lucky as us to have him as a life friend.

ZACH HUDSON

Zach Hudson was part of the 94BW (Boys White) team that David coached during his time at Sereno Soccer Club. He became best friends with David's oldest son, Mason, who also played with 94BW.

David Robertson – affectionately known as Davy – had a crucial influence on every player he coached at Sereno. There is no better proof of that than the results and success that followed. He got the most out of each and every player, taking teams places we never dreamed were possible.

David never subscribed to any given style. He knew that if he played to his players' strengths and opponents' weaknesses, we could compete in any match. No one game was the same, as each brought on new challenges. Although we had talented players, we would have never conquered these challenges without the brilliance of David's coaching.

David also differed from other coaching philosophies because he was the most hands-off coach I played for. David allowed his players to play at practice; no drills, no excessive fitness, just some cones, bibs and a ball was all we needed. David knew that we were better off learning how to problem-solve for ourselves, and that situational instincts are more important than mastering any given play or drill.

Lastly, I would say David was not just our leader, he was the heart and soul of our team. He held us to the highest of standards and taught us to believe in ourselves. He was known for his energy and foul language (when necessary), and, like I said, he always got the most from his players.

We were nothing but grateful for David, and we owe our success to him. I think it goes without saying that he was the best coach we ever had.

KRISTI, TRACI AND MITCH HAMMER

Kristi and Traci's son, Mitch, was part of the 99BW team that David coached. Firstly, Kristi and Traci share their memories of David before Mitch gives an insight into what it was like as a player in one of David's teams.

Davy is one of a kind; a coach, a leader, and, more importantly, a great friend to our family. As a coach he was a driver, challenging players to be their best and inspired them, being a former great in the beautiful game, but also by his 'colourful' choice of motivating words with that accent which reminds me of Sean Connery. He was very patient with the team. Very humble too. It was fun when the football aficionados recognised him as one of the finest to ever take the pitch with Rangers. Mostly he is a man of amazing character who really cares about the success of each and every one of his players. You don't find many like Davy.

He is a wonderful family man, a great friend and impacted the lives of hundreds of players fortunate enough to call him their leader.

I was so blessed to have David coach me for a few years at Sereno. It's almost surreal that a player of his calibre was my coach, but he was also a great friend to our family. At least two nights a week I would ask him if I could stay and do a second practice. I learned so much from him. He was so patient, and he cared so much about my success. I am currently playing D1 at college and in my senior year. I credit so much of my success to David. He taught me how to be the player I am today. I sure do miss him and his family as we have stayed wonderful friends. I am looking forward to going to Scotland to visit next summer once the pandemic is over.

Thank you for all of your hard work and dedication to all of us young players who were lucky enough to have been a part of your coaching success.

LESLIE JOHNSON

Leslie was the executive director for Arizona Youth Soccer from 1995 to 2018. She oversaw and ran the whole of Arizona youth soccer, which had over 50,000 boys and girls playing, and was in charge of setting standard for youth soccer clubs.

I have known David Robertson professionally and personally for over ten years.

The first time I met David was eye-opening for me. As the executive director for Arizona Youth Soccer, I had the pleasure of attending the US Youth National Championships as the state representative for the West Region's U14B champion, which happened to be David's team from Arizona. The road to the US Youth National Championships is not easy or indeed short. It is a culmination of winning your own State Championship, competing and winning the Regional Championship and then on to the nationals. The competition spans four months, with over 10,000 teams competing for the top award.

David's team performed well, and as runners-up that meant they were one of the top two teams in the United States. That was an amazing achievement but that is not what impressed me. During the week-long competition I witnessed something I had never seen in my 25 years of soccer. This coach, the man with so many championships, awards and accolades from his own impressive career, this man who loves to win, this fierce competitor – he made sure every child on his roster had time on the pitch, ensuring every young man had an opportunity to compete in the National Championships. Imagine that, you are coaching at the US National Championships, wanting to be the best U14B team in the United States and you choose to put your young men first! David expects hard work and dedication from his players, and he made sure they saw the reward for their hard work. To say I was stunned is an understatement. What a character-building moment for every young man on that team!

I knew at that moment I needed David to not only continue coaching, but I needed him in leadership at board of director level. And it wasn't just his knowledge and experience I was looking for, I needed his sense of honesty, loyalty and fairness too.

David was easily elected to our board of directors where his vast knowledge and expertise improved and expanded the landscape of soccer in the state of Arizona. Because of his experience he was able to help us see the 'bigger picture', which in turn helped us change and modify some of our competition policies, ensuring a better product for our members. Many quickly learned that if you were making decisions based on what is right for the players you were going to be okay, if not, David would let you know!

As David continued to coach and help shape our association, his reputation was noticed by many outside Arizona as well and that culminated with David being chosen as Competitive Coach of the Year for our region, which was quite an accomplishment.

On a personal side, I enjoyed watching David the family man. He loves his family with the same intensity he showed during his playing days. David and Kym clearly adore each other. I miss their get-togethers. David and Kym make everyone feel so welcome in their home, and you are constantly laughing when you are with them.

The entire Robertson family is warm, friendly, funny and extremely close. We loved having them in Arizona and would love for them to come back. My home will always be open to them.

It is an absolute honour to call David and Kym my friends, and I'll be forever grateful for David's leadership in Arizona soccer.

DARLA SIPOLT

Darla Sipolt, managing director of Goldman Sachs, was the president of Sereno Soccer Club when David was director of coaching. Her two children, Amanda and David, played for teams that David coached.

At the time I was president at Sereno Soccer Club, David was director of coaching. Sereno was the premier youth soccer club in Arizona. The club had over $1m in annual revenues and over 1,000 kids in programmes from recreation to elite competitive travelling teams. I met David when he and his family moved to Arizona and I learned about his storied professional experience. David was an understated friend who could be found smiling in the background, but he transformed once on the soccer sidelines where he was anything but understated. You could easily hear David from the sideline although you could rarely understand what he was saying due to his thick Scottish accent. He coached not only the top boys' team at Sereno but also younger, less competitive teams. David's philosophy was about teaching and sharing his love for the game.

I wish I could have seen David play in his youth, but I feel fortunate to have met him and was able to see his impact on the boys and many teams he coached. What he's doing for Real Kashmir is astonishing but not surprising and it baffles me that a European team hasn't offered him a professional coaching job. His love for the game and his desire to teach and train is in full illustration.

MIKE LAVELLE

A graduate of the prestigious Columbia University, Mike Lavelle was firstly vice-president then president at Sereno Soccer Club when David was there. His two daughters, Emma and Olivia, were coached by David and have since gone on to play top-level college soccer.

What always stood out for me with Davy was that every year whatever teams he had always ended up competing for the State Cup or even the national title, and it didn't matter what team it was. He would take over a team, and it might be one of the weaker age groups yet by the end of the year the team was competing for the championship and the next year they were winning it, and usually competing nationally. And he did it without fundamentally changing the roster.

I can remember other coaches would complain that Davy got the best teams to coach. I would laugh as a few years prior the coach who was complaining had either refused to coach that very team because it wasn't good enough for him or had actually been the coach! I don't think Davy's fellow coaches, both at Sereno and in Arizona, appreciated how talented he was, what they were experiencing, and who they were working with.

Likewise, I also remember that every year our rival club, DelSol, would be poaching players from all over Arizona and the surrounding states to create 'All-Star' teams to try and beat Davy's teams, and they couldn't do it. And it drove them nuts! I used to tell the Sereno board that what people said about Bear Bryant, a college football coach in the USA, was the same case with Davy: 'He could take his players and whip yours, or take your players and whip his.'

The other thing I remember is that Davy was all about the kids. I remember talking to him after he volunteered to take on one of the second teams for the 11- and 12-year-old kids because their coach left part way through the season. Here was the best coach in the state of Arizona, and he's giving himself the second team to coach. I remember asking him, 'How is it going with the Blue Team?' [the White team was the first team, while the Blue team was the second team] and he told me it was because they were great kids. I could tell he loved coaching them as much as he did the older kids who were competing at national level because he would tell me more stories about them than the older kids.

Similarly, I look back fondly on how he used to come to me when I was president of the club and ask for us to help a kid who couldn't make the payments. Times were difficult financially for the club during and after the US financial crisis and great recession of 2008–2009 so the majority of the time I would have to say no. Yet somehow Davy always got those kids taken care of financially. Davy has such a great heart and to him every kid was basically a good kid who deserved a break.

TIM DONALD

Tim Donald, a successful Canadian businessman, worked with David during his time in charge of Phoenix FC. Together they tried to rescue the ailing club and developed a great relationship despite the difficult circumstances they found themselves in.

I had played soccer for years in Canada but when I came in at Phoenix FC, the sport was still growing in the US, so it was a great business opportunity. Unless you were mega-rich, buying a basketball, hockey or football team was out of reach so with Phoenix FC it was a chance to come in at grassroots level. But for me the main reason I came on board and helped fund things at the club was because of David.

You couldn't fail to see his passion for soccer and also the expertise he brought. He was the cornerstone and I saw immediately how well he balanced his professionalism and passion. He knows exactly when to use his emotions and when not to overdo it such that the players tune out. Having been involved in sports leadership for a while, for me, I thought that was a really neat thing about him and I saw pretty quickly that the players respected him.

I knew a little bit about what David had achieved in his playing career but once I dug deeper I found out how well-respected he was and that was the icing on the cake. I was impressed and knew I had not only a great guy as my head coach but also someone with a bit of clout when we were talking to people about players too.

Originally, I came into the club to help with the marketing side but pretty soon I was getting asked to put some money in. It all turned out to be a bit of a scam, which left me with a choice to either clear things up or walk away. I chose the former as I still thought it was a great opportunity. But it was evident fairly quickly that the debts were mounting up and, as much as we tried to 'band aid' them, we were eventually putting in sums in excess of six figures just to get the team through the season.

We achieved that and David was doing a great job keeping the players motivated so we were all set to go again for the next season. My intention was to bring in a core of local business guys as they were better connected than me in the area. At that time the USL were happy to offer the franchise to us – they had taken a deposit cheque – but some of the guys who came in gazumped us and we were accused of defaulting on payments. This was later proven to be false but that didn't matter, we were ousted.

Litigation followed and some of that is still ongoing. As all of this was going on David was trying to prepare the team for the new season and why wouldn't he? Throughout the whole fiasco we couldn't see any red flags. From our perspective we were either moving ahead on our own or with the new guys on board. We had the players in place and a deal arranged to rent a stadium, so everything looked good.

But the new partner we introduced took the deal for his own, and he and the league split the benefit of the franchise fee that had been credited to us between them. That made the deal irresistible for the both of them

The team we had helped save were eventually dissolved and, although David was originally meant to be kept on by the new guys to coach the new incarnation, he soon found himself out too. I think those involved didn't want anyone from the previous regime involved and I felt sorry for David as he got played a lot by them. Because of the kind of guy he is, he was doing everything in good faith as he just wanted to keep the soccer team going.

When I look back, David Robertson was the main reason why I wanted to invest in the club. As I have said, there was a big opportunity to create a soccer franchise in a market that didn't have one but you would never do that if you didn't have a coach on board who had the strength and character that David did. I was aware of what he had achieved at Sereno and, in my opinion, that club was never better than it was when he was there. Coming from Scotland, he wasn't aware of all of the politics involved – it wasn't about developing soccer in the state, it was about developing a business – yet he saw past that and was extremely successful there. And with Phoenix FC he put his money where his mouth was too and invested, that's how much he wanted the club to succeed.

David has now moved on and has had great success in Kashmir. I'm not surprised as his passion for soccer is unsurpassed. I am privileged to call him a friend.

SANDEEP CHATTOO

In 2016, Sandeep Chattoo founded Real Kashmir FC in one of the most hostile environments in India. He needed someone with strength of character to manage the club in these most challenging circumstances and he identified David was the man for the job.

When we started the club, we were looking for someone who would agree to come to Kashmir as manager. At that time Kashmir was not particularly stable so we were looking for someone who would be able to come and adapt to that. We therefore needed a strong person with a strong personality, a complete professional who was well-qualified. And when we looked at David's profile and the experience he had, we thought he would be fantastic for the football club. During our discussions something just clicked, and I knew when he came over it would be the right decision for us.

When David came to Kashmir for the first time, he did so in the midst of one of the harshest winters. When his plane landed at the airport in Srinagar it was snowing, and he was exhausted. There was no electricity, no internet and I wouldn't have blamed him if he made up his mind at that point to go back home. We managed to persuade him to give it a try and I'm glad we did.

In addition to coaching the team, David was instrumental in the basic structuring of the club. Everything revolved around him. We managed to get entry into the second division and it was really unexpected when we won it in 2017/18. We did it without losing a game too. We were the underdogs, but if I had any doubts that David was the right man to manage Real Kashmir, they vanished at that point. David's dedication, motivation, professionalism and strategies were all first class and I have had no problems with him.

We have now had two seasons in the top league although the second season was stopped early because of COVID-19. In the first season we finished third but could have won the league had it not been for a very unfortunate incident when a CRV was blown up and 40 people were killed. No teams were allowed to come to Kashmir after that so two of our home games were postponed. One match against East Bengal had to be played in Delhi while the other against Minerva Punjab never took place. Had that incident not happened I believe that David would have guided us to the league title.

With the suspension of the league – we were fourth, one point behind second-placed East Bengal and we had a game in hand – it has made it very tough. But after lockdown David and I were together in Kashmir for a month and a half before he was allowed to go back to Scotland, so we have managed to work out all the details for next season.

At the time of writing the league was due to recommence at the end of November 2020. David and the team will have had to face a big challenge as the games will only have been played at one venue, most likely in Calcutta. Not having any home fixtures will be a big challenge as we have a fantastic following in Kashmir, probably the best in the country. But I have trust and confidence in David that we can meet these challenges.

I have no regrets over bringing David to Kashmir and he has exceeded my expectations. I have an excellent, dedicated coach training my team. He has risen to all the challenges that he has been faced with and his commitment is immense. And as well as that, David is a fantastic human being. We are lucky to have him at Real Kashmir.

JONATHAN CRAIG

Hailing from Edinburgh, Jonathan started his career in grassroots football, working with the likes of Dalkeith Thistle and Hutchison Vale. He spent seven years working as a goalkeeping coach at Hearts and had spells with East Fife, Berwick Rangers and Hibernian. Jonathan has worked at international level too, having been part of the SFA Performance school in Edinburgh and also with the Scottish Women's under-19 side. After a successful stint as the head goalkeeping coach in the academy at Barnsley, it was time for a change, and he joined David's coaching staff at Real Kashmir ahead of the 2019/20 season.

I am a Rangers supporter and David was a big part of the successful team I grew up watching. I recall he was a hardy player, a brilliant overlapping full-back, but I have to say, as someone who aspired to be a goalkeeper, my focus was on the likes of Andy Goram at that time. But I didn't know David personally, so I was surprised when I got a phone call out the blue from his assistant manager at Real Kashmir, Jimmy Lindsay. I had worked with Jimmy when I was at Hearts but by now I was at Barnsley. But I was coming to the end of my time as goalkeeping coach there and I was looking for another opportunity.

Arrangements were made for me to come back to Scotland and meet David and, after we met, I took some time to think about the move. During that period, I watched the first of the BBC documentaries and it got me excited. I felt if I could prepare myself mentally to deal with the challenges living and working in Kashmir brought then it would be a good move for me. David also assured me I would be safe as the hotel we would be staying in was in the most protected area of Kashmir as it overlooked the army barracks. And I have to be honest, not at any stage have I felt unsafe during my time there.

Once I got out to Kashmir, I found out very quickly that David was a fantastic coach and an excellent man-manager. He has learnt from the very best having played under Sir Alex Ferguson, Walter Smith and George Graham, and to have achieved what he has done under the circumstances he has faced is unbelievable.

The way he deals with each individual player is different class. He knows what he wants from each individual player from the goalkeeper through to the centre-forwards and he puts his message across brilliantly. The way he analyses games and our opponents under very difficult circumstances is excellent too. In Kashmir we don't have access to all the state-of-the-art technology to watch other teams play and getting to games means either an arduous bus journey or an internal flight. But David is undeterred and always manages to gather the data he needs for each game we play.

He also has a good eye for a goalkeeper. The current first-choice goalkeeper at Real Kashmir, Phurba Tempa Lachenpa, is in the top three I have ever worked with. He so good in fact that if I was ever to get a job back in the UK, I would be looking to take Phurba with me. Our second-choice goalkeeper is Tenzin Samdup, who is a Tibetan international. Technically he is very good but tactically during games he isn't yet at the standard of Phurba.

David and I had already spoken about what he looked for from his goalkeepers in and out of possession and he made it clear that from day one I was to be fully in charge of the goalkeepers. But pretty soon he involved me in absolutely everything, even asking my opinion during games on substitutions to make. That was an amazing feeling for me as it showed he trusted me.

My dad hasn't always kept the best of health and after our first game of the season against East Bengal he called me to say he was going in for an operation. When I had spoken to him about going to India, he hadn't mentioned it, so I made my mind up that I was going back home to be with him. But then the gaffer stepped in. It turned out my mum had spoken to Kym, who had spoken to David, and he pulled me to one side and said that if I ever needed to speak to him about anything outside of football, he was there for me. And from that moment on I have spoken to David about everything. Just like he does with the players, he makes me feel great and, when you feel like that, you will not only do your best for the club but for him as well.

I have already mentioned watching the first of the BBC documentaries and I was part of the second one. But I don't feel they fully portrayed what David is like as they didn't show how he deals with the players and how he deals with all the challenges he faces on a daily basis. He is an unbelievable guy and I cannot understand why no club in Scotland has approached him to be their manager.

Even a worldwide pandemic couldn't stop him! We were stuck in the hotel for 49 days after the first lockdown and it was horrendous. Kym was instrumental in eventually getting us out, but David, while he was focussed on getting home safely, he also never wavered when it came to the job in hand.

Once it became apparent that the current season was ending, he turned his attention to preparing for 2020/21. One of the first things he did was get me to sign a new contract and he also asked me to identify goalkeepers I wanted to bring. There were times too when David, Jimmy and I would sit and watch games to see if we could pick players out who would improve the team. I reckon he managed to sign around 95 per cent of the players he wanted in unprecedented circumstances and that, for me, just sums up the character of the man.

I would like to think I can call David a friend for life. I have been involved in professional football for almost 20 years and David is right up there as one of the best managers I have worked with. I can't wait to get back out to Kashmir and get started again.

THE LAST WORD

In a book such as this it's fitting that the closing comments are attributed to someone close to the subject, so it's over to my wonderful wife. We have known each other since 1985 and are best friends. Kym is the rock of the family and worries about us all, so much so that she puts everyone before herself. She is a fantastic wife and mother and Chelsea, Mason, Jordan and myself would not be the people we are today if it wasn't for her.

She makes me laugh when I'm down, particularly when my playing career came to an end. She got me through it. We laugh a lot together and I have been so fortunate to have a supporting wife that has sacrificed to allow me to follow my football dreams.

Quite simply, I'm a lucky man to be able to call Kym Diana Robertson my wife. This is her side of my story.

David and I started dating on 1 May 1985. We both went to Harlaw Academy, and at the time David was playing in the Aberdeen reserves. We didn't know each other to speak to as he was in the year above me, but we did get the same bus to school. Growing up, my dad had played in the Highland League and at a young age I would occasionally be dragged to go and watch him play. Becoming a footballer's wife was the last thing on my mind! My mother would always tell me that if I married a footballer, she would disown me!

David was different, though, and we started going steady. I went to as many of his games as I could, taking two buses to Pittodrie, as I was still at school studying for my Highers and had a Saturday job. I can remember standing in the foyer at Pittodrie with the doormen, Alan and Stan, as initially I was too shy to go into the players' lounge. I was only 17 years old and in there were the likes of Claire Miller, Jill McLeish and, latterly, Claire Nicholas. But we did strike up a friendship with Theo Snelders and his wife, Mirjam, when they came to Aberdeen. They moved into a house in the same street as my mum and dad so we saw a lot of them and would look after their dog, Toby.

David and I got married on 9 June 1990 – I am happy to report that Mum didn't disown me – and we recently celebrated our pearl wedding anniversary. Less than a year after that, we made what would be the first of several house moves when David joined Rangers. We lived initially in the Moathouse Hotel before we moved to our new house in Erskine. It was a really exciting time for us, as we found out I was pregnant with Chelsea, and David and I spent all our time together when he wasn't training or playing. We got on really well with the hotel manager, Douglas Waddell, and his wife, Margaret, and they were so lovely to us. We had our bearded collie, Kozbi, with us and he would lie in the middle of the foyer at reception being petted and fed apples by the guests. He was classified as the honorary guard dog there.

I was 22 when David signed for Rangers, so I wasn't quite as shy as I had been at Aberdeen. We were both more mature and wiser. David was still the youngest in the Rangers team but we were closer in age to the other players and wives so we built up good relationships, particularly with Stuart McCall and his wife. Stuart had signed for Rangers at the same time as David. They stayed at the Moathouse also and I remember them coming round and helping us unpack when we moved to Erskine.

Chelsea was born in 1992 with Mason arriving two years later. When Mason was two weeks old, we moved to Newton Mearns, but when the day came for the movers to come, David was lying in bed at a hotel in preparation for a pre-season tournament at Ibrox! Thankfully my mum and our good friends, Graham and Janette, came to help. Jordan arrived in 1995, completing our family. We had great times in Glasgow with so many special memories made.

When David decided to leave Rangers in 1997, he had several offers from clubs across the UK and Europe. When it comes to changing jobs or employers you sit down and weigh up the pros and cons of each option; however, when it came to football decisions, I left the final call-up to David. He had to be happy where he was playing, and I was supportive of his decision to join Leeds United.

But due to the issues David had with his knee, his time at Leeds was pretty miserable for him. As soon as he found out, at his medical, that he didn't have an ACL in his left knee it became psychological as it was always at the back of his mind when he was training and playing games. He was in a lot of discomfort that previously had gone unnoticed. The mind is a very powerful tool and we often wonder what would have happened had he not had the knowledge about the knee. That was a big deal for David, and it is probably the unhappiest period in his career.

When he wasn't able to play, David assisted with the school runs and the kids' after-school activities. This was huge for him as it kept him preoccupied. He was going through hell as he wanted to play and make a contribution to the team but was unable to do what he loved most. Eventually, David had his biggest fear realised when the surgeon advised that he could no longer play at the top level. He had to come to terms with the fact it was over, and it was a difficult time for us as he could no longer play the game that he is so committed to and passionate about.

He tried to make a comeback with Montrose and the family had moved back up to Aberdeen by the time he ruptured his Achilles tendon, an injury that brought a definite end to his playing career. But I knew he wouldn't be out the game for long and he joined Elgin City as manager, enjoying some success during his time there. After David finished with Elgin, he had a brief spell back at Montrose.

But he felt he needed a new challenge and that's how our move to Phoenix, Arizona, came about. David and his pal Derek Thom went out to Los Angeles to visit another of their friends, Neil Talbot. Neil told David about the opportunities that were available in the US and when he came back from his boys' holiday, the decision was made: we were heading Stateside!

The move was hard for the kids as they were leaving their friends behind and Chelsea, in particular, wasn't keen to go. She was about to sit her exams at school, so we weren't sure whether or not to leave her behind to complete them or take her out when we all went. In the end she came with us – I recall her hating us at the time – and all three kids soon fell into the American lifestyle. In fact, Chelsea was the first to adopt the American accent. That had been accelerated when she had been asked to do an announcement at school. She refused to do it and within months she had the accent down to a tee. She enjoyed her time out there so much that she didn't want to come home!

I don't think we realised just how full on the job at Sereno was going to be. When David commits to something, he always gives 100 per cent but this was 24/7. But he started well and took Mason's team to the national finals for the first time and that made him like a god to the parents. Going to tournaments like that really put kids on show for college recruitment and we were all so proud of David as he played such a significant role in making that happen.

Even now David feels working in youth football at Sereno shaped how he is as a manager and how he deals with his players. He knows how to get the best out of each and every one of his players as he knows what works for one player doesn't necessarily work for others. He can identify the ones who need the arm round the shoulder and the ones who need a bollocking every now and then. And that's what's earned him respect. His players adored him and he was so highly thought of by the parents of the kids in the team he was working with at Sereno that they arranged for a Scottish piper to play ahead of the last practice session he took.

After nine years in Phoenix, things turned sour within Sereno Soccer Club and David moved on to a club in Austin, Texas. By now Mason was at the University of Washington, Chelsea had graduated from the University of Arizona and was in the process of moving back to the UK, while Jordan was at St Mary's University in San Antonio. David told me that this was it, he was going to Austin to take a step back and relax. The job appeared to be a lot less pressurised than the one at Sereno and it looked like we would get to spend more time together.

Not for the first time David sold the move to me, and while he rented an apartment in Texas, I was back home in Arizona trying to sell our 4,600-square-foot house. Out of the blue David called to say he had been offered a job in Kashmir, India. My answer was categorically 'no'. He had come back to Phoenix to spend some time with us over Christmas and New Year but when he decided to go to India, we barely spoke. I even refused to take him to the airport to catch his flight.

While David embarked on his three-day journey to Kashmir, I was left to conclude the sale of the house, but I had no idea where we were going. Was it to Texas? Back to the UK? I had no idea. I didn't know where our belongings were going and on top of that we had three dogs – Sammy, Dexter and Roxy – and a cat, Cali, to contend with. The uncertainty over our destination meant the way our belongings were wrapped for transportation had to be taken into account as this is different if you are travelling internationally rather than internally. And in addition to transporting our belongings I had another car to move, too. I sorted that out by convincing the removal company I used to take one of the cars in their truck!

The sale of the house was eventually concluded but that brought about more issues. Both David and I had to sign the paperwork but as you'll have read, there were communication issues in India. The only solution was to send the paperwork to David who then printed it off, signed it, had to find a way of having it notarised and sent back using FedEx. As you can imagine this rigmarole did nothing for my mood at the time!

I eventually found a house to rent in Austin, a couple of days before I was due to arrive, but to get there I had to undertake a 16-hour gruelling road trip which included a stopover in a hotel.

My friend Sylvia came along for the ride and I am so pleased she did as I don't think I could have done it without her. The cat cried in the car for the duration of the journey and I was caught speeding en route. Meantime, I haven't heard anything from David who I thought must be living it up in India oblivious to what he had left behind.

We were only permitted one pet in the house in Austin, so I had to get Jordan to come from San Antonio to get the keys from the realtor, so I didn't arrive with all these pets. That meant I could sneak all the others in, but as Sylvia had to get back to Phoenix, I was left alone in this strange house, not knowing anyone, surrounded by our belongings, not knowing whether or not I should unpack.

The bold hero eventually returned in February. I was relieved to see him if I'm honest and after we talked it was clear just how much this job in India meant to David. I didn't want him being in the job in Texas if he was going to be miserable, but since David would no longer be working in the States, we all had to come back to the UK. I flew back and forth for about six months as we had signed a rental agreement for the house in Austin and had some loose ends to tie up back in Arizona. During that time, David was in Scotland looking for a house in Aberdeen and he also went back to India too as the new season had started.

Although I initially had my reservations, I am so proud of what David has achieved in his short time in Kashmir. He does struggle with the poor communications as he's a home bird. There have been numerous times when he's called and the signal has frustratingly dropped midway through the call but, rather than call back another time, he keeps on going. After 15 or 20 attempts I'm ready to throw my phone against a wall but David keeps trying because he wants to stay in contact as often as possible.

He's actually a really sensitive soul and that's not a side of him many people see. For example, he's never really come to terms with the loss of our dog Sammy who had to be put down about six months after we got back from the States. Losing a pet can be like losing a family member, but even now when his name comes up in conversation, you can see a tear running down David's face.

I have been to Kashmir now three times and it's only once you're out there that you appreciate what David has to go through on a daily basis. You don't go to Kashmir to go on holiday although I have to say that the scenery is stunning. But it's a completely different world and I can see why David gets so frustrated. A lot of emphasis has been placed on the amount of swearing David did during the two BBC documentaries but if you saw the circumstances he is working in you would completely understand how he gets so exasperated.

But we didn't get to see the other side of David, the one where he takes the players to one side and talks to them one to one. And all bias aside, I have seen him deal with players when we were in America and he is one of the most empathetic people I know. He listens and takes on board what each player needs to be successful. He admits he's a better coach now than he was in the beginning at Elgin due to the experiences he has had. No one expected Real Kashmir to have had the success they have had under David. To have done what they have done – something that many regraded as almost impossible – is remarkable.

To sum up our time together, I have to say that David makes life interesting! I don't think I could have chosen a better father for our kids, but he keeps me on my toes and I often joke with people that I have five kids, with David being two of them. I tell him regularly that it's good he makes me laugh otherwise he would drive me mad. In fact, he's my version of Frank Spencer. Some of the things he has done are pure slapstick and it makes me laugh just thinking about them.

There was one time out in Phoenix when he fell fully clothed into our swimming pool trying to retrieve a stone that the dog had dropped in. The first I knew about it was when I encountered him at the door, dripping wet from head to toe. When I asked him what had happened he told me that as he reached in to get the stone he could feel his mobile phone falling out of his pocket. And as he tried to prevent his phone going into the water, he lost his balance and into the pool he went.

There were more recent episodes too. We were having some work done on our house in Aberdeen and David was helping the guys load guttering into their van. As he was backing out, he tripped over the tow bar and ended up flying out the van with his arms flailing in the air. It was all caught on camera too and everyone we have sent the video to has been in hysterics because it could only happen to David.

And before he left to go back to India in November, he went to tidy up the dining room and the next thing I knew he was coming through with paint on his trousers and shoes. As he had been tidying, he had managed to spill a tin of paint but, rather than get himself hung up about it, he just laughed it off. And that's something he does often, he is very self-deprecating. But to know him is to love him and that's what I have done for just over 30 years. The kids and I are lucky to have such a great guy in our lives.

STATISTICS

Playing Honours

BP Scottish Youth Cup (2): 1984/85, 1985/86
Scottish League Premier Division (6): 1991/92, 1992/93, 1993/94, 1994/95, 1995/96, 1996/97
Scottish Cup (4): 1989/90, 1991/92, 1992/93, 1995/96
Scottish League Cup (4): 1989/90, 1992/93, 1993/94, 1996/97
Tennents Sixes (1): 1987
Forfarshire Cup (1): 2002

Managerial Honours

North of Scotland Cup (1): 2003/04
USA State Championships (9): 94BW, 6; 95BW, 1; 96BW, 1; 99BW, 1
Hero I-League Second Division (1): 2017/18
IFA Shield (1): 2020

Appearance Record

Aberdeen (1985–1991)
197 appearances, 4 goals

League	135 appearances, 2 goals
Scottish Cup	10 appearances, 0 goals
Scottish League Cup	21 appearances, 1 goal
Europe	10 appearances, 0 goals
Other	21 appearances, 1 goal

Rangers (1991–1997)
267 appearances, 21 goals

League	183 appearances, 15 goals
Scottish Cup	26 appearances, 3 goals
Scottish League Cup	19 appearances, 1 goal
Europe	22 appearances, 0 goals
Other	17 appearances, 2 goals

Leeds United (1997–2001)
36 appearances, 0 goals

League	26 appearances, 0 goals
FA Cup	1 appearance, 0 goals
English League Cup	4 appearances, 0 goals
Europe	0 appearances, 0 goals
Other	5 appearances, 0 goals

Montrose (2002)
13 appearances, 1 goal

League	8 appearances, 0 goals
Scottish Cup	0 appearances, 0 goals
Scottish League Cup	1 appearance, 1 goal
Other	4 appearances, 0 goals

		League			Scottish/FA Cup			Scottish/English League Cup			Europe			Other		
		A	S	G	A	S	G	A	S	G	A	S	G	A	S	G
1985/86	Aberdeen	0	0	0	0	0	0	0	0	0	0	0	0	1	1	0
1986/87	Aberdeen	32	2	0	3	0	0	2	1	0	1	1	0	1	0	0
1987/88	Aberdeen	23	0	0	4	0	0	4	0	0	2	0	0	4	0	0
1988/89	Aberdeen	23	0	0	0	0	0	5	0	0	2	0	0	4	0	0
1989/90	Aberdeen	20	0	1	2	0	0	5	0	1	0	0	0	3	0	0
1990/91	Aberdeen	35	0	1	1	0	0	4	0	0	4	0	0	7	0	1
1991/92	Rangers	42	0	1	5	0	0	4	0	1	2	0	0	4	0	1
1992/93	Rangers	39	0	3	5	0	0	5	0	0	9	0	0	4	0	1
1993/94	Rangers	32	0	1	6	0	1	4	0	0	1	0	0	0	0	0
1994/95	Rangers	23	0	3	2	0	0	1	0	0	2	0	0	4	0	0
1995/96	Rangers	25	0	3	5	0	1	3	0	0	5	0	0	4	0	0
1996/97	Rangers	21	1	4	3	0	1	1	1	0	3	0	0	0	0	0
1997/98	Leeds United	24	2	0	1	0	0	4	0	0	0	0	0	5	0	0
1998/99	Leeds United	0	0	0	0	0	0	0	0	0	0	0	0	0	0	0
1999/2000	Leeds United	0	0	0	0	0	0	0	0	0	0	0	0	0	0	0
2000/01	Leeds United	0	0	0	0	0	0	0	0	0	0	0	0	0	0	0
2002/03	Montrose	8	0	0	0	0	0	1	0	1	0	0	0	4	0	0

Also available at all good book stores

9781785316470

9781785313929

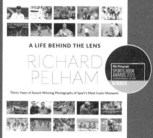

9781785315466

9781908051332

9781905411245

9781785316180

9781785315275

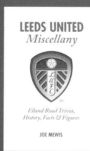

9781905411962

9781905411832